ANGELS WITH TAILS

SPREAD YOUR WINGS LITTLE DARLINGS

Copyright@Chantelle Jacqueline (2025)

The right of Chantelle Jacqueline to be identified as author of this work has been asserted by her in accordance with section 77 and 78 of the Copyright, Designs and Patents Act 1988.

All rights reserved. No part of this publication may be reproduced, stored in a retrieval system, or transmitted in any form or by any means, electronic, mechanical, photocopying, recording, or otherwise, without the prior permission of the publishers.

Any person who commits any unauthorised act in relation to this publication may be liable to criminal prosecution and civil claims for damages.

ISBN 978-0-6484085-4-3 (Paperback)
ISBN 978-0-6484085-3-6 (Hardback)
ISBN 978-0-6484085-5-0 (E-Book)

First Published (2025)

Part One: Where am I?

-Atlas-

I WAKE UP sleepily after a nap, stretching my paws. My ears prick up. Someone's been calling my name. I hope it's daddy telling me that it's time to get up and play fetch outside. I love it when it's playtime. But this isn't my home; it doesn't look or smell right. My home smells sweet and warm from the strawberry-scented candles. There's almost no smell here, and I'm not in the comfort of my own bed. I know my house like the back of my paw.

I've had a wonderful and happy life with the Trembley's. Ever since they adopted me as a puppy, they've cared for me and played with me. And as soon as I hear my daddy's voice call out my name in a cheerful, happy voice, I know it's playtime.

I run over to him and sit by his feet. He holds something behind his back while beaming a smile at me. The anticipation is killing me, so I bound up and down, my tail wagging. He teases me at first by showing an empty hand, but then he pulls out the other one from behind his back, and my tail goes crazy! I jump up and down when I see that daddy's holding the lime and grey-coloured pull rope clutched between his fingers.

'Is it playtime?' he asks me in an ecstatic voice, as I bound up and down, my tail flicking around crazily. I stand on my hind legs, my front paws on his boyish chest. He teases me more by holding the pull rope just out of reach, and then he swings it from side to side, laughing at me, trying to get it. When I do get it, I'm mindful not to bite him (because that would have resulted in me being taken away and surrendered to the pound). I snatch it from his hands as he laughs. I shake the pull-rope around like it's one of the Master's old socks, and daddy laughs harder. He calls me a silly boy, and I'm inclined to throw the pull-rope up in the air, where it lands on the other side of the lawn. I run after it and scoop it up in my mouth again. I see the Master standing in the doorway, holding a bag of Canadian Natural's dry dog food. I drop the pull rope. He waves his hand as he calls to my daddy while shaking the bag of food, another one of my favourite things about the Trembleys. 'Colin, bring Atlas inside. It's dinnertime'.

FOOD!

I try to follow the Master and Daddy inside, but that's when I realise that I'm not home anymore; my feet stay still. I can't smell anything. Everything around me is white. I don't move from my resting position; I simply gaze around at the area before me. The place seems safe enough... there's nothing dangerous around here and I feel somewhat calm, though I'm not ready to trust it just yet.

There's no smell, and I can tell this place isn't home. Something's off about it, but I can't quite work out what it is. The walls and ground which I lay upon are soft, almost as smooth as my bed back home. They're different shades of white and grey, which look like those puffy white things often seen in the sky; I think humans call them "clouds". But there's no way I'm in the clouds. Maybe my family has decided to take me to a theme park that's covered in cloudy structures and surfaces as a surprise. But I can't see any of my family anywhere. I can't see Master Mason or Mistress Victoria; even Daddy Colin is nowhere to be found. If they aren't here, where are they? Where can they be?

I start to worry.

What if they've left me here? What if they're in danger and I was too far into sleep to realise? I want to get up and find them, but something in my belly tells me not to get up. I ignore it and get up anyway, but I'm not standing up for long; the pain of a sharp, stinging feeling in my belly makes me fall back to the ground again.

I start to cry, howling out their names in clear distress. If my family is in danger, I have to be with them and protect them.

***

Finally awake, I see?' I hear a voice say. It sounds different from the one I heard before waking up in this strange place. But it doesn't sound like anyone I recognised. I peer over, and I see another dog about my size. The dog's medium-length fur appeared unkempt. She's female, and her coat is a mixture of tan and black, like mine. She has a smooth, caring voice that makes me feel somewhat at ease. However, I'm still wary of her because she could've done something to my family, and for that reason alone, I don't trust her, even if she speaks gently like how the Mistress talks to me, using it as a way of reassuring me.

The stranger has a beautiful-looking face, but I can't shake away those red bumps on the bottom of her eyes that appear swollen and look like mini tumours. I can't help but wonder how on earth she can see with them in the way. I want to ask her about it but decide that would be a topic for another day. Right now, I just want to know where I am and where my family is.

I tilt my head as I look at her. 'Who are you?' I ask her, and she replies, panting with her tongue, 'My name's Shelby. And you are Atlas.' She seems pleasant enough, I think to myself, but I still don't trust her. I need more information about this place and why I'm here instead of being at home with the people who love me. 'What is this place? Where am I, and how do you know my name?'

She gives me a reassuring look as if she expected me to ask her that. 'I know the names of all the pets here, yes, even you.

But don't be scared, Atlas; I was in the exact situation you're in right now. We all were.'.

I don't know what to say to that. I try to sit up, my tail between my legs, but the stinging feeling in my belly comes back, and I'm forced to lie on the soft surface below me. 'Oh, goodness!' Shelby yelps, her eyes on my paunches. She looks frightened herself. Shelby attempts to walk over to me, but I stand my ground. I lower my head to her, growl, and tell her to back off because I don't trust her.

'Please, Atlas, your wounds still haven't healed. Let me lick them, and the pain should go away,' she says with sympathy. She's trying to get me to lower my guard, but I'm not going to, not until I have an explanation as to where I am and what's going on.

'I don't know you, therefore, I don't trust you', I say with a growl. 'Tell me where my family is and where I am'. Shelby then lowers her head in a submissive gesture. 'Will you at least let me lick you and stop the pain if I tell you?' I think about it, but the pain in my belly is too much, and I can't live with not being able to move or sit up.

I roll onto my back, permitting her access to my exposed belly. Head still lowered and tail between her legs, she walks over to me, and she gently licks my wound, being careful not to cause even more harm to me.

I get up, feeling like I do when Daddy leaves the gate open. I look at Shelby intently, waiting for an answer to my question. I'm shaking; it suddenly feels cold here, or maybe that's because I'm scared.

'Your family is still in the Land of the Living, and you are in hea…'

'Land of the Living!' I shout in denial. 'What do you mean, Land of the Living? I don't understand. My family should be here. I should be with my family. Where are they? Why am I not here with them?'

'Please, Atlas, let me finish' Shelby says patiently. I sit down and stay silent, letting her finish. Shelby lowers her head for a moment, takes a deep breath before she looks me in the eyes, and what she says next makes my heart sink. 'You're in heaven for animals.'

I yelp as if I've stepped on a piece of glass, and I fall backwards, landing on my back. I get up and back away from her. My tail's cowering between my legs, my head's lowered submissively, and I'm trembling.

I shake my head, not wanting to believe her... *I... can't be dea*— I remember hearing the Master and the Mistress sitting in the kitchen with bowls of chicken soup. I'd already started my dinner, chewing on a lamb bone from last week's roast. Everything had been going wonderfully. But then I started to notice something off about the Mistress's tone. I'd stopped chewing on my bone to sit by her side. I looked at her imploringly and put a paw on her knee, asking if she was okay. She'd dismissed me at first, which made me sad. Placing a foot on the knee always cheered Daddy up when he came home from school and his face was covered in water. So, I couldn't understand why it hadn't worked on the Mistress. Was I doing it wrong?

'Colin,' the Mistress leaned in and whispered to Daddy, who looked at the Mistress from his side of the table; his face was a mixture of confusion and sadness. I didn't like to see him like that. I prayed desperately for things to cheer up and that I'd be able to see Daddy smile again. Then I heard the Mistress say something about Freddie. My ears perked up at the mention of Fred. He was a paraplegic, from what the Master said, from a motorcycle accident that had left him unable to use his legs, so he had to sit in a chair with wheels. Fred was always good to me when he visited us; he'd always have a bag of Dog Delights for me. I could tell when he was over because he'd whistle and shake the bag of treats, and I'd immediately be at the foot of his wheelchair, jovially panting.

'He's in the hospital from...', Daddy said.

'A fall,' the master adds sadly. Hearing that Fred had an accident made me whimper. I looked at both Master and Mistress, wanting to know if Fred was okay.

They looked at each other for a brief moment before they left their seats walking over to Daddy, who was still in his chair, holding his spoon, looking concerned. Both the Master and Mistress hugged Daddy. The Mistress made noises that were the opposite of laughter... she was crying. It made me miserable. I went under the table, depressed by the sudden shift of mood, and placed my chin on Daddy's knees, whimpering. I heard the mistress in a teary voice say, 'Uncle Freddie died a few hours ago. He's in heaven with Grannie Martha.'

After Mistress Victoria had said that all four of us burst into a song of howls and cries.

***

Heaven's where the dead people go. And Shelby had mentioned that I'm in heaven for animals. That means that... that I'm... dead.

No! It isn't true; it can't be true. I'm not dead! I'm just dreaming. I have to wake up! Everything will be back to normal as soon as I wake up from this nightmare. I'll wake up to my dad holding me in his arms with his loving embrace. He'll pet my fur and give me smooches until my tail starts wagging, and I'll lick his face. He'll tell me to stop only when his face is moist, and he gently pushes my face away, saying that he has school and has to get up to shower and get changed.

Everything will be just like that when I wake up, everything will be alright, I'll be back with my family, and we'll continue with our daily routines. I close my eyes for a minute, and when I open them, my heart sinks. My ears lower. I'm still here, and Shelby continues to gawk at me as if I'm a sorry, depressing zoo exhibit.

I lie down sadly, head resting on my paws and my tail wrapped around my body like a cat. My eyes leaking with the same wet substance that I'd see in my family's eyes when they would mourn... was this what it felt like to cry?

'It can't be, I-I don't want to believe it... I've left my family behind,' I say miserably. 'It was my job to protect them, my job to save them from danger,' I cry. Shelby, witnessing my grief and knowing my pain, lies by my side, her mangy medium fur tangles against mine, warming me up. I feel her tongue rubbing against my coat as I whimper and cry because I'll never be able to see my family again.

'How did this happen? Why did this happen to me? I thought I was a good boy?' I look at Shelby with eyes that beg her to tell me that I was a good boy, but she just looks at me like she's confused, and I can't blame her; she's just met me, after all.

'Atlas, do you remember anything about that night, the night before you woke up here?' Shelby asks me. I look at her as if hearing the front door open and hearing the Master come from wherever he goes during the day. 'Not a lot,' I state.

'I'm sorry for making you remember something terrible, but try to remember what happened that night,' Shelby requests. And I look up into the never-ending sky, trying to remember what happened before I found myself here.

'Well, it started just like every other day, the Master and Mistress were at the place they call "work", and Daddy was at "school". I was alone for most of the day.'

'Perhaps not recalling every single detail. Just that night,' she explains carefully.

'I'll try.' My memories are a little foggy, but I close my eyes and try to remember them in detail.

After dinner, the Master and Mistress put their food leftovers in my bowl, and I ate them happily without much trouble. Daddy then walked to the pantry and shook the bag of Dog Delights to get my attention. It always did; in two seconds, I was already at Daddy's feet, prodding his foot with my paw. He smiled at me joyfully, dug his hand into the bag, and emerged with one of the flavoured beef sticks.

'Who's my good big boy?' he asked.

I bark back, 'ME! ME! I'M A GOOD BIG BOY!' He handed me the beef stick and pet me on the head and behind the ears. He always knew my comfortable spots, and I savoured every moment of being his pet.

'Colin, bedtime. School tomorrow,' the Mistress sang out.

'I know. I'm not five anymore, Mom', Daddy replied. 'Come on, Atlas', he addressed me, and I stayed close behind him as we descend the hallway into the bathroom so daddy could brush his teeth.

I wandered into his room, nudged the door open with my nose, and went inside. Regarding Daddy's room, I went to his clothes wardrobe and pulled off his Jurassic Park pyjamas from the hanger. I trotted happily into the bathroom and dropped them by his feet, panting.

'Thanks, boy,' he praised me with a stroke behind the ears. I loved it when he stroked me behind the ears. When Daddy finished cleaning his teeth, I accompanied him into his bedroom like I always did. But I could sense that something was very wrong, so I didn't go straight into my comfy dog bed like I usually did. My ears pricked up, and I could hear the Master and the Mistress talking, but there was another voice that I didn't know... and I'd met a wide variety of people during my walks with Daddy

and the Master, and I knew their voices well. But this voice didn't match any of those I'd met on walkies or visits to friends' houses.

I stared at Daddy's bedroom door, sensing something terrible. I stepped forward. 'Atlas?' Daddy called to me. But for the first time, I ignored him. I couldn't shake off the tension that something wasn't sitting right with me. So, I decided to investigate. I left Daddy's room and stood there for a bit, listening to the voices coming from the living room. The Master and the Mistress' voices sounded high-pitched and shaky, and the other unrecognisable voice sounded angry and impatient.

'Well, where are they? I don't see the money or the jewels,' snarled the strange voice. What would he want with the Master's valuable paper and the Mistress's pretty rocks? I had foolishly thought to myself.

'Okay, okay, I'll go get them, just put the gun down,' I heard the Master say. My feet started to carry me down the hallway towards the living room. I watched, puzzled and a little frightened, as the Master headed into the kitchen; the sound of the cutlery clinking around inside the drawers as the Master went through them. I saw the Master then rush back into the living room, waving his wallet in the air. What would he do that for? Why would he offer his pouch with his valuable-coloured paper to this stranger? I was so confused.

'Where are the jewels? I don't see the jewels!' The stranger shouted. Now, NOBODY shouts at the Master! It was something I wasn't going to let this stranger get away with. I made my appearance in the living room, standing behind the couch, and inspected the stranger. He was a middle-aged-looking man with curly blonde tufts of hair coming out from under his black beanie. He was dressed in black and was holding something that looked very similar to Daddy's cowboy toys.

'Look, mister, I'm handing you my wallet with $300. Isn't that enough? We don't have much in terms of riches. Just take the wallet, and please leave us alone,' the Master's voice quivered.

The stranger took a step toward the Master and for a minute, I thought he'd take Master Mason's wallet, but what the stranger did instead was unforgivable! Raising that metal L-shaped thingamajig, he thrust it across the Master's face, causing the Master to stagger and the Mistress to cry out his name.

'He was offering you his wallet! What the hell is wrong with you?!'

'Shut up, you black bitch,' the stranger raised the L-shaped thing again to hit the Mistress, but this time I leapt into action! This intruder wasn't going to hurt the Master and Mistress anymore! I'd make sure of that. It was my duty as the Trembley family dog. I'd ensure their protection and safety. I leapt out from behind the couch in front of the Master and Mistress. I growled, bared my teeth at the intruder, telling him to back off and leave my family alone!

'Atlas!' I heard the Mistress call out my name. Don't worry, Mistress Victoria and Master Mason, I'll protect you with my life!

'Bloody meat headed mutt!' the intruder insulted me without fear, and he aimed the L-shaped thing at me. I leapt onto his arm, the arm holding the thingamajig. I heard the Master yell out, 'Atlas, don't!' but that was one order I didn't want to obey. At that moment, I was going to drive this man away and make sure he left with an injury to prove that he was never welcome here again! Not while I, Atlas Trembley still guarded the house!

My teeth latched onto the intruder's arm, and I heard him cry out in pain. GOOD! I thought. Serves you right for hurting my family! The man tried shaking me and pushing me off, but I wouldn't budge. 'ATLAS, PLEASE!' Master Mason called, but I didn't listen. 'DOWN BOY!' I kept a firm grip on the man's arm;

that's when there was a flash, and a piercing sound came, seemingly from the L-shaped thing, and for some reason I felt a hard-shaped acorn inside my belly that hurt me.

'STOP IT! PLEASE' Mistress Victoria screamed, 'YOU CAN HAVE THE JEWELS, JUST LEAVE THE DOG ALONE! WE BEG YOU!' I yelped and was forced to let go, trying to figure out what had just happened; something hard had hit me in the belly. I shook it off; driving this bad man out of the house was my top priority, and I intended to follow it until the man turned tail and left! He hurt my family, and I wouldn't let him get away with it. Growling threateningly at the man, I leapt upon him again. This time, I latched onto the other hand and shook it sharply.

'Tori, call 911!' screamed Master Mason. I kept a hold of the man's arm, digging my teeth into his arm and tasting blood. The blinding light and booming noise erupted again, and I felt double the pain in my belly, but still, I didn't let up! I kept a powerful grip on the man's arm.

'Bloody meat-headed dog! Get off!' No! You'll pay for hitting the Master and Mistress! *I could feel the pressure of the intruder's thing hitting me hard on the head, but I still wouldn't let him go!* 'GET OFFA ME!' *I heard the booming noise and felt triple times the pain in my belly. As much as I wanted to bite this horrible human's arm off, I was forced to let go. And when I did, he smacked me to the ground with his metal thing, and I fell to the floor in a growing puddle of some red stuff.*

The intruder was also bleeding from a giant wound on his wrist. He stumbled back, holding it, watching as it bled. I tried getting back up to chase the man out, but I ended up falling back to the floor. I heard the sound of police sirens wailing outside the house. I wanted to smile, knowing that the bad man was going to be arrested and taken to where bad people go, but I could only feel an immensely sharp pain in my belly.

'Oh my... TORI, CALL THE VET!' I heard the Master call out.

'ATLAS!!!'

Daddy?

The pain was unbearable, but I managed to lift my head and see my daddy staring at me. His face was coated in water. I desperately wanted to get up so I could lick his face and reassure him that everything was going to be okay, but I fell down and whimpered in pain.

'C-Colin! Get behind me', I heard the Mistress say. She tried pushing Daddy away from me, but he broke free from her grasp and ran to where I was lying on the carpet. Hearing his saddened voice broke my heart. He patted the ground and lifted his hand; it was covered in blood that was coming from... me! It was my blood. Daddy was shaking his head; he threw his hands to his eyes and cried into them. I heaved my head at him and managed to lick his knee. The Master and the Mistress knelt by his side. My vision started to go fuzzy, and my sharp hearing became muffled. I laid my head down and whimpered on my dear daddy's leg.

'Atlas! Atlas, please don't leave me! Please wake up, buddy! I need you.' I could feel Daddy's small hands shaking my side and his muffled voice as I could hear my own breathing start to become less and less. I closed my eyes, and everything went black. I couldn't see anything, couldn't hear anything, and couldn't smell anything. Nothing...

I look up at Shelby, my eyes dripping with tears, and say, 'Am I bad that I can no longer protect them? Does my family hate me now?' I whimper, feeling the pain from those metal acorn-shaped things inside me again. Shelby's brown and pink eyes widen. She nudges her head against mine, putting her paws on mine, speaking to me comfortingly, which reminds me of when

Daddy had come home crying, and I had lain down next to him on his bed, with a paw on his knee licking the side of his face.

Shelby reminds me of the face Daddy would give me when he thanked me, grateful for being there for him and for not leaving his side. He was my daddy. I would never even think about forsaking his side for a second. I wish I could be with him now, but I can't.

'Atlas, don't you think for a second that you're a bad boy!' she licks my face. 'You saved your owners from being robbed and possibly getting shot themselves with those "acorns" and ending up in your position. You saved your owner's lives that night! Some dogs can't do that, but you, you valiantly charged head-on into battle despite being shot five times! You managed to drive the intruder away and saved your family and their possessions. You are definitely **not** a bad dog; you're a perfect example of a **good** dog, and you should be proud of what you did last night,' she says and licks me again, but I turn away from her; something is still eating me up like fleas.

'But what if they don't remember me? What if they get another dog and forget about me?'

Shelby pawed my face, telling me to look back at her. 'Atlas, you silly goofball, answer me this, why on earth would the Trembley's forget the good boy that saved their lives?'

'Because they'll have good times with their new dog?' I answer dumbly.

Shelby steps in front of my face again. 'Just because they laugh and have a good time with another dog doesn't mean they'll forget you. I know my owner misses me dearly. I also know that she loves me. Same with your family, you'll ALWAYS be in their hearts and souls. Think of it like this: You're their guardian angel, an angel with a wet nose and a tail. Same with every animal here, we're all Angels with Tails,' Shelby says as she steps back and gives me some time to think about her words.

I think about it—I still want to see my daddy again, but good things come to dogs who wait, and I realise that she's right. I glance at her, and my tail starts to wag nervously. 'Okay, Shelby, I understand'.

Shelby's tail perks up. 'Suppose I better give you a tour around the place', she tells me calmly, once again reassuring me that she isn't a threat.

'Yes, please', I say, watching Shelby turn around but tilt her head back in my direction, beckoning me to follow her. Her tail wags. I nervously stand and follow her through the clouds of heaven.

-Tiger-

I WAS HAVING a nice warm sleep, curled up in my usual position like I always do when I'm home alone or underneath the warm covers of my human's bed, but I can't shake the feeling of someone kneading on me. Not wanting to wake up, I stretch out my paws and continue to sleep soundlessly on the soft surface that feels like my bed, which in tow has been my human's bed. Along with the kneading, I can hear someone's muffled but rather warm voice calling to me. 'Tiger… Tiger, it's time to get up.'

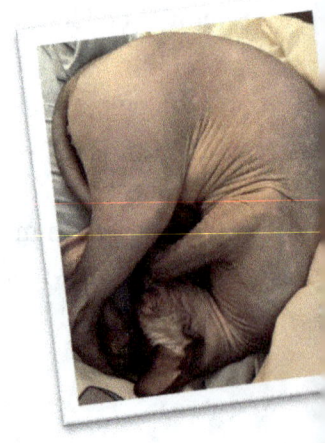

I'm tired, and I don't want to get up, not when I was having such a wonderful rest. I rule it out, thinking the voice simply belongs to Wolfgang Buchenwald; my elderly human owner, going about his daily endeavours to tell me to get up and eat my breakfast, which is usually a tin of GranataPet's DeliCATessen.

'Nein, Wolfgang, I'll get up soon. Right now, I'm too lazy to move. Just keep it room temperature and keep the flies off it, and I'll be out in a second or two,' I say into the blackness.

The kneading resumes, but it feels more arduous this time, as if whoever is doing it is more determined to get me up. I can feel my hairless body coil like the times my claws got stuck on the hand-made Persian carpet Wolfgang had purchased and imported from overseas from a carpet weaver in Afghanistan. Seeing the disappointment on his face as I clawed the carpet had brought some twisted joy to me; it was a game: how long would it take for the old man to notice his precious carpet being torn up? It had been all fun and games for me until I dug a claw deep into the fabric, try as I might, jumping and rolling around, I was unsuccessful in getting my claw free. However, I did try it for a prolonged amount of time until I noticed my human standing in the doorway staring at me. Wolfgang would give me a disgruntled look which said, *what am I going to do with you*, when I looked at him pleadingly, telling him that I had given up trying and that I could use a hand or two to free my paw.

Wolfgang would shake his head at me and say, 'I said you would get stuck one day. I told you not to tear up the carpet. You just can't help yourself.' I wanted to meow my protest, but my logical side knew that he was accurate, that I couldn't help myself when it came to comfortable mats just waiting to be clawed and kneaded upon.

Wolfgang walked over to me, shook his head, and muttered 'cats' under his breath. He knelt to me and picked up my pink paw and the piece of fabric my claw was stuck in. He unwound the fabric from my spur and unhooked it from the rug before putting both it and my paw down. He watched me while I bathe myself in front of him.

'Things are going to change around here, Mister Tiger, no more destroying expensive carpets or furniture. Tomorrow I'm going to buy a few things for you. I'll get the materials and build you a palace fit for a king such as yourself,' he told me. He picked me up, stroked me under the chin, which reminded me that I was his little boy. Oh, it was pure bliss whenever he'd scratch me under the chin.

You've got to love this man.

I remembered that Wolfgang had kept his promise on two things. I knew that he wouldn't have the strength or capacity to manually build a tower, let alone a cat palace, so my human had done the reasonable thing: he purchased a scratching post and a cat château, that he assembled; I loved that darn thing. I'd often sleep in its little cat-sized house or in its basket. But this didn't change the fact that my favourite bed—my real bed—— was inside Wolfgang's double bed.

Most nights when it was time to go to bed, he'd hold up the covers for me, and I would let myself inside. There, I'd snuggle up to him and purr as he put the covers down on me, patting me until we'd both fall asleep. Those moments were one word: wonderful.

'Wake up, Tiger', a faint, muffled voice speaks.

'No, I'm sleeping,' I mumble back. The voice sighs, and the last thing I can process before I'm so rudely awakened is the pricking feeling of another cat digging its claws into my skin. I was enjoying my sleep when the image suddenly takes a different turn, and I see people above me holding needles. I kick at the air and meow. When the claw touches me again, I wake up with a start. The first thing I see is another cat, with white luscious, neatly groomed fur, a short but pretty face, and big blue eyes. I identify the cat's breed as Persian. Those cats are world-renowned for having luscious fur and dazzling eyes. I take a moment to look at the floor and see it's beige coloured, and it feels good on my paws, but when I look down to smell it, it's funny because I can't smell anything. Confused, I look up at the Persian, who is sitting there with her fluffy tail around her front legs.

'Holy kittles, you sleep long,' she speaks to me with a peculiar accent and voice I don't recognise.

'Who are you, madam?' I ask politely.

The white cat snorts and bursts into trills of laughter. She rolls on the floor, kicking the air. I'm so confused. I take a moment to look around and see that everything's grey and white and appears soft and cloudy. Even the floor itself has the same level of softness and texture as the walls around me. The cat appears to blend in with the environment.

What is going on? Where am I?

I look at the Persian cat and demand to know what's so humorous.

'I can bypass the formalities, Tiger, but you said, madam. I'm not a girl; I'm a boy like you! So that makes me a sir!'

I stare at him. Well, judging by the neat state of his coat, he had to belong to a lovely, wealthy family. 'I'm sorry, but you don't look like one,' I say.

'Ayup! I am a born and bred male Persian, and don't worry, my good sir, you are definitely not the first to mistake me for female. Even my own humans had mistaken me for one too when I was handed over to them as a tiny little kitten. Maybe it's just the way I was groomed.'

The fluffy white cat stares at me, his tail flicks. He starts kneading the soft ground happily. 'I know what you must be thinking. What is this place? Why am I here instead of home?' He stole the words from my mouth, and all I can do is stare, tilting my head slightly.

'Well, first up, as a continuation of me being mistaken for a female, my first human, a little girl and daughter to a native New Zealand family named Rita, had named me Koretake.' Koretake, stops kneading and looks away, seeming to be embarrassed for some reason. I ask him what he's so ashamed of, and he quickly fills in the blanks and tells me the translation to his name. 'It's Māori for… Fluffy. I know, it's typical for a little girl around six to name a long-haired Persian like me a girl's name. But at least it's not Miss Kitty or Princess because that would just be humiliating for a boy like me.'

I stare at him and nod, jealous by all that fur to keep him nice and warm. If I want to get warm, I have to be under Wolfgang's bed covers or next to the heater or wait for Wolfgang to run a nice warm bubble bath for me—having no fur has its disadvantages.

'But this isn't about me. This is about you and explaining your purpose for being here and why you aren't with your human or owner, as the dogs like to call them.'

Taking another glance around me, I try to work the answer out, but nothing. My first thought is the vet, the last place I remember clearly before going to sleep and waking up here. But that's when I dismiss the idea of this being the vet, because the animal hospital, I remember, doesn't have a soft floor with clouds painted on it. However, it does remind me of the Schneider household; the place where I was born into a litter of six kittens, four sisters and one brother.

Wolfgang had adopted me at four months, and he'd been the best human a hairless cat like me could want. I was about to ask if I was back in the house where I was born but decide not to, as that would just sound dumb. So, I say nothing, waiting patiently for Koretake to fill in the gaps in my knowledge and provide me with the answers to my much-desired questions.

'What would you say if I told you that you are in heaven for animals?' Koretake suddenly asks me, flipping the conversation around. Now, it is me who is to answer the questions.

'Well, I wouldn't believe you, and I'd tell you to stop pulling my tail and tell me something truthful and not a fragmentation of human imagination.' I answer, and Koretake walks to me and sits by my side, his fluffy tail overlapping mine, making me think even more about him being a female and that he's just pretending to be male. 'Well, Tiger, heaven is indeed a real place, and we are both in it'.

I glance at him, puzzled and slightly insulted. I begin to step back from him, lowering my ears and swinging my tail around to show him my agitation. 'I don't want to believe you… Heaven's a place for the…'

'Dead. 'Fraid so, Tigger.'

'Tiger,' I correct him.

'Whatever, same thing.'

My eyes widen at what's been said to me. 'B-But what about Wolfgang? What's become of my human? Oh, please tell me he's still alive and didn't destroy himself from heartbreak,' I say, beginning to tear up. 'The man's already suffered enough heartbreak'. Koretake lowers his head and bunts me on the chin.

'Don't panic, Tiger, your human is still in the *Land of the Living*. Right now, we need to focus on you.'

My tail flicks around at an uncontrolled pace. 'N-No, I won't allow this to be true! Wolfgang needs me! I'm the only thing he has left! Can I at least see him? Even if it's for a second,' I beg, lowering my posture to him to appoint him the dominant one.

Koretake looks at me like I'd stare at a dog walking in the street, and says, 'I insist yo...'

'Just for a second. Please. He means the world to me,' I say, scared and frightened. I watch an opening in the opaque floor appear next to him. I apprehensively move closer to look into it, expecting Koretake to play a mean game and push me into, it like the one time I went for a walk outside the house and ran into an alley cat who fooled me into getting my head stuck in some smelly trash.

I peer into the opening in the floor, and I see Wolfgang, who's sitting on one of the vet's waiting chairs. Seeing him was enough to make my tail fly up, but when I radiate my ears and listen carefully, I hear him crying. A female human with long yellow hair tied up with some fabric is sitting next to him. She's rubbing his back and saying words of comfort to him. She wears a white overcoat, and I'm given the impression that she's one of the vets. Now that I think of it... she looks uncannily similar to the vet I've seen before falling asleep and before waking up here. That's when I remember: the reason for the vet visit and the reason for me waking up here in... heaven. That visit was my last one. I'd died at the vet and my owner Wolfgang is in the process of mourning me.

'Look at him down there. Gosh, it hurts seeing him like that,' I say sadly, shutting my eyes and looking away, not wanting to see Wolfgang in such a state. When I open them, Wolfgang and the vet are gone, and Koretake is sitting next to me, cuddling up to me. I lie on the soft, hazy floor and hide my face behind my paws.

'I remember everything that happened before waking up here, I say. 'I remember seeing the despair on Wolfgang's face when he noticed the changes in my behaviour. I wouldn't eat, barely moved and was always tired.'

'You were dying?' Koretake asks me sadly, even though I suspect he knows the answer. He can see it on Wolfgang's grieving face that it's evident that I wouldn't come out of the vet breathing.

'Yes.' I remember it all. Even the words the vet had said before the needle was placed in my paw, which made everything go dark within seconds.'

I could tell my life was reaching an end as my body deteriorated with each passing day. It was a few months after my ninetieth birthday. I'd lost all appetite for food; I just wasn't hungry for it. I would try to eat, but it would just fall out of my mouth and back into the bowl. I barely moved from Wolfgang's bed or spent most of my days lethargic, sleeping in the little house that was part of the cat condo he'd bought for me. I lost all my energy and motivation to play with toys, go to the litterbox to do my business. Even cuddling up to Wolfgang in bed was a struggle. My weight began to drop dramatically, which had alarmed Wolfgang; his beloved friend was getting old and dying, and it wouldn't be long until we both would have to say the hardest goodbye ever. At times, I wished I could just die, so the pain would stop, but I continued to cling to life and tolerate the pain because I felt for Wolfgang.

I tried to pretend I was okay and stay strong for him because he loved me dearly, and I knew that for him to see me in such a terrible state must've been splitting his heart into pieces.

'Please don't let it be true. Please let it be sickness. Oh, please don't be dying on me.' They'd been the words Wolfgang whispered on repeat as I lay on the floor, barely breathing and unable to move.

He packed me up in the pet carrier. I'd always hated the transport cage, but this time, I didn't complain or attempt to prevent Wolfgang from putting me in it. I was so weak and bathed in suffering that I couldn't do anything, only breathe heavily as Wolfgang sealed me inside the carrier and packed me inside his giant metal mouse to take me to the local Kleintirpraxis Frankfurt Veterinary clinic.

'Please let it just be minor,' I could hear Wolfgang plead repeatedly. He took me, still inside the carrier, inside the vet. I looked around weakly at the other humans sitting down with their animals, either in carriers or sitting by their sides.

At the counter at the vet, Wolfgang begged. 'Wolfgang Buchenwald, please, I need to see Dr. Wahner urgently! It's my cat, Tiger. I think he's really sick.' I could tell by the distress in his tone. He knew I was dying, but he didn't want to believe it or even mention the word "dying," so he painfully told himself that I was just sick and that Dr Suzanne Wahner would be able to fix me up because she'd done so many times before whenever Wolfgang took me to see her.

That's when I recognised the vet with the yellow hair. That was Suzanne Wahner.

'Please take a seat, Mr. Buchenwald. Dr. Wahner will be with you in a minute,' the woman behind the desk said. Panicked and stressed about what was to come, Wolfgang sat, trying to *reassure me that everything would be okay and that I was just really sick. 'I'm not okay, Wolfgang. You know that, but you tell yourself otherwise. You know that after this, I won't be going back home with you.'*

We didn't have to wait long, as Dr. Wahner had shown up right on time and calmly ushered Wolfgang into the operating room. Suzanne was a healthy-looking young woman in her middle thirties with beautiful sea-blue eyes.

Wolfgang put the carrier holding me on the silver table, Dr. Wahner unlocked it and gently took me out of it. She placed me on the table, touching me with her gloved fingers and with all the medical equipment that humans use to operate on sick or injured animals. I couldn't see Wolfgang, but I could hear his breathing. Unable to move, I listened in closely; my own heart beating slowly. Dr. Wahner sighed as she took those bud things out of her ears. She called Wolfgang over and explained the heartbreaking news to him.

'I'm sorry to say this to you, Wolfgang, but he's in a lot of pain. He's dying from lymphoma, and I'll have to put him down. I could give him antibiotics and medication to possibly keep him going for another few days. If you want my advice, I say you do the honourable thing and end his suffering. You had a good life with him. Just try to remember that.'

After that, my hearing went, and everything became a muffled blur, I could tell that Wolfgang chose for me to get euthanised because I saw those needles come out and the tear on his face, which I was grateful for because the pain I had felt was nothing short of unbearable. Then it just stopped and everything went black.

NOW AS I lay here with Koretake I realise how much I miss Wolfgang, and knowing that I can no longer cuddle and comfort him when no one else will, it just fills my heart with glass. Koretake bunts against my ears then licks them, grooming and comforting me.

'I honestly can't imagine what it must feel like to die at the vet,' he said. I didn't look at him as I muttered, 'Yeah, it's horrible to die, knowing that you're leaving your owners behind.'

'The important thing to remember is that we'll always have a place in our human's hearts. We're angels with tails, my friend, and that's all we need to think about. We gave our owners good memories, and we should feel good about that.'

'Yeah, you're right, Koretake. You're absolutely right,' I agree because his words are valid, and I'll miss Wolfgang daily. But like humans and animals, we all have to find a way to cope with the loved ones we've lost.

'Well, anyway, let's lighten the mood and go somewhere,' Koretake says as he stands and nudges me to do the same.

'Where?' I ask.

'There's an all-you-can-inhale catnip bar if you want to go and have fun with other cats like us,' Koretake's says, his tail standing straight up. I do like the sound of that, even though I'm still overwhelmed with the feeling of being separated from Wolfgang and still concerned about what will become of him as he mourns me.

I'm in need of cheering up, and having some catnip with Koretake seems like the perfect coping mechanism.

I get up. Shake my furless body and say. 'Yes, I'd like that very much, my good sir.' I smile and bunt up against him to show him that I'm eager to go with him and get high on catnip.

Koretake's eyes dilate like he's just seen a mouse scurry across the floor. Showing his beaming happiness along with his perked tail, he leads the way to this catnip bar, and I follow behind him.

-Lilly-

'MUM. MUMMY?! I' I call out in my dream upon hearing a voice. My eyes fly open blurry from waking up so suddenly, but I can still see around me. The area is beige and soft beneath my paws, and in seconds, I'm standing up after hearing someone call out my name and recognising the voice as my Mummy's.

I look around, trying to find her: left, right, up, and down, behind me, but I can't see her. She calls out my name, so it's my duty to find her so we can play together like we always do.

She probably has food ready for me, or the rest of the family might be coming over for dinner, or even better she got me another green ball to chase since my other one has strangely ended up in pieces. I can't decide! All three-options sound amazing! 'Mummy! Mummy? Where are you, Mummy?' I call out to her but was given no reply, so I call out again. 'Is the rest of the family coming over? Is dinner ready? Mummy?' I call out to her, tail wagging and panting happily.

That's when my eyes adjust even more, and I can see that I'm not at home, the park, or at any of my other family members' houses. I'm in a place I don't recognise one bit; everything is a mixture of white and grey or beige. I can't smell anything, but it feels soft and warm beneath my paws. It seems and looks like a friendly place with there being nothing scary or harmful, but none of this means a thing if I can't find my mummy. She has to be here with me; there isn't a single moment that I'm not by her side.

I'm her loyal Jack Russell, and it's my sworn duty to stick by her whatever the condition or situation is. That's the sole purpose of being a faithful dog: to protect and ensure the Master's happiness, especially when the Master is sad or feeling unwell. It's a dog's job to make sure they don't feel lonely, and I make sure I do that job to its fullest.

I never like leaving my mummy's side not even for a second, so when she'd go into the room with the word "Toilet" on the door, I'd try to follow her inside, but she'd tell me, 'No, Lilly'. I do as I'm told and leave her alone until she's done. Then, the first thing she's greeted with is me, sitting down in front of her, playfully wagging my tail and panting my tongue as if I know she's hiding the green ball behind her back and that it's almost playtime. It has to be playtime.

I start to worry. I keep calling out to Mummy, but there's no answer, nor did Mummy show herself to me. Did she abandon...? No! She didn't. She wouldn't! Mummy wouldn't even contemplate the idea of leaving me behind because she loves me just as much as I love her. I've been part of her family from the first moment she met me at the place of my birth in a place called Baghdad, in Tasmania, Australia, I think.

At the first meeting, I was still very young and had just opened my eyes along with the rest of my siblings, well, brothers. I was the only girl among five brothers. I'd also been the runt of the litter, so I was smaller and the youngest of my siblings. But that didn't bother any of my brothers and parents. We were still very young and had so much growing to do before we'd be sent away to separate homes, to live with a different family than our own. Because the people looking after us couldn't raise two adult Jack Russells and six puppies on their own, so we had to be sent away to different homes to live our lives with other forever families.

Like my brothers, I didn't like the thought of leaving my blood parents behind, and from the looks of them, they didn't like it either, but they'd tried their best to put on happy and brave faces for our sake.

'The Mistress and the young Masters can no longer look after us as a whole family, as much as I want you all by mine and your mother's side. We can't go against the Mistress's wishes.' Our father had carefully explained to us. 'Try to imagine what your new home could be like; think about how many friends you might make when you go on walks when you're older. We were just like you once. We were puppies like you.' I didn't forget my mother's kind words. Then came my adoption day, and I was introduced to the best dog mum ever!

'Lilly,' there's that familiar voice again! My ears perk, and my tail is back into the daily wagging routine. 'I hear you, Mummy! Just come out, and we can go back home together!' I call out to her again, expecting Mummy to come out and greet me with loving arms.

'Your owner isn't here, I'm sorry to say,' the strange voice tells me.

'Huh?' I look behind me and see a towering black Great Dane sitting before me, looking sad, as if she's lost her favourite toy or, worse, her owner. Feeling no fear towards this giant dog, I simply stand and stare up at this dog's height.

'My name is Alexia,' she says. 'You're probably wondering where you are and what's going on,' she says gently.

'If Mummy isn't here, do you know where she is?' I ask her as if I haven't heard what she'd said before about where I was and what was going on. But the main thing I want to know is the whereabouts of Paula Lahey: my mummy.

'I will get to that soon, dear Lilly, but first, I need you to listen to me. What I am about to tell you will be one of, if not the worst thing your ears will ever hear.'

'I've run out of little green balls?'

'No... not exactly,' Alexia says and drops her head low to show that she's about to say something far worse than me losing all my prized green balls. What could possibly be worse than losing my favourite stash of little green balls? I remember when I lost one; I felt lost and incomplete until it was found in the drawer in Beth's room.

My eyes widen when it comes to me, the worst possible thing in the history of dog-kind!

'DID MUMMY DIE?!' I yelp, staring pleadingly into the giant dog's brown eyes.

Alexia looks flabbergasted. 'No! Goodness no! Your owner is still alive and well. It's you who died. Not your owner, Paula.'

I am speechless at first, unsure how to react to this news. My body is frozen; my mouth hangs open. I stare aimlessly at Alexia, trying to process the words she's told me.

I've died instead of Mummy? I don't know how to react to this at first. But when I do... I stare at Alexia, shaking my head, both in denial and in sorrow.

legs. I begin whimpering and yelping as if I've stepped on another piece of glass that was left on the ground, like I did when Uncle Jacob had accidentally knocked over a glass cup on the kitchen table, causing it to break upon hitting the ground. It had been cleaned up, of course, but some really tiny pieces remained. I happened to step on one. I was taken to the emergency vet shortly after.

I've always hated going to the vet. They'd injected me with this pointy thing that would always put me to sleep, and I hated it when they put that thing in me, because it stung, but when I would wake up and was allowed to go home, I kept falling over and I had no idea why.

Uncle Jacob had always found it amusing when I'd stumble and fall over, and as long as he and Cousin Jackie were smiling and having a blast, nothing else mattered. I love making my family happy as much as I love playing and chasing after those little green balls. So, to hear that I've died and knowing for a fact that I'm never going to see them again makes me sad and depressed. Nothing else has mattered in this world other than my family's happiness. They are my world, my life.

What is my family doing now? How are they coping with knowing that they can no longer rely on me to make their day better? Are they thinking about me? No! Alexia's lying! She has to be! I'm not dead! I can't be dead! I'm alive and just having one of those awful dreams. 'This is all a dream, and when I wake up, everything will be back to normal, and I'll be welcomed into Mummy's loving arms again. I have to be in her arms again; I have to be on her lap as she knits, I have to be! I'll wake up, and Mummy will be overjoyed. Just wait and see; she'll envelop her arms around me and hug me! She'll say goodbye to the vet take me home and let me sleep in her bed.

'Lilly plea…'

'NO! NOT TRUE! LIES! I WON'T BELIEVE IT!' I yelp. I back away from the big dog, bring my paw to my mouth, and start biting it in a last moment attempt to wake up and return back to my mummy's loving, warm arms.

'LILLY, STOP IT!' barks Alexia, but she isn't my Mummy, so I don't stop. I continue to bite my own paw until it hurts, and I can taste my own blood. 'WAKE UP!' I yelp. 'I'm coming, Mummy! I'm coming home!' I keep telling myself until Alexia approaches, smacks me on the head with her oversized paw, forcing me to stop hurting myself. She lies down and covers my paws with her own, preventing me from chewing them. 'Stop it!' I wail to her. 'I want to go home! I want to see Mummy again!'

'You can't! That's what I'm trying to tell you. You died. That's why you're here. There are other pets here that have gone through the same thing you're going through right now. Biting yourself won't take you back. As much as you want to deny it, you cannot return back to the Land of the Living. I'm really sorry to tell you this,' Alexia says to me.

I look at her, feeling a strange wetness trickle from my eyes and down my fur. 'Bu-But I want to see Mummy again. I didn't even get a chance to say goodbye,' I tell her, and Alexia stands to join me by my side where she puts a paw around me.

'I know you want to see your owner again. We all do. But we just have to come to terms with the fact we have to do without them for a while.'

'For a while?' You're saying I can see her again?' I ask her earnestly. Alexia looks down at me sadly, but I can see some signs of hope inside her eyes.

'Well, yes... when they eventually die themselves, because nothing lives forever.'

My tail slowly begins to wag at the thought that I will one day be reunited with Mummy. I lick Alexia's leg, and she lowers her head and licks me on the head. My tail wags more at the feeling of Alexia licking me on the head.

'Now I know this is not the time to ask this of you because you've only just calmed down after I explained your situation, but heaven needs a record, in your own words, of your last moments before waking up here. So, could you tell me what happened the night before you went to sleep and woke up here? I know it will be hard for you to recollect the events leading to your passing, but try to stay strong and tell me.'

Darn it, why did she have to ruin the pleasure of the moment for something so heartbreaking and something I would much like to forget. I want to say something that would distance her from the question, but I don't know what to say. So, I sigh. I know I won't be able to puppy-eye my way out of this, even though it always worked with the humans. I'll have to tell her what I remember about that night and try not to burst into howls at the thoughts.

It takes quite a bit to reach the events of last night before waking up here because most of the memories I had with my human family were good and were nowhere near considered sad. Well, maybe aside from that one time. I stepped on that piece of glass and had to be sent to the vet, so it could be removed with professional, gentle hands. They had to put me under this thing they called "anaesthesia" to make me fall asleep and send me back to the land of bones and tennis balls.

That's when I find it; the memories of my last moments. Recalling the emotions I sensed when the pain from the shard of glass wedged in my paw, and the dread I'd felt when Uncle Jacob took me in Mummy's car to the vet. I remember it like the time I was rolling in the grass, and a bee happened to be in the way. I got stung on the back. I remember it like that and already want to forget it because it was a particularly unpleasant and embarrassing chapter in my life that I don't want to acknowledge in my essentially positive and happy life with the Lahey family. Bees are annoying. But now that the memories are in my head, I suppose I have to share this with Alexia.

The last nights before that one night hadn't been so happy either, which I honestly hated. I hated feeling sad because if I was sad, I wouldn't have the motivation to eat, play or do anything. And when I was like that, it would make Mummy miserable. I hated it; I never liked seeing her with an upside-down smile. I would just lie in one spot and listen sadly to words Mummy would say to Uncle Jacob on her small rectangular thing.

'She's not eating, she won't move, she won't even go out for walkies with Beth like she used to,' I heard Mummy say the magic "W"-word. I wanted to get up and fight this thing that was

holding me back, but my legs wouldn't let me stand, and I just ended up falling back to a lying position, whimpering that I couldn't go for walkies with Mummy's daughter Beth, Uncle Jacob's sister.

I looked up and noticed Mummy looking over in my direction with water leaking out of her eyes. 'Don't cry, Mummy, if you cry, then I'll cry,' *I wanted to say to her but didn't have the strength to even bark.*

'I'm at a loss, Jacob. I don't know what's going on with her,' *I heard Mummy tell Uncle Jacob. He tells her to take me to the vet and see what they think.* Not another vet visit, *I'd thought to myself. And soon after Mummy had said goodbye to Uncle Jacob on the rectangle thing, she came over to me, knelt down and patted me around the ears. My tail wagged at the feeling, but nothing else.*

'Beth, can you get Lilly's harness and strap her in? I'm going to take her to the vet,' *Mummy asked Beth, who looked at me sadly from across the room as if she'd also wanted to cry before leaving my line of view for a minute, only to come back with my pink harness.*

Mummy stood up, went back into the kitchen and picked up her rectangle thing again, and this time, I hear the voice of Dr. Elliot Prendergast, my vet. Beth tenderly picked me up and, put me into the pink harness, and buckled me in. After she did that, she carried me and my feet dangled in the air. Mummy then lowered her rectangle thing, walked over to the kitchen table, reclaimed her handbag and put the rectangle thing in it. She swapped it for her keys, which, hearing them jingle, meant I was getting a car ride. Little did I know that this would be the very last car ride I would ever have with Mummy and Beth.

During the vet trip, I tried to think of the positives I'd had during my life. The first day as a Lahey and seeing Uncle Jacob and Cousin Jackie for the first time. My, time does fly, *I'd thought to myself. I was still a puppy when I'd met the rest of Mummy's big family; Jackie was a little girl when I first met her; she's now an adult. Jackie would spoil me with treats every time she'd come to our house. She was a joy to be around because she'd play with me with the tennis balls that she'd tie inside old socks for me to chew and play with. I can only imagine how she'd react if she saw me in this state.*

At the vet, Beth carried me, Mummy signed me in, and we sat down in the waiting room with other sick or injured animals. It was a greyish-coloured room with a reception desk, chairs and pictures of cats and dogs stuck to the walls. I looked over from where Beth held me and saw a medium-sized dog that looked like it was a crossbreed of a Staffy and a Kelpie. I saw Chelsea on the name tag hanging from the collar and was given the impression that Chelsea was a female. I looked at her owner, well owners (how lucky for Chelsea to have two owners, she must've gotten twice as much love and playtime), two females with short hair were holding hands, one of them crying into the shoulder of the other, while the other one comforted.

'Lilly.' Dr. Prendergast called out my name. I looked at Mummy, who looked down at me. Beth shuddered. She picked me up, carried me into the operating room, and placed me gently on the cold metal table at the doctor's command.

Dr. Elliot Prendergast was a short, stubby man with no hair on his head and faint wrinkles. He wore blue glasses and often liked to carry a piece of paper clipped to a purple board. While on the table, Dr. Prendergast prodded me with all these cold silver things that vets use making me flinch and whimper from these things touching me when all I really wanted was to go home. He rubbed this circle thing over my fur to feel my heartbeat. When it was over, he studied me with a face that I never liked seeing on humans; it was sadness, and that frown on his face told me that he was about to say something terrible.

He removed his glasses and took plugs out of his ears so he could talk to Mummy and Beth, who'd been standing with their backs to the wall, hoping that I was going to be okay. Meanwhile, I was left confused as to why the doctor had taken off his glasses. 'What are you doing, Doc?' *I whimpered, confused.* If you need them to see, why are you taking them off?

'We'll need to do a thorough examination of Lilly,' he said. 'She's going to have to stay here for a few nights. We might be able to slow down what's wrong with her for a few days, and hopefully we'll be able to get her to eat something. But I'll say this, her kidneys are gone... I just hope you're okay with this, Paula. But if you want my advice, I'd say do the honourable thing,' Dr. Prendergast said to Mummy. Mummy nodded in response.

'Yes, you have my permission, Elliot. Do whatever it takes to make Lilly at least eat a doggy biscuit or just something...anything. Do whatever! Just please tell me if she's eating again and if she's ready to come back home.'

But I'm ready to go home now. I don't want to stay there at the vet alone.

Dr. Prendergast nodded, 'We'll let you know if there are any changes in her behaviour and diet,' *he told Mummy, and she looked at him with pleading eyes and her hands cupped together, holding a piece of fabric up to her eyes.*

But Mummy, I want to go home now! I don't want to leave you or Beth, Mummy! Can you please tell Dr. Prendergast that I want to come home now! *I whimpered, and as if hearing me, Mummy came to me on the cold table, leant her wrinkled face over and kissed me on the head before she pet me along the side and bid me farewell.* No! Mummy! Don't leave me!

'Thank you, Elliot,' *she said and after that, she left with Beth. Feeling some strength return to me, I cried loudly, even as Dr Prendergast and some other vets picked me up and gently put me inside of this cage, placed me on top of this colourful, comfy blanket gave me three different toys to play with, a bowl of water and two bowls of wet and dry food.*

'Stay strong, Lilly,' a female vet with short blonde hair and a sad smile said to me. But her words didn't mean a thing to me. How was I possibly supposed to stay strong when I knew that I wasn't going to see Mummy or Beth for the rest of the day.

'Sounds to me like your body was slowly deteriorating from the inside. Did the vets find out what was wrong in the end?' Alexia says glumly to me. I look down at my paws and tell her that I don't know what was wrong with me, and I don't think the vets knew either, just that I was very sick. I explain very clearly to Alexia that each one of those days that I was locked up in that cage had been some of the loneliest days of my life because up until then, I'd never left my Mummy or Beth's sight. I always woke up to either Mummy or Beth opening their eyes to the morning sunshine peering through the window. One of them would then go into the kitchen to open a tin of kangaroo-flavoured My Dog or open a bag of Schmackos and throw one on the floor for me to eat. That hadn't happened at the vet; the only light source I got was the lights in the operating room where I was kept. I rarely left the cage; the only times I was taken out was when the vets worked on me, poking me with those sharp things and putting me to sleep.

I wanted to go home. And when I looked into the faces of those who operated on me, they knew that I did too —by the way I whimpered and cried and tried so desperately to eat the food that I wasn't hungry for—and I could read it in their faces that they didn't want to keep me there and they'd aspired to send me home, but because I was too sick, they couldn't. And it was hurting them just as much as it was hurting me.

Life at the vet wasn't only lonely but boring too. Barely anything happened. Vets came and went, along with other dogs, cats, birds, rabbits, rats and even some lizards. I was alone in my cage. Another dog was in the cell next to me, but we never tried to communicate. I was so physically exhausted and wanted to be left alone, wishing that I could just go home. So, we both were alone and wanted our owners.

One day, the vets gave me a shot of something that'd built up some of my lost energy, and I was able to eat and drink again. I ate the food they prepared for me. I even started occupying myself with the toys they'd left for me, but because they weren't the ones from home, I wasn't as enthused about playing with them because they weren't my toys, and they didn't smell of home. I also didn't have anyone to play with, which only added to my increasing sense of loneliness and longing for home.

There were days I'd hear Dr. Prendergast talking with people on his own rectangle thing, and sometimes I'd listen to him talking to Mummy or Beth. But there was still hope for me because once on day three I even got a visit from Mummy who I was really excited about seeing, forcing my tail to wag. Dr. Prendergast told her that I was eating again, so she'd brought me a bag of Schmackos strips. She put her hand in the bag and took one out for me, and I took it gently from her fingers and chewed on it soundlessly, finally feeling a shred of lost happiness at seeing Mummy's face again and getting to eat one of my favourite treats.

When I was done, I stood up and walked to the door of the cage and stared pleadingly into Mummy's eyes, asking if I could go home. She looked at Dr. Prendergast, who shook his head and slowly patted me through the cage's bars.

'No, I'm afraid I still can't take you home, but it's good to know that you're eating again,' Mummy told me, patting me around the ears as my tail wagged. Then, she told me that she'd see me again and left me alone with those vets again.

'Why can't they understand that I want to go home,' I had mumbled to myself. 'Why don't they see that I don't belong here?' Luckily for me, the next day Mummy came and brought the Schmackos over to cheer me up and reward me for gaining the ability to eat again. Beth had come into the operating room. She had Cousin Jackie by her side. I'd felt my heart leap upon seeing Jackie's elated face in seeing me again, but underneath that smile, I could almost smell her salty tears; it killed her to see me like this, I could tell.

'Hey, Lilly,' she'd greeted me, unlocking the cage, and putting her hand inside to gently pet me across the head and side. 'Look what I brought over for you,' Jackie said, and held up one of my favourite squeaky toys: a carrot with a friendly-looking smile. I stared at the toy, and she put it inside the cage, placing it right in front of me.

'Thought you might want something from home to keep you company,' she said, patting me on the head as I looked at her, thanking her for bringing me something familiar. Her smile then began to quiver and tremble, and I could see water trickling down her cheeks. Beth moved to Jackie's side and gently started to pull her away from me as one of the female vets closed the cage.

'Thinking of you, Lilly. Hopefully, you'll be able to come home again,' Jackie said to me, wiping at her eyes with her hands. I managed to stand and started whimpering after just seeing her and Beth again.

'Dammit, Lilly, don't cry, you'll make me cry,' Jackie said as she wiped at her eyes. Beth was silent by her side, gently tugged at her arm as I cried out for them not to go, not to leave me alone again. 'I miss you, and I hope to see you again soon, Lilly,' she said as her and Jackie left.

The last thing I heard was Jackie's hysteric voice, saying, 'She wants to come home. You can see it in her eyes. She wants to *come home!'* After she left, all I heard were the distant voices and chirps of birds, and I was once again alone, but at least I had Mr Carrot here with me to remind me of home, so I supposed that was a plus.

After that visit I went backwards instead of forwards. My body got worse over the next two days. I went back to not eating; even the Schmackos remained untouched, and I couldn't move or do anything. I'd come to terms with the fact that I wasn't going to go home, so I just moped in my small cage, shutting myself from the world until the time came, and I was taken out of my cage and placed on the table for the final time.

'You sure you're able to do this, Cindy?' came the muffled voice of Dr. Prendergast. The black-haired female vet holding my paw hadn't said anything. She just bit her lip and nodded. Her face was strained. Dr. Elliot Prendergast stood by her side and gave her a reassuring pat on the back as the vet named Cindy brought the sharp nail-like thing to my paw. It pierced through my skin, and because I was already in so much pain, I felt no reaction to the pricking feeling. I looked on as Cindy pushed down on the stick that stood out of the cylinder-nail thing, and this clear liquid was injected into me. Soon after that, all my mobility was lost, and I closed my eyes.

***

I look up at Alexia's eyes. She stares at me in silence before reaching down and licking me on the head, to which I thanked her. 'It's always hard recalling our final moments, but it has to be done,' Alexia says.

'I understand,' I say slowly. Alexia nods, agreeing with me. 'Well, hopefully, you will enjoy your new home here in heaven. I'll stay here in case others such as yourself arrive. Ember here will escort you through heaven and introduce you to the other dogs and the other angels with tails,' Alexia says and steps out of the way. Another dog joins us. This one is medium-sized and is a crossbreed of Kelpie and Spaniel with a beautiful brown and white coat, fluffy tufts on the ears and an even fluffier tail. This new dog named Ember looks over at me, and her tail wags, happy to meet me.

'Hello Lilly, I'm Ember. It's a pleasure to meet you! Welcome to heaven. Now, would you please follow me?' she asks. I look at her, slightly scared, and ask her where we'll go. Ember's tail continues to wag.

Ember starts to pant, her tongue lapping at the air, 'Alexia tells me you love little green bouncy balls.'

'Yeah, I do love tennis balls,' I say as my feet slowly begin carrying me in the direction of Ember, leaving Alexia behind. I'm a little hesitant, but the idea of doing something with tennis balls is appealing to me.

'Well, where we're going, think of it as tennis ball paradise.'

My eyes light up, and my tails starts to wag. 'Will there be lots of balls to play with?' I ask a little sheepishly.

Ember's tail wags even more. 'Heaps! All the balls you could want!'

I go down on my front paws to exhibit the play bow as my tail wags like there's no tomorrow. Ember does the same before we both get up and continue on our way. Onward to Tennis Ball Paradise!

-Mittens-

'STAHP! THAT TICKLES!' I mew happily in my sleep, pawing at the air. Someone's playing with my belly, and it tickles! I feel something sharp but also soft rubbing against my belly. I try to turn around on my paunch, but the tickling doesn't stop. It moves to my back as I laugh, trying to roll over to stop whoever's tickling me!

'Pwease! No more, I get up!' My eyes open, and I see that I'm in a place that I only know from my dreams, of birds and butterflies, and imagining what it would be like to fly with them; floating in the air, laughing with them until I catch up to them, catching them in my mouth.

The ground is very soft, like my bed; it's a light pink, and from what I had remembered hearing from someone, it was called white, or beige?

I don't know much of the world around me because I'm still growing; a kitten of five months old, so everything is still very new, and everything that moves, or is small enough is a toy for me to play with. Even a leaf is fun to play with; knocking it up into the air and swatting at it with my tiny, fuzzy paws is so much fun, and I don't want such a fun thing to end! It's just as fun as chasing flies inside the house, and butterflies in the garden that flutter around the flowerbeds and trees.

I love going down low and stalking the butterflies. I pounce into the air, swatting them. I love playing! But one other thing I enjoy a lot is exploring my surroundings, seeing if there are new things to investigate and find.

I once found a grasshopper in the garden, stalked it and caught it with my paws. It tried getting away, but I picked it up in my mouth and happily took it inside, where I gave it as a present to the small hooman who looks after me. It was my way of saying 'thank you' for taking care of me.

Speaking of hooman, I wonder where she is now. The last thing I remember about her was her conversation with the taller hooman's about wanting to get another kitten to serve as a friend for me when they're out doing what hooman's do throughout the day.

I wonder if they're out getting that friend for me.

'Oh my!' a voice calls. 'One so young to end up here.' I don't recognise the voice, and it's speaking something I don't understand. I'm curious about the voice, and I think this is something good to investigate.

'Pardon?' I mew, spinning around and seeing a dark-coloured cat, bigger than me, sitting with its tail wrapped around its legs, slowly flicking from side to side. Was this the other cat that Hooman said she'd get for me? Looks a little too big for a kitten. Oh! Maybe it was going to be my big brother or sissa!

Regardless, I see this as a perfect moment to learn from watching Marian. I remember when Marian would invite another hooman into the house, Sheila, was the other hooman's name. So, learning from Marian and watching her with Sheila, I tried to make friends with this dark-coloured cat, with pretty-looking green eyes, nicely groomed fur, and a tail that looked fun to play with.

Hooman's always liked to greet each other with, "'Hello'", so I figure I should do that to win this other cat's friendship. I should also introduce myself while also asking to be friends. Yes! Be friendly and kind, and I'll surely make a new friend!

'Hello! My name is Mittens Kushner, and I'm five months old! I live in a house in a place called Edinburgh with a lovely garden full of butterflies to play with! I like to play with leaves and bugs that I find in the garden and at home. I love exploring the house and neighbourhood to see what I can find. Maybe you can come around the house sometime, and we can explore and play together as friends?' I chirp happily like those birds that I'd often see playing in the birdbath in the backyard. I stand looking pleased with my first attempt at making friends; my tail in the air, hopeful that this dark-coloured cat will agree to be my friend. But the dark-coloured cat just stares at me, its tail showing no sign of going up, making my tail fall and my hope disappear. I think I may have said something wrong to upset the cat.

'What wrong? You don't want to be friends?' I ask the dark-coloured cat.

'So young. So naive,' the dark-coloured cat says to me.

I don't understand what the cat's trying to get at. I know I'm young, but what does the cat mean about me being "naive"? I don't understand. I'm so confused. The cat is meowing in words I don't quite understand yet. What does naïve mean? Where am I? Who's this pretty dark-coloured cat? Is the cat just as confused as I am? Is the cat not seeking friends? These are some of the questions that I want to ask, but I don't because I don't want to pester the dark-coloured cat and seem annoying, because by what I can tell by the cat's tail movements, I *am* annoying it. Still, it won't hurt if I ask for the cat's name. Looking up at the cat, I ask for a name while carefully walking a few little steps towards the cat to sniff it. The cat looks down at me and paws me gently on the head as if telling me to look up at it as it tells me its name and answers my question.

'I'm a female Bombay. My name is Noir; it's French for black, matching my coat. I never thought I'd see a kitten as young as you here in heaven,' the cat called Noir tells me, only adding another question to my small, silly mind.

'What is Heff Vin?'

'No, heaven: it's a place where pets and humans alike go when we pass away.' Another puzzle piece was added, which meant more questions and more confusion.

'Pass away? Like going to another home or passing a toy over to another?' I ask Noir, not really giving it any thought and not thinking outside the backyard when it comes to working things out for myself. Which, now that I think of it, did remind me of something I had found before everything went dark, and before waking up here and having a never-ending load of questions to ask Noir in front of me.

Noir's tail flicks, and I step back from her. 'Still so young and inexperienced. You parted from the world at such a young age. Oh dear, oh dear, oh dear. How am I going to explain your situation to you in the best way possible? Think Noir think,' Noir says and holds her head up high as if catching some of the morning sunlight. She closes her eyes to think.

While she does that, I sit down and take a moment to glance at my surroundings, taking in the peaceful environment. I see a portion of the floor stand up like a piece of string from one of the carpets back home; it starts to slowly fly from side to side, like one of the flowers blowing in the direction of the wind. Seeing it as a way to cheer me up and take my mind off the questions that I had for Noir, I start to play with it. I swat at it with my paws, smack it, bite it, and knock it up into the air so I can chase it as it blows peacefully in the sky, me following behind, and my tail perked. Using my legs I bound off the ground so I can swat at it like it's a pesky fly that would buzz around my food if I didn't eat it.

'Mittens?' Noir suddenly calls out to me. I stop playing with the piece of fluff from the ground. My tail drops as I look over to the black cat and answer the call to my name. 'Now I realise that this is all too confusing for you. It is to everyone when they first arrive here and have no idea where they are and why they're here. But don't worry, I'll try my best to explain it in the best way possible. But first, I must ask something of you.'

I look at her with bewilderment. I don't know why she'd want to ask me anything. I won't be of much help to her. I'm young, and I don't know much about anything— just some things that are in my home and the names of some of the hooman's that come by the house, like Marian's friend Sheila and the taller female hooman's mum, whose name is Diana, and of course, Marian, the hooman who looks after me.

'Do you remember what happened to you before you blacked out and woke up here soon after?'

I need some understanding of exactly what she's asking of me, and what kind of stuff she wants me to remember about last night. 'Like what I did, ate, and what toys I played with?' I ask her. Noir shakes her head patiently; tells me I don't need to give her every single little detail about yesterday. She calmly tells me to remember just the essential bits.

'Is it okay if I go to sleep? It helps me remember things more clearly when I'm dreaming,' I ask, looking up at Noir as if she's Marian, and I'm begging her to refill my bowl with more Whiskas dry food.

'Yes, that's fine,' Noir says. 'Your dreams will be projected onto the wall behind you, so I will be able to see them and will grasp an understanding of what happened to you... how you died.'

I don't really understand the last part; I can't hear it properly. 'Okay!' I sing, going to lie on the floor, curling my tail around my body which would usually make Sheila and Marian put their hands to their faces and squeal in happiness, saying that I was the cutest kitten in all of Scotland. That's another thing I've loved about living with the Kushner family. They praise me just for being cute.

'Goodnight!' I mew happily at Noir as I drop my head into my little fuzzy paws and close my eyes, aiming to go to sleep again, and try to do what Noir had asked me.

Not long after I've closed my eyes and fallen to sleep, the dreaming begins. I can see the world once again through my own eyes, as I wake up to the memory of yesterday, with the sun spilling through the box-shaped holes, in the warmth of my little house on what the tall male hooman calls the cat tower. Seeing through yesterday's eyes, I watch myself stretch out my paws and let out a big yawn, ready to start the day. I get up, arched my back to a morning stretch and left the comfort of my soft little house, where I hopped off the platform and wandered into my hooman's room to wake her up by jumping on her bed, paw at her face and mew for her to fill my fish-shaped bowl with some Whiskas kitten food.

The day started just like any other day, me waking up and begging Marian or the tall female hooman for food. It was a fine start to a dream and one that I would want to remember for quite some time. Marian followed me into the kitchen, picked up the bag with the grey coloured kitten on it and opened it. She tipped the bag over the bowl, and the dry food spilled out like what hooman's call "fountains."

I then saw myself eat the food, and I wondered if Noir could see it too. If so, was she getting bored of seeing me eat my food, or was it wonderful to her? Maybe Noir had never tasted Whiskas dry food before—part of me wanted to wake up and tell her just how marvellous and delicious Whiskas is, both wet and dry. But I know that she wouldn't want to hear a tiny kitten talk on and on about food, so I keep dreaming of the events of yesterday, doing what Noir had asked of me.

After I ate my food and drink the bowl of kitty milk Marian had also given me, I decided to do my daily routine, exploring my home and the backyard and playing with the white butterflies that fluttered around the flower garden. I'd been living the life of a kitten to its fullest, and I didn't want it to end. Living like this with the best hooman's ever was so much fun, and Marian was the best hooman to play with!

I left the kitchen and headed straight for the back door, where I mewed, scratched and pawed on the door, begging to be let outside so I could do what all kittens like me do, according to the tall male hooman: explore and get into "trouble."

'You want to go out?' The tall female hooman asked upon coming around the corner with a bowl of rabbit food in her hands. She saw me with a paw on the door, looking up at her pleadingly. I mewed at her, something that always worked on Marian, making her do what I wanted, whenever I wanted it she smiled at me, charmed by my small fuzzy face, walked over in my direction, glanced down and said, 'Such a cutie you are, Mittens,' she told me. She placed her hand on the door, her eyes not leaving mine as I blinked at her, standing up on two legs and putting both front paws on the door as I mewed at her again, insisting on being let outside, so I could play and explore.

'Outside. I want to play outside with the butterflies,' I mew to the tall female hooman, begging to be let outside, so I could play and explore and hopefully bring her, the tall male hooman and Marian a present. The tall female hooman bit her lip and smiled as if trying not to let herself fall victim to my adorableness, but how could she resist looking at a cute little fuzzball like me?

'If I let you out, no more bringing in bugs from the garden and definitely no birds and mice.'

'Aw, but I like bringing you all presents to show how much I love you,' I mewed to her as she turned the door knob and held it open slightly, just enough for me to weasel my way out, so I could enjoy the things I loved so much. 'Hello, backyard!' I mewed cheerfully as I sat on the porch and gazed dreamily up

into the sky, seeing the blinding sun and the blue-coloured sky and the clouds, meaning that the day was going to be another good day for Mittens the kitten doing what Mittens the kitten does best! Exploring and playing with anything that moves. 'Oh dear, I have a feeling I know where this is going,' I hear Noir mumble.

The first place I went to was the birdbath, and I saw some wrens playing in the water and puffing up their feathers. I also saw one blue wren that I hadn't seen before.

'Hello, Mr Bird!' The bird hopped on the edge of the birdbath and stared down at me. 'My name is Mittens', I say to the blue bird. 'I haven't seen you before. Want to come down and play with me?'

'Fat chance, Tabs. You just want to eat me.' The blue wren tweeted at me, turning around and showing me its tail feathers and sending a rod of bird poop at me, which, luckily, I'd dodged.

'Hey! That wasn't very nice, Mr Bird,' I yell out, going down on my front and arching my back up, ready to pounce.

'Oh, that's cute, real cute. Hey ladies, look at this tiny kitten. It thinks it can pounce and jump up here to catch us.' The birds burst into song, saying mean things about me, when I simply asked to be their friend, and if they'd wanted to play with me. Those wrens were meanies, and they weren't worth my time. I gave up trying to pounce and catch them because the birdbath was too big, and my legs were still very small, and I wouldn't be able to make the jump anyway, so I wandered away from the birdbath to explore something else.

Hmm, where haven't I investigated yet? I thought to myself as I sat down under the shade of the blueberry bushes near the backyard fence. I trotted along the fence line until I came to a small opening; a piece of the fence had become unstuck from the ground, standing a few inches apart from where it was meant to stand, creating a gap. How could I not have noticed this before? I wondered to myself. I'd explored the backyard a dozen times. How come I just saw this now? Apparently, I hadn't been paying attention to my surroundings. I had been so focused on chasing those butterflies that I hadn't noticed this until now. No matter! It led into a completely new area. I decided to take the chance to explore it while I could because if the tall hooman's saw this, they'd cover it up, so I'd no longer be able to use it for further explorations.

I squeezed my little body through the gap, my legs pushing me from behind until I flew out, landing flat on my belly. I blinked, gazing up in wonderment at what I was seeing. I was outside the backyard! Outside the Kushner house! Now what stood before me was a massive garden full of enormous trees, with leaves on the top but no flowers surrounding them and no butterflies fluttering around, which made me feel slightly uneasy. The place looked a bit spooky because it looked like I could get lost in there, but nonetheless, it was a new area that I had to investigate, and that's precisely what I'd done.

I trotted through the tall grass, my tail raised, and my eyes set on reaching those massive trees so I could look up at them and admire their sheer size and scale. 'Wow,' I'd mumbled to myself upon seeing something so tall. Was everything outside the backyard this big? I could only imagine the size of the butterflies and birds around here; would they be just as big or even bigger? Part of me wanted to find out, the other part didn't and just wanted to explore the trees and the massive garden they stood inside.

I didn't reach very far when all of a sudden, the nice dream had become very scary, and I didn't like terrifying things. I looked up and noticed the lovely, friendly sun was now gone, hidden behind the puffy white stuff in the sky. My tail went up, my ears flattened, and I lowered myself to the ground. I could feel my fur begin to fuzz up as I took a step backward, and I tried hissing, but it just sounded silly and small.

I started feeling a stream of regret and started feeling very scared. My fur was frizzled up. I began feeling cold when I peered over and heard the sound of running feet coming my way! I wanted to back up, but my little legs wouldn't take me anywhere; they were stuck! So, I watched, really scared, as a large animal resembling a cat bounded before me; its mouth was open, making it look frightening.

'St-Stap! Mu-Mummy!' I cried out, but the giant cat didn't stop, and just as suddenly, the sun disappeared behind the puffy white things and everything went dark.

***

I wake up from the dream, yowling and shaking, paws in the air and ears flat, my fur all puffed up. I start hissing at what I'd dreamt up. I'd never seen anything so scary in my whole life, and I didn't want to see anything like that again. Something like that was far too frightening. No kitten or puppy should have to see it. I want to go home. Where's Mummy? I want my Mummy. I want my Marian to hold me in her arms and cuddle me until I can calm down enough to sleep with her in our bed.

Suddenly, I feel someone touching me, so I zip around, claws out and smack whoever is touching me. It's Noir! She's licking me to calm me down.

'Oh my! I... I SO SOWWY! I didn't know you there!' I squeal, feeling sorry for hurting her in any way.

Noir continues to lick me on the head. I can see water dripping down her black fur.

'Come here, rub yourself against me,' Noir tells me gently, and I do as I'm commanded, walking over to her, and dropping onto her feet, shaking.

'I never could've imagined such a sweet little tabby kitten to have such a horrible end like that,' she says, taking her paws out from underneath me and using them on me, rubbing them against my fur, before laying down herself, resting her paws over me and proceeding to warm my cold, frightened little body up.

'N-Noir?' I mew shakily.

Noir looks down at me. 'Yes?'

'Where's mummy?' I ask her. Noir simply stares at me, not knowing how to answer.

'I don't know, dear Mittens.'

'I want to go home. I want my Mummy. Can I go home now?' Noir blinks her eyes, and looks at me with sadness.

'No, I'm afraid you can't go home.'

Wh-What? What does she mean that I can't go home? I want to go home and be in the arms of the hooman's who looked after and cared for me. Why can't she see that I'm scared and that I want to be with Marian?

'Why?' I ask.

'Because you're dead. Do you know why everything went black as soon as that big scary cat touched you?'

I don't want to think about that big scary cat in that scary dream again.

'Because that mean scary cat killed you. Your curiosity got the better of you, you wandered too far from home and ended up paying for it,' she said resting her head on me. I feel her body starting to shake. 'I'm so sorry, Mittens. I'm so sorry that you went out so horribly.'

It feels like Noir has been comforting me forever, and this strange idea comes to me that I'd always known her, like she was there when I was born twenty-one weeks ago, but I can't work it out. Maybe it's because she's an adult cat and has tended to me with care and she reminds me of my Mummy, not Marian, but my real Mummy. I do feel a lot safer around Noir since that bad dream, and since she'd started to comfort me and make sure that I'm okay.

'You feeling better now, Mittens?' Noir asks me.

I look up at her and nod. I want to call her Mummy, but I can't forget the hooman's who cared for me. But I suppose Noir could be a third mum to me. Marian is number one, real Mummy is number two, and Noir could be number three.

'Are you ready to get up and go somewhere nicer and get some food? You must be hungry for some Whiskas.'

That was something I wasn't going to stray away from. I was actually starving for some Whiskas, and it would be a way of reminding me of home, so I was glad that Noir had mentioned it.

'Yes, please, Noir. I would like that very much,' I tell her, making Noir stand up, being careful not to hit or bump me with her paws. 'Come on then, young Mittens, let's get you something to eat,' she says with a cheerier voice as her tail flicks up.

I get up and stretch my back before going over to her side to follow her. But then I stop, which causes Noir to look back with concern. I remember one of the first questions I had asked her when I first saw her. By looking at her straight tail, did this mean that she...?

'Wait, does this mean that you'll be my friend?' I ask her. Noir's tail tip curls slightly.

'I'll be whatever you want me to be, young Mittens. So, in other words: yes, I'll be your friend.'

I've never been so happy to hear those words. I've always wanted a friend to play with.

Now full of the bubbling joy that I was always known for, I follow happily by Noir's side as she leads me to a place where I can gorge myself on kitty milk and Whiskas's dry food, living the life of a happy kitten again!

Part Two: Hour of Mourning

-Colin Trembley-

2019

'ATLAS! ATLAS!'

'He's gone, Colin…,' said Dad.

'NOO!!' I wail. 'He's badly hurt! Bleeding! We have to get him to the vet. Mom, call the vet. We have to help him!' I scream at Mom, begging her. I try to shake my dog awake.

I look over at Mom, who has the phone in her hand, which tells me that she's already called the vet, but she has a look in her eyes that I don't like. It says that she knows something that I don't, something that I don't want to believe.

I feel Dad beside me, putting his hand on my shoulder and trying to call out to me in a voice that I barely hear over the sound of my own sobbing. I heave and push my dog over, and I gasp when I see the holes… and blood spilling out of them.

I want to try my own version of CPR on him, but I'm scared that I'll push more blood out of him, and I don't want to do that. I don't want to cause Atlas even more pain. I try looking at Dad and try to ask him why he isn't opening his eyes to look at me, but he just shakes his head and keeps telling me that Atlas is gone.

I don't want to believe him, so I shake my head and continue to shove and shake at the dog who has filled a large portion of my life with love and laughter. Atlas isn't just any old rottweiler; he's my dog, my best friend, my family, and I don't want to lose him: the cause of most of my happiness.

It doesn't matter how hard I shake him; my boy won't move. He won't even open his eyes or growl like he'd always done whenever someone tried to wake him or whenever I tried taking one of his chew toys away. I won't accept the fact that Atlas is dead because he can't be! Atlas is built like a tank. He can handle anything and enjoys it when people play rough with him. So why is he choosing not to get up?

'Mom! We must take him to the vet; he's badly hurt and needs the vet, otherwise, he'll die!'

'He already is... look at all the blood he's lost,' Mom says to me, holding her phone in her hands. I feel Dad's grip tighten on my shoulder. I zip my head around to look at him and wipe my eyes.

'Dad, please, he won't move,' I place my hand on his chest and lie my head down, checking for a heartbeat... nothing.

'He's dead, Colin. I'm sorry; there's nothing the vet or we can do. He was shot five times. No dog would be able to survive being shot three times,' Dad says.

'But... but...' I stammer. How am I supposed to do anything without my loving best friend by my side? He needs me. I need him.

Dad's grip tightens. I feel my face tighten and my lips tremble. 'He truly is an amazing dog and doesn't deserve to die like this,' Dad says to me, putting his arm around my shoulders to comfort me while looking at the body of my dog lying on the floor, in his own blood, and all I can do is stare helplessly, hoping that by some miracle, he'll wake up and everything will be alright.

I hear footsteps and look over to see Mom has come over. She kneels beside me. 'Tomorrow, I'll tell your school and say that there's been a death in the family. Christ, it's a miracle that none of us were shot. How are we expected to make our home safer, Mason?' Mom says to me before saying the last part to Dad.

'Good idea, Tori. Colin doesn't need school to put more pressure on him, and I don't know Tori. We'll just have to think about how we can make our home more secure,' Dad says to

Mom before telling me that once I'm ready, we'll go online and look at other dogs to adopt, creating new memories, but only once I'm ready and when the house is safer, so we don't have any other run-ins with bad people.

But the trouble is, I don't think I'll ever be ready to get another dog. Atlas was such a big part of my life, and I don't know what I'll do without him. He isn't just my dog; he's my best friend. He always sat by the front door, his tail wagging, waiting for me to come home from school, which I treasured, because most days at school were bad, and by a bad day at school, I mean I'm a frequent punching bag for some boys older than me.

They push me around every chance they get, trip me, causing me to drop my books, and sometimes, during recess and lunch, they grab me and drag me into one of the boys' toilets and bash me, punching me to the ground where they kick me and laugh, calling me names and mocking me. But because it was a common occurrence for me to be chosen and beaten up in the boy's bathroom, I'd become used to being dragged out of sight and beat up just so these older boys could have a laugh at picking on a skinny little African-Canadian boy with no friends. I didn't bother trying to fight them off, I just endured it, wishing school would just end so I could go home to those who treated me with kindness and love.

They'd do this until another boy who wasn't part of their group would run off and call one of the male teachers, saying, 'Cole Waterson and his friends are bashing up Colin Trembley again in the bathroom next to the gym.' The teacher would then send them home for bullying, even threatening to suspend or expel them if they didn't lay off me.

I'd be taken off to the sick room soon after my visit with the teacher, where I would sit and wait for either Mom or Dad to come and pick me up to take me home, covered in bruises and sometimes with a bloody nose. Thankfully, the teachers were understanding, and I was grateful that some of the kids had the power in them to stand up for me and call the teachers on Cole and his friends.

I hated the fuss of being sent home but I hated it more when Mom or Dad had to take time out of work to pick me up, but I loved coming home, because despite being covered in bruises, I knew that I'd be coming home to a pleased Atlas, waiting at the door for me and ready to smother me with licks and nudges.

He'd bring his favourite pull-rope toy over and drop it in my lap, asking me to play with him. Atlas, indeed, was the best dog a boy like me could have, and he never once failed to cheer me up. Most of the time, I would pick up the pull-rope and play tug-of-war with him, but there were other times I'd give him a pet around the ears and quietly tell him 'no'. Atlas had always understood whenever I'd say 'no.' He'd whine and tilt his head at first, then he'd lick me on the face, lay down and rest his head on my lap, lick my hand whenever I placed it on my knee.

And the times when I came home crying from a terrible day at school, Atlas was always around; the only time he left my sight was to go outside and to his business.

I loved Atlas so much. He was always there for me when I needed him.

'Want me to tell Auntie Esme?' Dad asks me, and I nod without looking at him, my eyes heavy with tears.

I look down at Atlas's unmoving body, place my hand on his belly, and rub it. My hands are shaking, and I can feel my lips are trembling. I can't feel his heartbeat and his stomach is already starting to go cold… meaning that he was well and truly dead. My dog and best friend is gone, and there's nothing the vet or we can do to help him.

Upon coming to that final realisation and letting it sink in that my boy's dead, I throw myself into Dad's chest and hug him.

The sound of my crying is muffled. I can feel Dad rubbing my back as I cry into his chest, saying Atlas's name over and over, praying for a miracle: for Atlas's wounds to be magically healed so he'd wake up with a bark and a whine from seeing us cry.

But that isn't going to happen: I'm never going to see Atlas's happy tail wagging. I'm going to come home after school to an empty house, one where I won't be greeted by the cheerful barks of a happy dog outside the door. Life isn't going to be the same without Atlas... I just know it; he's been by my side since I was two years old.

Although I don't remember much of the first few years; I go by what my parents tell me. My parents said they'd adopted him when he was only a few months old and that he was an adorable puppy.

We did everything together: played together, went on walkies, played at the beach, rolled down hills and even bathed together. Atlas was incredibly loyal and protective of my parents and me. One day, Uncle Freddie tried to sneak up and pretend to rob Mom's purse for a joke, but he was quickly stopped when Atlas saw him acting strangely and barked at him, showing his teeth and growling, before Freddie dropped the act and brought out a bag of treats from inside his vest. Atlas's mood had changed immediately. There were times when Atlas would charge at people who'd looked at us wrong or tried to hurt us, chasing them off before coming back and continuing with our walk.

It's going to be very lonely without him by my side. And the days—because Cole Waterson and his stupid friends bully me—are going to be twice as hard because I won't have a dog to play with, lick my face or cheer me up whenever life gets me down.

***

Should be bury or get him cremated?' Mom asks dad, who sounds closer to where I am, suggesting she's joined us on the floor; Dad still hugging me, rubbing my back and hair.

Dad sighs sadly, 'We'll decide that later, Tori, it's best not to rush things. Right now, we'll mourn the loss of our beloved Atlas,' he tells her before gently pulling me away from the hug and staring right into my teary eyes.

Mom's on her knees next to him. She reaches out a hand to wipe the tears from my eyes. Her breath is shaky as she comforts me. I can tell by the way she wipes under my eyes that she doesn't like seeing me this hurt. I can tell that she's missing Atlas as much as I am.

'Don't worry about going to school tomorrow or for the rest of the week, Colin. Your father and I will sort it out in the morning,' Mom says, putting a hand on my cheek. It looks like they're both struggling to hold in their tears.

'Your Mom is right, Col. Cry as many tears as you want over the week; there's nothing wrong with crying over losing someone you love, plus the shock of being burgled. We'll sort everything out tomorrow morning, okay?'

Mom rubs her fingers through my short black hair, 'We're really sorry about Atlas. If we could do anything to save him, we would. It was that horrible man who killed Atlas.'

'I'll never forgive him... I hope the cops are beating him,' I say bitterly, clenching my fists, feeling an intense bitterness for that man who'd taken my best friend from me.

'I know it's going to be really hard without Atlas, but try to think of all the good times you spent with him. Can you do that?' Dad asks me, but I don't answer him because, in truth, I don't know if I can force my brain to think of all the good times I would have without Atlas, because even if I did think of Atlas, it would just be sad and I would cry even harder. My mind would just show me Atlas's dead boy, lying there on the floor, surrounded by a pool of his own blood. I might even have a nightmare of seeing Atlas die again, seeing him getting shot over and over while I'd be powerless to do anything to stop it. Only left to watch as my dog was killed again.

'Mason, why don't we let him sleep with us? Don't let him sleep alone,' Mom asks Dad. '

'Alright, Col, you hop into bed, we'll be in shortly,' Dad leans over and kisses me tenderly on the forehead, followed by Mom wiping her eyes soon after.

I stand up and begin to head up to their room, but before leaving the living room, I turn my head around, taking one final glance at Atlas's lifeless body, willing him to wake up. He doesn't, and I sniffle, wiping my eyes, and slowly making my way to my parent's room, softly crying.

Thinking of Atlas along the way...

-Wolfgang Buchenwald-

2013

AS I DRIVE back home to Frankfurt, I can't help but play Dr. Suzanne Wahner's fateful words, 'You'll have to put him down,' again and again like a record in my head that's scratched and keeps skipping and repeating the same verse.

The thought haunted the very essence of my soul. Dr. Wehner told me this right before giving me the devastating ultimatum: of paying pricey vet bill after pricey vet bill or doing the hard, but kind thing and allowing my little boy to be euthanised to put an end to his suffering. Suzanne Wahner saw Tiger and me a lot, to know us as regular patients at the vet; to understand that I had wanted the best for Tiger, and that my love for him was unquenchable. Even when he got something stuck in his paw, or eaten something he shouldn't have, it was always Suzanne who'd been assigned to work with Tiger. She knew more than anyone else just how much Tiger meant to me and how devastated and heartbroken I'd be if I were ever to lose my beloved Sphynx cat. But even so, she knew that I'd pick the option that would cause all his pain to end. So, without saying anything and putting a hand over my mouth, I closed my eyes and nodded, telling her that I'd given her permission to go along with the procedure.

I sighed heavily, biting my lip behind my hand and squeezing my eyes shut. She knew that Tiger was the only one keeping my heart together since my family had decided long ago they no longer wanted me in their lives because I was, quote, "naive and stuck in the past".

My two daughters, Carina, and Doreatha, disowned and abandoned me in 2004. Carina and her husband moved to Sweden, and Doreatha and her husband to Italy. My wife Irene also left me for her co-worker Gerald Brandt in 1996. It's now 2013, and I haven't heard anything from them since they left all those years ago. I don't know if it's something I did to them which caused them to leave me. It's the same with my old friend Erwin Feld. We were close until 2010, when he moved away to the top of the country in Kiel. He told me he'd call me and give me his phone number, when he settled in, but he never did. Maybe he forgot, or perhaps I'd done something to push him away. I don't know what I did or if I had done anything at all. I like to think that the reason Erwin didn't call me was because he forgot.

    Tiger was the only one who'd kept my heart at peace and kept me from spiralling into a severe case of depression.

    I adopted Tiger all the way back in 1999 after my wife left and I struggled to keep in contact with the girls on my own; I needed Irene for that.

    I started reading through the newspapers to see if there were any pet adoption ads. Most were dogs, and I was considering getting one, but the listing address: Berlin and Hamburg was too far from where I lived, but I didn't give up; I'd take what I could get as long as it wasn't far from Frankfurt. Then I remembered finding an ad for Sphynx kittens in Mannheim. Perfect! The kittens were hairless, but I hadn't cared for appearances; the new kitten would be my companion, and as long as I raised it right and it filled the empty space in my heart, that was more than acceptable.

    I went to Mannheim, and I left one hundred euros lighter and with a blue and yellow-eyed, seven-month-old male kitten. I'd named the kitten Tiger, thinking that it would fit him because of his strong and fiery attitude. And since then, whenever I made that trip to Mannheim, Tiger was my faithful companion, growing up into a beautiful, wrinkled boy who could always sense when I was feeling down.

He'd announce his presence with a meow or a trill, and he'd jump and knead on my lap before sleeping there, warming up my legs in the process. Tiger has fulfilled his purpose and mended my broken heart. And although he was a cat and they aren't as excitable as dogs, Tiger was just as loyal as a dog, and he loved attention.

A few times, I've actually broken down in happy tears while Tiger's s been sleeping on my lap, so when he'd wake up, he'd see a smile beaming on my face. I'd hug him and thank him for being such a positive influence in my shattered life and for not leaving.

I can't describe just how grateful I was to have Tiger in my life. He's done so much for my mental health that I almost forgot about my family disowning me. As long as I had my little wrinkly boy beside me, I was happy.

They'd been two of the saddest days of my life. Because I'd think and talk with myself about just how much of a failed husband and father I was, remembering one of the last things that she ever said to me, 'You never had time for any of us, it was always work, work, work or some other excuse, and Christ, your house is a bloody museum, get accustomed to the modern world, Dad. Oh, and another thing, did you even love any of us? No, I don't think so, It's always Erwin. You're either at work or with Erwin. ' Basically saying that I'd caused my family to shatter and abandon me. The truth was that I *did* love them. I was just... busy, a lot more then I am now. I'd try to contact my daughters by ringing them and texting them, but I wouldn't get a reply, and my calls would instantly go to voicemail or the answering machine, so I came to the conclusion that my own two daughters, just like their mother, wanted nothing to do with me.

If I didn't have Tiger to comfort me and ease my sorrows, I might've spiralled into depression and become suicidal. Realising that without my family or anyone to talk to during difficult times, there was just no purpose in living. I did have Erwin, but he didn't have a phone.

    Would it be like that now? Is my family still avoiding me even if Tiger is gone? Highly reckon so. The last I'd ever heard from either of them was back in 2004. I doubt they'd even acknowledge my existence, and if they did, they probably still view me as a burden, holding them away from their dreams because I was 'a simple old fart who couldn't accept change' (Carina's words before leaving). They probably wouldn't even bat an eyelid if word got out that I'd hung myself from a ceiling fan. I can imagine them saying things like, 'It's no big loss that he's dead; he was a fossil anyway.'

    I'd tried so hard to be the man my family wanted and needed, tried to give Carina and Doreatha a happy childhood. But in the end, they just followed in their mother Irene's footsteps, and I was left behind to wallow on the sins I'd committed as a husband and father; the sins of being too busy with work and having Erwin as a friend; my ex-wife didn't like or trust Erwin because he was an alcoholic who apparently groped her.

    I pull up onto the driveway of the house that I've lived in my whole life, but I don't get out. I sit in the driver's seat thinking, pondering my mistakes as a human being and the things I could've done better. I look to my side and see the empty carrier, realising that Tiger's absent. His body probably undergoing the process of cremation. I know that I should've been there for my boy during his final moments, but I just couldn't; I couldn't stay there and watch the life leave his eyes. With this thought I throw my head onto the steering wheel and bawl at the idea that I'm now going to live the rest of my life without Tiger.

    Everything is only going to get worse, I can predict myself losing it and succumbing to depression, where I become self-destructive, which will lead to me tying a noose around my neck.

My family had disowned me. Tiger is gone.

I'm all alone.

Alone and afraid of what I might do.

I eventually take the keys out of the ignition, leave the coolness of my car to step out into the heat and lock the car behind me. I trudge sadly into the house, putting my navy-blue trench coat on the hook and kicking off my boots.

Not bothering to clean my tear-stained face, I wander into the living room, not knowing why at first, just standing in the middle of the room, softly sobbing to myself while staring down at the carpet that has pieces of fabric poking out of it like new strings of grass. I clench my fists and look up from the carpet because I don't see the familiar and welcoming sight of a hairless cat kneading on it. I see the photos on the mantelpiece before me, and the landscape painting that my parents had bought years before I was born.

I walk over to the mantelpiece and examine the pictures. Most of them are family photos of myself when I was twenty-seven years younger, when my youngest daughter, Carina, was born back in 1976. I look happy in the pictures. Doreatha was two when Carina was born. Irene is smiling alongside me. She holds baby Carina while I stand beside her, holding Doreatha's hand, smiling broadly while pointing to Carina.

Shrugging off the images of my old family, my eyes dart over to one particular image, and that's when the tears start to form again. I pick up the photo and hold it with both hands, studying the subject immortalised in the frame. It's one of the first pictures I'd ever taken of Tiger, when he was still an inquisitive little boy with baby blue eyes and wrinkled skin. I look at the photo of Tiger as a kitten, my hands shaking as I stare at the curious look on his little face.

I look back up at the mantel, pick up another picture frame, and hold it over the first picture. Again Tiger as the subject; he's older in the second photo and is sleeping on my bed, curled up and looking positively adorable. Even without hair, Tiger had sure kept me warm when he'd snuggle up next to me in bed.

Now, those blissful nights are just memories, and nights are going to be cold and lonely without Tiger sleeping and purring by my side. And I just know that my dreams aren't going to be pleasant ones because I don't have my lovely little boy to comfort me when times are rough, or when my mind wanders off into the harsh memories of my family—the things they'd say or might think about me.

These photographs of Tiger are painful to look at. Still, at the same time, they have provided me with peaceful comfort, knowing that I'd chosen right by not letting him suffer for another minute longer. If Tiger's in heaven, he won't be suffering anymore, the pain he would've felt throughout the recent nights is gone, and he'll be living a life of bliss with other cats like him. And while it's comforting to know that Tiger is no longer suffering, it's painful knowing that he's no longer with me. But I guess it was going to happen sooner or later. Tiger was going to die one way or another. It's the same with everyone else: no one lives forever, and as much as we may think our pets are going to stay with us forever, we all know that they don't.

'I miss you so much, Tiger. You'll always be my little boy,' I sob while staring at both of the photos, holding them together and hugging them, refusing to part with them.

Keeping the pictures to my chest, I venture up the stairs to my now empty room, trying my best to ignore the many scratching posts, toys and condos that I'd bought for Tiger over the years.

While in my room, I peer at the pictures again, inconsolable sobbing at the images of kitten Tiger staring curiously into the camera and sleeping in his usual bagel position.

I set the photographs down on each side of my bedstand so the first thing I see when I wake up is either baby Tiger staring at me or adult Tiger sleeping.

It will take me a while to get over Tiger's death, but waking up to these photos in the morning will at least give me solace, just seeing his lively face, absent of pain is enough to soothe my nerves.

That's when I think about work. I should call and inform them that Tiger passed away and that I wouldn't be there for a few days. Admittedly, my boss, Stefan Gunner, would understand. He's always treated me well at work because Stefan knows that things were hard for me ever since my divorce in 1995 and my two daughters cutting contact with me. He also knows of the strong bond I had with Tiger.

I should ring him and let him know of the current turn of events.

Forcing distance between myself and the lovely photos of my precious boy, I go downstairs to fetch my phone from my bag and dial Stefan's number. Sniffling, I try my best to hold back the tears because it won't sound professional to ring my boss in tears. So, I strive to hold them back until after the call is over.

The receiver remains blank for a few seconds, which I can understand. I'm patient and not in any hurry. In the past, if Stefan didn't pick up instantly, I'd hit the redial button and he'd eventually pick up. And if it's me who's calling, he knows it's essential or urgent.

Finally, Stefan's voice came on. 'Hello? Wolfgang?'

'Hello, Mr Gunner,' I say, trying my hardest to hide my tears and sniffles.

'Good heavens, man, you feeling alright? You sound upset.'

'I...,' I sigh, 'I'm not in the best state right now. I-I was wondering if I could have some time off?' I say, wiping my eyes with my fingers.

'What happened?'

'There's been a death in the family,' I tell him. I hear shock and sadness in his voice before he asks me who's departed.

'My cat, Tiger had to be put down about an hour and a half ago,' I tell him sadly, clenching my eyes, feeling the sting as the tears beg to fall.

'Oh shi-crap...,' he exclaims. 'I know how much Tiger meant to you. Geez, man, I'm so sorry. My condolences, dear friend,' he tells me in a comforting, understanding way. I knew he would. Stefan Gunner wasn't like most bosses; he was kind and generous.

'Thank you,' I simply say.

***

Stefan Gunner spoke gently with Wolfgang Buchenwald. He could understand what the man was going through as Stefan had lost his own pet dog to canine babesiosis all the way back in 2002. So Stefan knew Wolfgang's pain perfectly. Stefan knew how much Tiger had meant to him since Wolfgang often gushed about his hairless cat at the office and how his family had decided to just up and abandon him as if he was a deformed child they didn't want.

Stefan could never correctly understand why Wolfgang's family disowned him. Based on all the years he'd worked with the elderly man. he discovered Wolfgang Buchenwald to be an honest and generous man who only sought to help others rather than himself. He was a kind-hearted, thoughtful man who always strived to do his best for those around him. Stefan could never understand why his wife and two daughters had cut contact with him, considering everything he would do for them, he wasn't poor, he lived in a reasonably pricy house and lived off a reasonable salary, so like Wolfgang, Stefan just couldn't understand why his family hated him and couldn't understand why Irene told him to end his friendship with Erwin, he and Erwin had always been good friends, Stefan had met and liked him, and he couldn't understand why Irene didn't.

***

'The most I can give you is a week. You know that, right?' Stefan confirmed.

"Yes," I say.

'And as soon as that week is over, I want you back here in the office?' he explains.

'Yes, I know. A week is all I need. Thank you, Stefan. Thank you for understanding,' I say, trying and forcing myself to sound pleased, but my feeble attempts falter. I just can't do it. The grief and expanding loneliness are just too much.

'It's my job to look after my employees, Wolfgang. You be sure to look after yourself, alright?' Stefan says heartily.

I sigh again, close my eyes, and let out a breath, finding some relief in knowing that I have a week of uninterrupted mourning and praying for a miracle to get through it.

-Paula Lahey-
2020

MINE AND BETH'S hands are shaking with anticipation. Both of us are waiting for Dr. Prendergast to ring and tell us the news about our dear Lilly. Waiting for the words telling us that Lilly is okay and that we can collect her tomorrow and take her home and, not only will I and my daughter Beth— who's going to be sixty soon, — love to see Lilly healthy again, but my son Jacob and his daughter Jackie would sure love to see the little bundle of joy jumping from couch to couch and chasing after tennis balls.

Beth and I sit around the kitchen table, staring at the phone on the dining table, crossing our hearts, breathing heavily while I bit my lip and shake my fists, hoping Elliot can fix Lilly. It's sunny outside which I take as a sign that things are going to be okay.

After an agonising minute of waiting, the phone rings. I picked it up in a flash, answer it, and bring the phone to my ear, speaking hesitantly and shakily.

'Yes? Elliot? Any news on Lilly?' I ask with hopeful anticipation, waiting for him to tell me the good news, that Lilly would be fit to come home. I look at Beth's face, which, like mine, is webbed with age.

There's a heavy sigh, 'I'm so sorry Paula, there was nothing we could do; Lilly passed away a few minutes ago. I'm really, really sorry, but putting her down was the only way to grant her peace and put an end to all her pain. My team and I tried to save her, but there wasn't anything we could do. I'm so sorry.'

I almost drop the phone… I feel as if I could die of a heart attack because of his words.

'You did the right thing by giving us permission to euthanise her if things didn't go according to plan because I can tell you, at least Lilly isn't suffering.'

I comb my fingers through my white, thinning hair, my hand shaking. I remember giving the doctor permission to do anything necessary, because I didn't want her to suffer. Even if it meant ending her life, I was willing to not let my precious dog suffer anymore and was more than willing to allow Dr. Prendergast to do anything in his power to ensure she was eating and drinking.

I want to reply to Dr. Prendergast, to thank him for telling me and for doing the right thing, but my mouth is dry, and the words won't come out.

So instinctively, I hand the phone to Beth, who can tell by my facial animations that the news was the worst for any dog owner to hear. I sit frozen, my wrinkled hands trembling; hearing this news of Lilly's passing is just so raw and heavy. I wonder if I'll experience another stroke, so I clench my heart, feeling its rapid beats. That's when the memories of Lilly playing with tennis balls and running amuck around the house (especially after the baths) comes crashing into my head, causing my heart immense pain. My mind floods with all those once happy, heart-warming memories that had brought me joy and were now painful and heart-breaking.

It was even more of a struggle to think of something else because most of the good ones were based on all the other dogs I've owned over the years: all dead (Mindy: old age. Molly: run over. Chloe: mauled). The eleven years with Lilly were some of the best moments of my life because she was such a special dog. I know that I'll never be able to see and create more memories like that with Lilly ever again.

I can't imagine a life without her. I clutch at my throbbing heart just as Beth hangs up the phone. She returns it to me, hands shaking, and her eyes stare ahead, unblinking in disbelief. I can see her eyes starting to water up as if the fact that Lilly is gone was only beginning to sink in. I can't blame her; I'm doing the same.

'Oh my,' I hear her whimper as she excuses herself from the table to wander into the living room. I watch Beth from the corner of my eye, seeing her approach one particular corner between the couch and the armchair. Beth leans over, reaching out to grab something.

'Oh!' I squeak, putting my hands to my mouth upon seeing one of the first toys we'd bought for her when she was a puppy; it was the stuffed white rabbit squeaker with long arms and legs that Beth had bought for her all the way back in 2009. It was honestly amazing that she didn't wreck it like her other plush toys.

I watch Beth hold the rabbit toy, staring at it without making a sound, she then embraces it. 'It still has her fur over it,' she says, her voice breaking, making me cry even more.

While Beth hugs the white rabbit toy, I pick up the phone before me. While hesitant at first, I know I have to tell him, so I ring Jacob's number. He quickly picks up soon after, his voice concerned.

'Mum, everything alright? How's Lilly?' It's going to be hard, but I know I have to tell him the news. He loves Lilly as much as his daughter Jackie does and those who've had the pleasure of meeting her.

I don't even try to hold back the tears as I tell him the heart-splitting news.

'Lilly's dead,' I say.

As expected, Jacob's tone becomes distraught in a matter of seconds. 'No… no…' he sniffles. I tell him about how Dr. Prendergast had informed me a few nights before that Lilly was eating again but was still in bad shape and that her kidneys were gone. I explained that I'd given Elliot Prendergast my permission to do whatever was necessary to make sure Lilly didn't suffer. But because Lilly was just so full of life and love, I guess I'd tormented myself into thinking that she'd live forever, and nothing would ever be able to take away her dedication towards the Lahey family.

One thing is definite: I'm going to miss Lilly a lot because as naughty as she might've been, she's family, and it's always depressing to say goodbye to a family member. Especially when it's a dog with the purest of hearts. She's so full of love; she even had an upside-down love heart shape on the side of her.

'Was she in pain?' Jacob asks. I can hear the struggle in his voice as he tries to control himself and speaks with me in a much more precise tone.

'No,' I tell him simply. 'Dr Prendergast said that she didn't suffer and that she's forever free from the pain. He also said to me that I did the right thing by not choosing to keep her alive.'

'That's good... as long as she didn't suffer. Now I'll have to tell Jackie. After that, do you want us to come over and give you and Beth some emotional support?' I was going to turn him down when I thought of Jackie and how she'd react to hearing the news regarding Lilly's passing, but then I revoke the idea and decide it'd be good to see my son and granddaughter again. Beth and I would need the extra support from both Jacob and Jackie, so seeing them would be nice for us both.

'Yes, we'd like that very much,' I say to him. Okay, we'll be there shortly. I'm really sorry about Lilly. Stay strong, Mum. Goodbye.'

'Bye,' I say miserably as the call ends.

I glance over at Beth, sitting on the couch, still clutching the rabbit to her chest. I tell her that Jacob and Jackie will be coming over soon, and Beth simply nods, not saying anything as she goes back to hugging the rabbit toy. I venture into the living room to join her, take the rabbit from her, and embrace it so I can feel and smell Lilly's fur.

But that's when I look over, glancing at the DVD shelf next to the TV. I see a silver frame with a signed drawing of Lilly happily panting—the drawing Jackie had done for me for my eighty-fourth birthday, two years ago.

I stare at the picture for a few seconds, stunned by how much detail the drawing has and how Jackie's captured Lilly's beautiful essence so well, despite having no colour. It's as if Lilly is staring right at me, happily telling me not to worry and that she's in heaven. It's as if she's trying to say to me that she'd had a wonderful life and that she was happy to be my dog. My lips tremble, my eyes become heavy. I pick up the framed drawing of Lilly and sob heavily whilst holding it. I keep it to my chest and cry, my knees threatening to drop, so I heave myself over to the other couch and sit down, caressing the signed drawing like a priceless treasure.

'Beth,' I call, she looks up from the rabbit to me. I hold the picture of Lilly smiling up at her. 'Remember when she'd look like this whenever a little green thing was involved?' Beth stares at the picture, holding her hand out, beckoning me to give it to her. I did. She studies it carefully, putting the rabbit toy on the arm of the chair beside her, stroking the glass over the picture. I watch in sorrow as Beth examines the drawing of Lilly. She then puts her hand to her mouth and makes a choked sound right before handing it back to me and holding her mouth with both hands as she starts sniffling.

'I'm going to miss that face so much, Mum. Her little yap when we'd hold the ball in front of her always made me happy,' she says before reclaiming the rabbit by the arm and holding it close to her heart once again. All the while, I continue to sit on my chair and helplessly stare at the jovial drawing of Lilly. Then, I stand and put the sketch back on the shelf where it belongs. I sit back down on the armchair, hands to my eyes, and bawl into them.

My quaint little house isn't going to feel the same anymore; it will feel lifeless and dull without a little four-legged friend running around like she has the zoomies. And it's only going to get worse when we receive Lilly's ashes in one of those little bags with her name, date of birth and date of death. However, a good outcome of getting her ashes is that we can put them with the ashes of the other dogs we've owned and loved. While Lilly may not be physically with us, we can take some comfort in knowing that she's being looked after and is no longer suffering.

A few minutes later, there's a slow knock at the door, followed by its opening. Jacob, dressed in his tan work attire, grey boots, and a black belt around his waist. Jackie's dressed in a knee-length black and white dress and black sneakers. They both enter the house, daughter behind father.

I see Jacob's face is red; he's been crying but is soon able to control himself, wiping tears away from his cheeks. By his side is Jackie, and my word, her face appeared five times worse than Beth's. Seeing my daughter cry is already painful because it's rare, but to see my granddaughter Jackie crying like this is heartbreaking.

I glance at them both, brushing the tears from my cheeks. Jacob sees me trying to sweep the tears from my face and approaches. I get off the couch, but my body feels heavy, and I feel I'm about to fall, but Jacob helps me by throwing his arms around me. I have to stand on my toes so my weak, frail arms can reach over him and hug him.

'Thank you,' I squeak.

While hugging me, Jacob tells me multiple times that he's sorry for our loss and that Lilly was a lovable dog that didn't bite, didn't get into any fights and was always around when people needed her. I tell him he isn't wrong, that Lilly was one of the best dogs Beth and I had ever owned, and that there would never be another Lilly.

Lilly was always special, even as a puppy. Now, she's going to be engraved in all our hearts as a legend.

***

Jacob Lahey embraced his mother, exchanging soothing words, expressing his utmost displeasure at losing their dear friend and family pet. Jacob felt like his heart had been ripped right out of his chest when Paula had informed him of the egregious news. Knowing that he'd have to pass down the same bit of information to Jackie was going to be twice the struggle for him because underneath her cocky, wonderous talent to generate laughter by just opening her mouth and saying a simple quip, Jackie Lahey is a compassionate and emotional young woman who—if the news is dire, like Lilly's passing—will become a weeping mess, likely to cry herself to sleep at night. And all efforts to cheer her up would be fruitless.

Luckily for Jacob, he didn't need to directly tell Jackie what Paula had told him because Jackie was already in the room when he received the call from Paula. Jackie knew that something disastrous had happened just by listening to her father's vocal tone. When the line ended, Jackie approached Jacob, her eyes starting to lose their cheery sparkle, she asked just three words: 'Did Lilly die?' With lips trembling and eyes leaking, Jacob replied with a nod.

Jacob asked Jackie if she wanted to see how Paula and Beth were coping, and she said yes. Despite knowing what to expect, both father and daughter went to Paula's house to provide her and Beth with some much-needed comfort. At the house, Jackie hugs Beth and Jacob hugs his mother. The roles swap after two minutes of a sympathetic yet bittersweet embrace. Beth goes over to tightly clutch her older brother (by two years) while Paula hugs her granddaughter. Jackie is much like her father has been, apologising repeatedly about how sorry she is that Lilly couldn't be fixed and how the vets were forced to pull the plug to put an end to the pain she was feeling. Jackie gushes about how Lilly had helped her cope during one of her most challenging years when her great-grandmother, on her mother Katie's side had passed away at ninety-two, leaving Katie and Jackie emotional wrecks.

'I only just got out of that very tough year that was 2016, and then Grandma Sophia passed away in 2017. I remember Dad ringing you about it, and you offered to bring Lilly down, which was really helpful and just what I needed. Lilly saw the sadness and loss in my eyes and could tell that I was deeply hurting, so she jumped up on my lap and started licking my hands while also giving me those adorable puppy eyes as I patted her head, making her tail wag. She was one of a kind, a truly wonderful dog. God, I'll miss her, but at least Sophia will look after her, same with my good friend Cassandra's dog Shelby; they'll look after her and make sure she's okay,' Jackie says to Paula, who keeps her arms around her granddaughter, hugging her and not wanting to let go, fearing that if she lets go, she will lose her too.

'I know, she was a lovely dog with a friendly personality,' Paula tells her. Overwhelmed, Jackie places her head on Paula's shoulder, softly sobbing into it, trying hard to stay strong for her grieving grandmother. 'Think of Lilly becoming your guardian angel,' she tells her through tears. Paula slowly nods. It will be challenging, but Paula makes that mental promise to herself that she'll do as Jackie asks her to and try to think of her beloved Jack Russell Terrier as her guardian angel.

-Marian Kushner-
2017

AFTER WE DROVE my best friend, Sheila Leidy back home to Dundee, we returned home shortly after 2pm. Sheila and I had spent the day at the park before it was time to head home so Mum could prepare an early dinner. Once home, I get out of Dad's car and open the gate to the backyard. I begin to look for my white tabby kitten, whom I named Mittens.

'Mittens? I'm home!' I call out. But I don't hear my kitten's playful mew, just the familiar sound of the birds tweeting above me.

Maybe Mittens is asleep, I think to myself. I have to look for her. Oh, goody, a game of hide and seek! My parents and I may have only had her for about four weeks, but I obsessed over the tiny feline.

I play with her every day after school, carry her to bed, and let her sleep in my bed with me because her fur is just so cuddly and fuzzy. We're in love with each other.

Mittens follows me everywhere! Even when I have to go to the toilet, Mittens pushes herself into the bathroom and watches me.

When I call for her, Mittens comes to me. Whenever it's dinner, playtime, or simple cuddle time, I call out to Mittens, and she mews before running to join me.

But this afternoon, I don't get a reply, which is weird; Mittens is nowhere to be seen. At first, I just assume Mittens hasn't heard me, so I call out again, this time louder.

'MITTENS! MUMMY'S HOME! TIME FOR CUDDLES!' Again, I don't hear the familiar and adorable mewing noise that usually comes from Mittens, the only sounds being the birds playing in the birdbath, neighbours chattering, cars whizzing past, and the TV inside. But no familiar mew or sight from Mittens.

'Mittens? Where are you? Why aren't you answering me?' I wonder out loud. I start to look for her around the backyard, under chairs, in the garden, peering through bushes and flowerbeds, searching the yard for my kitten, all while calling out her name. Each time I call, the same silence is present, which is beginning to frighten me.

I can't help shake the scary feeling that something might've happened to Mittens and I know I won't be able to rest until I know my kitten's okay. I have to find her and see if she's alright.

'She's probably sleeping somewhere under the house. Come inside, Marian, you know how Mittens is when she's asleep; nothing can wake her. Sure, she comes when called, but remember she's a cat and cats love to sleep, so expect her not to come all the time,' Dad calls out to me from the kitchen. He's helping Mum cook dinner; a simple vegetable with gravy dish. We always have vegetables with gravy dressing at least once a week.

'But Dad, she would've woken up if she'd heard me calling out to her asking for cuddles,' I whimper, remembering all the times she'd be at my feet in two minutes, mewing happily and playfully, waiting to be picked up and cuddled.

'Do you suppose she got out and something happened to her?' I ask Dad. He's quiet for a few seconds before telling me that it's unlikely since the fence around the house is very strong wood and the gaps are tiny and doubted that Mittens could squeeze her tiny little body through.

I want to believe him, but because I can't hear or see Mittens anywhere, my mind is travelling to the worst-case situations, and I don't think the thoughts will be leaving any time soon. As long as I know Mittens is okay, I'm okay.

But I don't know if she's okay because she won't answer my calls and won't come running to my feet, demanding cuddles. I want more than ever to hold Mittens. I want to feel her fuzzy fur under my fingers and the soft padding of her paws. I want...

'Tea-time!' Mum calls out to me. I won't be able to stay outside looking for Mittens, because my parents will get angry if I don't come inside for tea. So I go inside, take my usual place at the dinner table near the window. There, I sit still and quiet waiting for my plate of veggies to be served.

For some strange reason, I keep finding myself staring at the yellow fish-shaped bowl on the floor in the kitchen near the hallway. It was one of the first things my parents bought for Mittens when they'd told me the news; saying that because I'd been a good girl, had done well in school, and got good grades, they were going to reward me with a kitten of my choice. That fish-shaped pet bowl was one of the first things they'd bought. The other things were a scratching post, a fluffy pink and blue checkerboard patterned pet bed, a plastic bag full of cheap assorted cat toys and two cans of Felix kitten food.

I stare at the bowl as if it were the Barbie doll I'd always wanted. I watch as Mum picks it up, places it on the table counter, and already with a can of Felix in her hand, she scoops half of the can into one of the sides of the bowl before sealing the can of Felix up with some glad wrap so that it won't go off. I say nothing as I watch Mum closely as she puts the half-empty can of Felix back in the fridge. She then put the bowl back onto the floor, hoping Mittens will come in after being drawn to the smell of food.

Dad comes over with my plate of steaming cooked vegetables topped with brown gravy. He set the plate in front of me, but I don't pick up my spoon or fork to dig in like I usually would. I just stare at the serving of food, not hungry. Then he and Mum take their seats opposite me. They start chatting about work (they both work for a real estate company called Hamish's Houses), while eating the food off their plates.

Meanwhile, I continue to sit in my chair, bringing my shoulders in and grasping the tips of my blue dress, staring at the steaming gravy that had been spilled over the mashed potato and peas. My belly is talking, but I personally didn't feel like eating. I honestly just want to go to bed and cry. I miss Mittens greatl, and not knowing where she is or if something has happened to her is making me scared, making me lose my appetite for my dinner.

'You're not eating, Marian?' From the corner of my eye I can see Mum looking at me. She kneels down beside me and gives me a hug, asking me if I'm okay. I shake my head, not taking my eyes off Mitten's fish bowl. I can see both Mum and Dad look over at where I'm looking, and they both make a sad sighing noise. Dad then puts his hand on my shoulder to comfort me and tell me that everything will be alright, and that Mittens will come back. I really want to believe him... but my belly and imagination tell me otherwise, and I can't shake them away to think of something better.

'You know how little kittens are, Marian: they tend to focus on exploring their surroundings. I'm sure she'll come back. She's only lived here for a few weeks, remember? Everything is still very new to her.'

'Your dad's right. Try to cheer up, Marian. Mittens will come back. It might not be tonight, but she'll come back; just think about the good things that will happen tomorrow. I think that she's snuck into one of the neighbours' yards and is sleeping there. Try not to worry dear, who knows, Mrs Dane or Mr Caterwaul might come knocking by tomorrow morning with Mittens in their hands,' Mum tells me, hoping to cheer me up and put a smile on my face. It does, but it isn't my usual cheerful one. It's the one that I make whenever I know something terrible is going to happen.

I manage to shift my eyes away from Mittens' food bowl and instead start to eat my food. I eat what is on my plate until only a few splodges of gravy and potato are left on it. After this, I decide to go to bed early, despite my parents telling me it's only six o'clock. I personally just want to sleep and have an early night. I tell them, and they sigh before allowing me to get up and leave. I get into my pyjamas and lie in bed, forcing myself to go to sleep and dream that Mittens will come home and be happy to see me.

The next morning I've overslept and am awoken by the sound of Mum and Dad talking with Mr Caterwaul downstairs of our two story-house. Dad *was* telling the truth! Our neighbour Angus Caterwaul has found Mittens and is returning her back home! I can't contain the fizzing excitement in my body as I fling the covers off my body, grab my lime-green dressing gown from the hook on my door, put it on and tie the strap around me. I fling the door open— my heart pounding as I skip through the hallway of photos, past the kitchen and living room and finally to the front door where my parents and Mr Caterwaul are standing. But when I see the tip of Mittens' fur poking up from Mr Caterwaul's hands, my feet stop, causing them to skid a few inches on the shiny wooden floor.

'Thank you, Angus,' I hear Dad say, but his voice isn't a tone of bubbling excitement. He sounds sad, very sad. It's the same with Mum: she too speaks in a voice that sounds like she's about to cry or is at least trying to hold back tears.

'I'm really sorry that I couldn't return her back alive, Mr and Mrs Kushner. I know how much this kitten meant to you,' Mr Caterwaul says to my parents.

What does he mean by "return her back alive?" (Wait!) It takes me about five seconds to figure out what Angus Caterwaul means about returning her alive.

'Marian's going to be heartbroken.'

(No...)

'I can imagine. For a little girl to suddenly lose her pet cat, it would be hard on anyone' speaks Mr Caterwaul.

(No!)

Then Mr Caterwaul sees me from behind Mum and Dad, and he tilts his hat to cover his face. 'I do apologise, Zack and Edith, but I believe I have overstayed my welcome. God bless you three,' he says before handing what I suppose is Mittens over to my parents. Then he steps out of the doorway and closes the door on himself. My parents stare at the door for a few seconds before they both turn around to face me.

My kitten, who I've named Mittens, is lying in both their hands, but she isn't moving... and... and she had patches of blood on her white fur, she isn't even making any noises to show the discomfort and pain she's in, meaning she... is... dead.

I don't need my parents to explain what death is to me; I learnt about it in school when a boy named Scott McDenvers spoke about his uncle's best friend dying of this thing called Leukemia and when Dad's older brother Jordon had died in a car accident. So, yeah, I know what death is. But just to confirm, I ask them through teary eyes, they reply with a simple nod.

I'm lost for words.

I want to ask them what happened, but my throat feels dry, and I can't make any noise; even if I want to, my mouth can't make any clear noise. I push my way through the gap between my parents and look at the tiny fury body. I reach out a hand to touch it, feel it and... and... she feels warm. But she isn't moving, her death is... recent. (she died yesterday, so wouldn't be warm)

My parents know that seeing Mittens lying lifeless in their hands is hurting me badly, and they know that I want to know what happened to my Mittens.

'How had she di... ' I ask returning my hand to my body as quickly as if I've just touched a cactus.

'Marian… I think it would be best…,' Dad says.

'I want to know!' I manage to shout in a croaky voice. My knees become weak, and I can no longer support my own weight. I end up falling to the ground, sitting on my knees. I cup my hands like I'm in church, praying to God. I look up into the sad faces of my parents as they hold the lifeless body of my little kitten, not knowing if they should tell me what Mr Caterwaul had told them about what had happened to Mittens and where he found her.

Mum looks at Dad, and he looks back at her. They both make loud sighing noises before Dad tells me to go into the lounge room, sit on the couch and wait for them because they're going to put Mittens down somewhere. I do what I'm told without question and go into the lounge room, sit down, and look at my hands, waiting for my parents to come to talk to me about what happened and what we're going to do with her body.

As I wait for them, listening to the sound of my own sobbing, I remember something happy; how I'd felt on the day Dad had driven us up to the Thomson house to pick Mittens out from a litter of seven.

Dad had picked me up from school, which, from memory, had been another one of those boring days with the teacher that no one liked: Mr Liam Morden. Everyone just calls him Mr Boredom because he speaks in a robotic voice, and drags out his lessons with his slow, emotionless voice. He's just a boring teacher who never makes his classes fun, unlike our English teacher, Mrs Rainbird.

But anyway, Sheila and I had been dying of boredom while in Mr Boredom's math class, when the school bell rang, and the class flew themselves out the doors like a stampede of rhinos. I waved bye to Sheila as her adult brother Aaron Leidy came to pick her up. At the same time, I happily went over to meet Dad, who sat in the car park waiting for me with a grin on his face.

Dad asked me how school was, and I told him it was boring because we had Mr Boredom for pretty much the entire day, making the day drag on and on. He quoted the common saying that school is what I make it, and I tell him that I know because he and Mum say that every time I complain in some way about school and how the lessons bored the heck out of me.

Dad elbowed me in the arm, I looked at him, wondering why on earth Dad had done that. He smiled and winked, asking me if I knew what day it was and where we were going to go before home. I remember I stared at him and shook my head slowly and asked him where, but he didn't tell me. He just smiled at the road, leaving me in the dark because he obviously wanted to surprise me. And he definitely did, because the Thomson's don't live far from where we lived: around the corner and a few houses from where we are, so in about twenty or so minutes we're outside of their home with Mr and Mrs Thomson waiting for us, jolly smiles on their faces. They both walk over to greet Dad like old friends with a 'Hello' and a kindly handshake.

Meanwhile, I stood outside the car, holding the fringe of my uniform's dress. Mrs Thomson saw me, and grinned in a friendly, loving way before approaching me, the lovely smile never leaving her face.

'You must be, Marian? Zack and Edith have told me that you like cats?' she teases. '"Especially kittens?"' I looked at her and nodded shyly before realising that Dad had taken me there to pick out a kitten since I'd done well with my grades and had gotten a good ranking on my school report.

'Do you have kittens?' I asked her brightly, and she'd smiled sweetly at me then and told her husband, Mr Thomson, that she'd take me out back to see Ruby and her litter of five kittens.

When I first looked at those mewing little babies, my heart felt like it had become a puddle of melted ice cream. They were just the cutest little things I have ever seen, and choosing just one was going to be a real job, even more of a chore than cleaning up my room whenever it got messy—the joys of being a kid. There was a total of seven kittens: two completely brown, two mixed with brown and white and three white. The mother cat was a fluffy brown and white tabby with beautiful green eyes. One of the brown and white kittens was a little smaller than the others and that one had been the one I'd chosen, that one had been Mittens.

I was about to relive my memories when both of my parents step into the lounge room, getting me away from that comforting memory of first meeting Mittens and the day we'd taken her home. They have the same grieving expression on their faces as they moved about the room, coming and sitting on opposite sides of me on the couch. Mum puts her arm on my shoulder, and Dad begins to explain to me what Angus Caterwaul had told him and Mum. I listen eagerly, wanting to know, even though it will break my heart.

'Marian... you see... Angus... he...' Dad stammers, unable to get his words out. It breaks my heart even more to see my usually confident dad stutter and trip over his own words like this.

'What your dad is trying to say, sweetie... is that Angus actually doesn't know what happened to Mittens... he was just going on a gut feeling.'

'Yes,' Dad adds. 'He mentioned that he was out doing some gardening, pulling out the weeds, when he heard some yowling: the sound cats make when they fight. After that, he went to investigate, leaving his backyard to go into the area that leads into the forest out back. You know what I'm talking about, right Marian?'

I nod slowly, remembering that outside our backyard is a big scary-looking forest where according to Dad and our other neighbour Mrs Dane the nutcases and smokies go to fool around. It's also the place where a lot of wild animals and feral cats roam.

'Well, Angus said he went over there to see what was going on. He claimed that as soon as he stepped outside, he saw some feral black and tabby cats run away and disappear into the forest. And...'

'And... that's when... he saw...' Mum says. 'The small motionless body of a white tabby kitten. Angus said he went over to investigate closer, and was horrified to find that it was... it was...'

'Mi-Mittens...' Dad says.

I'm lost for words. So, the only thing I can do is to put my hands to my mouth and stare into the faces of my parents as they both looked at me. Mum is silent while Dad is by my side rubbing my shoulder, both telling me they're sorry.

'Mi-Mittens…' I blubber as both my parents throw their arms around me and hug me close as I burst into tears. All while crying out Mittens' name, because I know that my kitten, who I tried to look after and raise, had wandered off and gotten herself killed by another animal while we were out.

Oh, why did you have to wander off Mittens? Why did you have to leave me so quickly? I'll miss you so much...

Part Three – Adjusting

-Atlas-

ADJUSTING TO MY new lifestyle is precisely how I thought it would be: hard. I don't have Daddy Colin to help me along with this journey like he'd always been - ever since I was a puppy. He isn't by my side to reassure me that things will be okay and that nothing terrible's going to happen because he's around to make me feel warm and safe.

Despite being a rottweiler who overpowered him and most of the dogs I'd pass when Colin took me for walks, I always felt a surge of comfort and safety whenever I was around either Daddy Colin or the Master and Mistress.

But now I'm alone in this weird place.

Well, not entirely alone; I have Shelby by my side to hold my paw, and answer any of the questions I have for her; questions about this place that she calls "Heaven".

One of the questions I have for Shelby is if there's a daily routine that animals have to follow: routines like waking up; eating breakfast; going for daily walks; playing with toys; having dinner, and finally, going to sleep. But one of the biggest questions I've saved for Shelby regarded seeing my family and whether I was ever able to see them again in Heaven or if I could at least return back to the Land of the Living to check up on them and see how they're doing. Particularly, to see how Colin's doing? But I suppose that question will come later when things aren't so stressful and overwhelming and when I've become used to the idea of me being… dead.

Following closely behind Shelby, I follow her out of the clouded area to an open space with luscious green grass and a beautiful blue sky with a bright sun shining over the grass. My eyes widen, and my tail stands still. I stare in amazement when I notice there are other animals on the grass that are interacting and playing with each other, not just dogs and cats, but birds of all kinds: horses, rats and mice, and lizards— and fish that are swimming in the air and not in the water! I hear a tiny black and tan-coated chihuahua chasing a big Alaskan Malamute with a beautiful white and silver coat, squeak out in a high voice, 'I'm gonna git ya Aspen!' to which the Alaskan Malamute replies cheerfully with, 'Not with those teeny legs, Jackie!'

I glance at Shelby, who in return glances at me, her tail wagging softly. I don't know what I'm thinking at this time, but Shelby just nods and speaks pleasantly to me and says, 'everyone is your friend, even the cats and other animals here. Everyone is a friend to everyone.'

'But what if the animals hated each other in life?' I finally speak up. Shelby's tail wags a bit more as if she's been waiting for me to ask this question.

'Sometimes arch-rivals can settle their differences and find companionship in Heaven.'

'I'm still not quite sure if I follow you, Shelby,' I say.

'And that's completely understandable, Atlas. Most new angel pets don't understand why this has happened to them and what Heaven really is, but believe me, you'll come to understand soon enough. After you make some friends and learn your way around the place, Heaven will be like your new home.'

I don't think anything would be able to top the incredible memories I had with my real home in Quebec with the Trembley's. But I guess it won't hurt to try and adjust to my new life as an "Angel Pet," whatever that is.

'Heaven is basically designed for the departed to live their lives again, but one without sadness or violence. Its sole purpose is to make its residents feel at peace,' Shelby says.

'Okay... seems nice enough but I'll be the judge if Heaven is truly worthy of being called "home."

'Take as much time as you need to adjust. Every Angel Pet before you has done the same, I did when I first arrived here.'

'Hey! Look!' I hear a male-sounding German Shepard from the middle of the never-ending grass yard. He's staring at me next to Shelby. 'Another recruit is joining us!'

'Ooooh!' meowed a small white and brown fuzzy (looks like a ragdoll) female-sounding cat laying underneath his front paws. 'A Rottweiler, by the looks of it, seems like someone with a story to tell, am I right, Colonel Barkins?' The female cat says to the German Shepard named Colonel Barkins.

'Oi Shelby! Why don't you come and introduce the new recruit to Smudge and I?' Colonel Barkins barks to Shelby, and she barks back with, 'Of course, Colonel, be right over!'

The next thing I know is Shelby's leading me down steps made of the same soft fluffy clouds that I'd first woken up on, and we're heading in the direction of Colonel Barkins or the Colonel as the fluffy cat named Smudge had named him.

'My, my, isn't this one a handsome fellow,' Smudge, the cat, purrs upon seeing my appearance up close. She was then lightly and playfully kicked on the side by Colonel Barkins's foot, stood up straight, looking rightly proud of himself.

'No fawning over the new recruits until I can confirm that they're good pets!' objected the Colonel. This action causes Smudge to turn her head away simply, and she begins to lick at her paws and say, 'Ugh, so Millie Terry, Barkins; your duties were relieved years ago. Just look at the poor boy: he's confused out of his mind.'

Smudge walks toward me, her bushy tail hangs in a straight line in the air as she approaches my paws and starts to sniff them. I stare at the small fluffy cat awkwardly and step away from her, more confused than frightened at this point by this strange cat and her equally odd behaviour.

'Uh… Miss cat, I would prefer…' I say.

'A dog's nose! There! See Smudge, the new recruit wants to be assessed by someone from the Canine USA unit!' barked the Colonel.

Shelby steps before me to save me from the arguing dog and cat. 'Now, now you two, take a step back and give him some space. Remember, Atlas is new, so try not to bombard him, especially you, Colonel Barkins. Don't hassle him about your days in the army, like with most new recruits. Take it slow and ask simple questions about him. As for you, Smudge, yes, he may be a male dog, and I know that you fancy big, strong male dogs, but please, for the life of him, don't groom him until he gives you permission,' she tells them.

'Told you so,' Smudge cheekily says to the Colonel, her tail flicks up. She resumes sniffing my feet while the Colonel sits down and lowers his head submissively towards Shelby.

This makes me think, did Shelby come to him when he arrived in the same way that she had come to me when I'd arrived? Is that why he's submissive towards her? Does Colonel Barkins admire her because of her calm and gentle nature; how she appears more than willing to help those in need —those who are lost and confused like me?

'Yes, of course, Shelby,' he says before he puts his paw up in the air and says something that sounds like something out of those "war" flicks that the Master would watch on the TV back at home (Master…home…). What were they called again? Pledges?

'I swear on mine and my owner's badge that I, Colonel Barkins, will only go on about the glory days of the Canine Unit No. 32 if the new recruit asks for me to disclose such pieces of information.'

I watch as Shelby's tail starts to wag at the Colonel's pledge. This just leaves me more confused as to what's happening and who this dog and cat are.

'Good boy.' She says. She walks over to the German Shepherd and gives him a little lick across the face. This action causes the Colonel's tail to start wagging. And I can't blame him; I'd have loved to be called a good boy again, just like my daddy would call me.

'Well then, suppose proper introductions are in order?' Colonel Barkins asks, dropping the whole Millie Terry attitude thing. *Millie Terry? Doesn't she mean military?*

'Yes, indeed they are because I like this one, and so will you, Colonel Barkins,' comes the small but formal voice of the fluffy cat who's now lying curled up on one of my paws. I've forgotten entirely that the cat named Smudge was even there, totally forgetting that she'd come over to sniff me. But this time, I don't move her away because her soft, fluffy coat is nice and warm. It feels as if I'm in a field of sheep, their woollen fur brushing up against my short, silky fur. It's nice, like the times Daddy would invite me into his bed and cuddle up to me under the covers to keep me warm whenever it was winter and the weather conditions would get really cold.

It gives me some comfort and helps ease some of the homesickness and nervousness that I'm feeling. So, instead of moving, I look down and stare at the cat as she starts to stretch out her fuzzy paws before tucking them back under her body; she looks like something the Master and Mistress would bring home from the store; something wrapped in a plastic bag that was tied with this plastic tag thing. The thing that smelt of wheat inside was cut into thin pieces and often used to make the sandwiches that Daddy would take with him to school. I think I remember hearing the Master call it a loaf of bread, which is what Smudge looks like as she rests on my paw: she looks like a loaf of bread.

'Oh really,' asks the Colonel curiously, wondering why Smudge had told him that she likes me and that he'll like me too. 'Why's that?'

I look down and see Smudge sniffing my other paw, her long, fluffy tail wraps around her petite body. I could swear I can hear the sound of her purring and feel the vibrating sensation emanating from her body. What is she doing? This isn't making any sense to me.

'He has the smell of a hero,' Smudge says.

My eyes widen, I tilt my head, dumbfounded: can she really smell that just from my paws? Can she really smell what I'd done before coming here? I'd heard stuff about cats having good sniffers, but weren't the bloodhound breeds known for having the best dog nose? Do cats have noses like those bloodhounds? I suppose I'll learn a lot of things now that I have the chance to meet and greet with different pets and breeds, learning about their traits, family life and how they're adjusting to life without an owner taking them for walkies, feeding them, playing with them, or cuddling with them on the couch or in bed. I suppose I'll become one of these Angel Pets, and I'll learn to get used to life here in Heaven with other pets like me.

'In other words, he died saving a life. No, he died saving his family!' Shelby explains, standing proudly beside me, making me look down, not feeling proud about it.

'No way,' says Colonel Barkins. He approaches me cautiously, where he then proceeds to sniff around me and stares into my eyes. I take a moment to glance down and see his chained collar with a metal tag dangling beneath it with the engravement Colonel Barkins, Unit No. 32. It flips over to the other side, and it has a number on it: his owner's, I presume, as well as his home address, well… former home address before dying and coming here where he met Smudge, others like him and finally me.

I miss home.

Colonel Barkins stares at me intently, I gulp.

'Suppose I better leave you, boys, and one girl, alone, you seem to have everything under control *N-no! Shelby, wait! I-I don't know what to do!* I'll be at the Boneyard if you need me, ta-da!' And with that, Shelby departs from me. I want to call her back because I don't want her to go just yet but the way the Colonel's eyes are bearing down into mine makes me feel slightly intimidated; the way I'd felt whenever I knew that I'd broken something I wasn't meant to and that either the Master or Mistress would tell me off for it. I fear breaking my eyes away from his will result in something terrible, so I keep my eyes on the Colonels and stand my ground.

'You weren't joshing, Smudge. This fine recruit does have the smell of a hero.' Colonel Barkins then relaxes the sharp look in his eyes and sniffs my side before licking me on a particular spot as if drawn to it and the way it smells.

'Darn,' The Colonel says sadly.

'What does he taste like?' says Smudge, sounding like she's half asleep.

Colonel Barkins glances at the resting cat on my paw. 'For starters, these are the tears of a young boy, no older than ten or eleven.'

Can he also smell the red stuff that came out of me? I wonder.

'Oh ho?' says Smudge.

'My owner was a soldier in the United States Army named Corporal Tim McAndrews; while it seems that our friend Atlas here, had an owner who's a young boy.' He looks back at me, putting a paw on me as if asking for me to lie down and rest my standing legs. I do, and Smudge gets herself comfortable again on both my paws. I stare at the Colonel as he begins to ask me a series of questions about my family.

'Now, I understand if you may want to keep all information regarding your owners private. It's common for the new Angel Pets to not want to say anything as everything is still raw, and they are still confused and heavily distraught about what happened to them and why they're here. But you will be sure to let me or Smudge here know if a question is too confronting and you prefer not to answer it, okay?'

'Okay,' I answer. 'But before you do, can I ask you a question?'

'Sure,' both Smudge and the Colonel say together.

'What's the Boneyard?'

Smudge flicks her tail up to where it hit my bottom jaw like a feather duster. It's exactly what it sounds like.'

'Oh shush, Smudge. But it *is* basically what it sounds like. It's a big cylinder building with an enormous bone on the top. It's the place dogs like us go if we need something to chew, like chew toys and, of course, bones. Shelby's most likely chewing on this massive cow bone that she's been going at for the last few months,' says Colonel Barkins.

'Oh, okay, seems like a place I'd go to a lot,' I say. If it has pull-ropes there, I know that I'll immediately love the Boneyard because nothing makes me happier than playing with my favourite pull-rope toy with my daddy. But the sad thing is... who's going to play tug-of-war with me? Surely, I can't play tug-o-war with other dogs or a darn horse, for that matter. Suppose I can find out when I would get to the Boneyard sooner or later.

'The best part is that you can go as many times as you want, and broken toys will automatically repair themselves. The same goes for bones: they'll magically appear whenever a dog manages to break one,' says Colonel Barkins happily as I feel his tail beating against my bum.

'Heaven truly is a place of no boundaries, no violence, no rules, just you living out a happy, peaceful afterlife. However, I still prefer the Milkbar. Basically, it's a bar for us felines.' Smudge tells me as I glance down at her small fluffy body curled up on my front paws.

'Man, I'd kill for a sheep's bone right now,' the Colonel says dreamily, staring off into grassy terrain while licking his chops. 'But anyway! Back to business, enough about the Boneyard and back to you, Atlas and back to introductions. My name's Colonel Barkins, but feel free to call me The Colonel or just Barkins. I'm from Illinois in the USA. The lazy ragdoll snoozing on your paws is Smudge. She's from Yorkshire in England. And just in case you're wondering, Shelby is from Tasmania in Australia.'

'Atlas, and I'm from Quebec in Canada,' I inform them, getting the introductions out of the way so Barkins can proceed with asking the questions about my life as a Trembley.

'So, may I ask what your owner's name is?'

Phew! At first, I thought he'd ask about how I died considering that I'd just arrived here, wanting to know more details about the heroic thing I'd done for my family before waking up in Heaven. But thankfully, he didn't. I guess he's figured out that because I've only recently died, I'd prefer not to talk about my final minutes in the Land of the Living. I'm grateful; the way he nods seems to look like he's taken that into consideration, and instead, he decides to ask about my family in general. Although it does make me sad to talk about my owners because I know I might never get to see them again… I don't know; I'll have to ask Shelby or another dog that's been here a while and knows how things work.

For now, though, I can at least try to enjoy life here as an Angel Pet and meet new friends to play and eat food with. That will be really nice and will help comfort the loneliness I've felt with each passing second away from my family.

'My daddy's name is Colin Trembley, the Master's name is Mason Trembley, and the Mistress is called Victoria Trembley,' I say, replying to Colonel Barkins' question.

'Is Colin the boy? The one whose tears are soaked into your fur?' The Colonel asks. I look away from him, looking at the grassy patch between my front paws. I nod sadly. Smudge then wakes up to glance up at me. I close my eyes and softly start to whimper.

'Oh, dear,' I hear Smudge's voice, commenting on my gentle whimpers. I feel her get off my paws, her fluffy tail brushing against my chin as she moves away from me. But it isn't long until she comes back, jumping on my back, where she once again offers to make herself comfortable with the furs of my back. With Smudge now off my paws, I can now rest my chin on them and softly whimper. The very idea of knowing that my daddy's tears are stained on my coat is making me sad, and I want to express that sadness by crying.

The next thing I can feel is Colonel Barkins resting his body up to mine in hopes of comforting me. It's a nice gesture and makes me grasp some shared body warmth, but I'm still missing my owners dearly. I wish more than anything to see my family one last time. I want to wake up in front of them and give them one last lick on the cheek before I would have to say goodbye to them all over again.

'I want... ' I say.

'It's alright, Atlas. It's okay to whimper; we've all been in the exact position you're in,' Barkins tells me in a gentle, comforting way as he snuggles his head up against mine. 'Every single pet here has gone through the same thing that you're going through. The important thing to remember and to keep telling yourself is that while you may not be with them physically in the Land of the Living, your memory will always remain there because for humans to lose a pet is just like losing a human family member. It breaks them down to a degree that they feel like they'll never feel better, it's the same with the Colonel and I. When I'd peacefully died of old age, I was distraught leaving my human behind. I thought that I'd never be cheerful again and felt that I could never recover from losing my human. I thought that my human Fiona Arlington wouldn't remember me and that I'd just spend the end of my days moping around Heaven, sleeping and wishing I could die all over again, hoping that everything about me would disappear.

'But then I met Colonel Barkins here when he found me snoozing at the Milkbar with my face submerged in a bowl of milk. He asked me with a normal tone if I was okay and if I needed help. I told him to go away and leave me to die all over again. But he persisted because that's the charm of dogs: they pester you until you feel obligated to let them help you.'

'Oh, shut up, Smudge,' barked The Colonel

I open my eyes again and gazed into the beaming space where I can see other angel pets like me, playing together, tails wagging, horses galloping joyfully, cats having the zoomies, rabbits hopping around, and so much more.

'You see my point, Atlas? Even if you're dead and away from the humans that raised you, you'll always find help here because every pet in Heaven has died and gone through the exact same thing you're going through right now. As for your memory, I'm sure your family have stashes of photographs of your handsome face.'

I cross my paws and blink. Smudge then looks at the floor. 'Once I was sleeping, I got a chance to see Fiona again one time, and I saw her in bed asleep. *Is she implying that we can visit our owners again? In dreams?* She'd been obviously crying; her cheeks are covered with her dried tears. But in her arms, she was holding onto one of my photos that she'd taken some years before. You see, Atlas, your memory will always live on because you were an Angel Pet in life, and even though you died, you've unknowingly spread your wings, found your halo, and truly accepted you're one of us, an angel with a tail, and that's something to feel good about,' Smudge finished her speech.

I continue to stare at what's in front of me. The whimpering stopped. Now I think about Smudge's soothing words and how maybe one day, I might be able to see Daddy or the Master and Mistress again. The very thought has filled my heart with hope, and I lift my head to look over at Colonel Barkins lying next to me.

'Like it or not, Atlas, but we're not going anywhere anytime soon because we're your friends,' Colonel Barkins coos and I can hear the thumping of his tail wagging on the grass. My tail starts to join his, and Smudge comments. 'Welcome to the club, our newest recruit, Atlas Trembley!'

'Thanks, Smudge and Colonel Barkins,' I say and smile as my tail beats the ground even faster. I think I'll like it here in Heaven if Barkins and Smudge stay by my side as my friends. Because they've already made me feel slightly more comfortable about being here, and I'm grateful they even consider me as a friend. I like it. I only wish that Daddy was here to see it.

-Tiger-

IT REALLY IS a catnip bar! The structure outside is dome-shaped, with a giant catnip plant on the top, which seems to be beckoning all the neighbouring cats to come inside. As for the interior of the building, I can't see much of the furniture because it's completely submerged in gallons upon gallons of torn bags of catnip that spill out everywhere.

At first, I'm hesitant about interacting with the catnip piles out of a simple paranoia that something will jump up and give me a proper good fright, so I remain seated at the entrance, tail wrapped around me with my ears reared back.

Then Koretake comes up from behind me and gives me a light tap on the nose with his paw.

'The nip isn't gonna roll itself, Tiger. Come join me, get a real taste of bliss,' he says, trying to usher me over to join him in rolling around in the many mountain-sized piles of catnip and behaving as if we aren't, in fact... dead.

As tempting as it is to follow Koretake, I don't move; the feeling that something is going to jump out and scare me nags at the back of my mind, and I don't like being scared. How can I possibly roll around in catnip like I'd done many times before when I had the zoomies as a tiny kitten? I just can't do it... I can't just forget about Wolfgang Buchenwald and all the trouble he's gone through in his life. I can't goof off with a bunch of stranger-cats. I know that the cats want me to play with them to take my mind off what happened to me, but I'm just not feeling in the mood to play around; I just keep thinking of Wolfgang and how he'll be grieving me.

I love Wolfgang dearly, with all my heart, and I fear that he might contemplate tying a rope around his neck and jump from a tree branch, this would shatter my heart entirely. I wouldn't like the idea of Wolfgang being in a human Heaven so soon.

'Yo! Tiggr! Bring your hairless butt over here. I'd like you to meet someone special!' Koretake's voice calls out to me, and I leap backwards at a start. My back arches, just like I'd done when Wolfgang accidentally stepped on my tail when I was busy having a nice nap on the steps. I look up and see Koretake staring at me —with a short-haired tuxedo cat sitting next to him and grooming its paws, which looks like they have flakes of catnip on them.

'Quite a jumpy fellow, isn't he, *Fluffy*?' says the tuxedo cat in a distinctive female voice and an accent that my first impression hints at being a Spanish one. I watch the banter between the two cats play out in front of me as Koretake whips his head around to look at the black and white tuxedo cat disapprovingly.

'Oi, we've spoken about this before,' the tuxedo cat says.

'I know, but that still isn't gonna stop me from calling you Fluffy because you are, well, fluffy,' The female cat snorts, pawing Koretake on the nose. Koretake looks away from her, his tail gently swishing around in irritation. But his offence doesn't last long. When the female tuxedo cat finishes grooming herself and turns her face up to look at mine, she whispers something into Koretake's ear, which also immediately makes his tail stop swinging. Koretake turns his direction back towards me, his tail curls around his body.

'Hoy Tiger, what's that look for? Come over here and meet a dear friend of mine,' Koretake calls over to me again, and my tail unwinds itself this time. I slowly get up and shamble over to the two cats sitting by two mounds of catnip, waiting for me. My tail is low, and my head is drooped as a sign of submission, but my eyes remain fixed on the two cats before me.

\   Once there I sit down again, trying my hardest not to think of Wolfgang, because if I think of him, I won't be able to keep myself together. I look up into Koretake's blue eyes and the female tux's yellow ones, and I waste no time introducing myself.

'Tiger Buchenwald. I'm really sorry for the way I'm acting. I'm still missing my human dearly, so please forgive me.'

The female cat struts over to me and rubs herself on me. I watch her as she glances at Koretake for a second before returning her gaze towards me.

'You mind if I groom you?' she asks.

At first, I don't know if I want to be groomed by this stranger, but I revoke my doubts and hesitantly nod; being groomed seems nice right now, and I can do with the extra comfort of another cat.

'Well, ain't you gonna introduce yourself to our hairless friend here, Iris?' Koretake says.

'My apologies. My name is Íris De Armando but just call me Iris or Tux. I came from Natal in Brazil, but my adoptive family were originally from somewhere in Portugal. Now, please allow me to clean you as Sphynx cats are four degrees warmer than most of us cats as they tend to sweat from not having a coat. You're probably thinking, how the heck does this strange tuxedo cat know so much about my breed. Before I was found and adopted from the streets of Natal, one of my best friends was a grey sphynx like you. She was a stray who liked to call herself Luiza. I sometimes had to groom her so that she wouldn't sweat.'

I stare wide-eyed at the cat named Iris as she proceeds to groom my back. I look over at Koretake, who simply stares at me. I can hear him purring with contentment.

'I told you she's something special, Koretake says.

'Be a dear, would you, Fluffy, and please cut the jokes,' she says calling him Fluffy again. I knew this would result in an argument between the two cats, so I lie down, resting my head on my paws and stare ahead into the spilling bags of catnip: miserable and missing Wolfgang.

'Can you be a dear? Please stop calling me Fluffy, Iris. You know that my name's Koretake, the…'

'Māori translation, yes I know; you've told me plenty of times before,' Iris says.

'And I'll keep telling you, so you'll learn to call me by my actual name and not a girl's name.'

'Well, Fluffy has a better ring than Koretake,' Iris says, which then makes another cat pop its head out from underneath a pile of catnip. My eyes widen, and my head shoots up toward this other cat whose face is covered in flakes of catnip. The third cat has a beautiful short brown coat and a gentle appearance. The first thought that comes to mind upon seeing this cat is that its breed is an Abyssinian.

'Honestly, you two, you're in the presence of a scared and confused newborn angel here, and here you both are squabbling about Koretake's name being a girl one,' the third cat speaks in a masculine, formal tone with an accent that I pinpoint as being a mix of African and Indian. 'If you're going to continue arguing like a litter of kittens, please take it somewhere else and away from the sphynx,' he says before jumping out of the mountain of catnip. I see his beautiful brown coat and lean figure, which honestly makes me kind of envious of most of the cats here, who have fur to keep them warm.

Again, that was another thing I loved about Wolfgang Buchenwald and was missing greatly; I'd leap onto his lap whenever he sat on the couch or in the rocking or armchair. There, I'd get myself all nice and cosy on his lap until I'd fall asleep on him. The only times I was forced to move was when Wolfgang would gently push me off his lap so he could go and relieve himself in the bathroom. Then he'd come back a few minutes later, sit back down on the couch, return to where he left off in the book, or show he'd been watching on the small television in the living room.

I loved every moment I spent with my old human. I'd give anything to have at least one more day on his lap, just one day with him, to see that smile of joy he always had on his face whenever he'd see me. He'd always have that smile even if I was naughty.

'You two have no sense of humour,' I hear Iris say. Oh, that's right, I'm still stuck in the middle of these three cats arguing. I watch as she stands up and proceeds to strut away, tail up high like those beautiful female snowcats Wolfgang and I used to see on the television. I glance over at Koretake, who's darting his eyes, looking at the third cat and then me, the third cat, me, and so on.

'Hey, thanks for backing me up there,' Koretake speaks with the third cat, whose tail is mildly flicking around.

'I'll take it from here, Koretake. You should go meet Iris at the Milkbar. I'll send the new angel over when I finish with him,' the third cat tells Koretake politely and respectably to go away.

'Oh, okay.' Koretake turns to follow behind Iris but soon stops and turns back to the third cat with a suspecting glint in his blue-slitted eyes. 'You're not gonna mummify him, right?'

Mummify? Was Koretake bonkers? What did he mean by this cat wanting to mummify me? This is the 21st century, right?

'Koretake... leave,' the third cat says.

'Okay, okay, I'm outta here, but be sure to escort him to the Milkbar when you're done, as he won't know where it is.'

'Yes, I know, Koretake. I've been dead for a long, long time. I know what to do with newborn angels,' he says without much life in his voice. Koretake leaves.

***

The lean cat turns his face towards me, then sits down and puffs his chest. He clears his throat before speaking to me in the most formal way I'd ever thought possible for a cat. I think I've been a polite and respectable feline to socialise with, but this cat with the lean body and beautiful short coat has even beat me, honestly making me appear like a stray.

'Apologies for those two, good sir. My name is Pharaoh. I was the pet abyssinian of the local Egyptian archaeologist Samir Hassan in 1724. I died in my sleep in 1731, and who might you be?'

Darn, he wasn't kidding when he said he's been dead for a long time, he's ancient.

'I'm Tiger,' I say simply, not wanting to sound rude by letting the confusion mixed with my own hesitation get the better of me to the point where I'm left speechless. Thankfully, the cat named Pharaoh seems to understand. The way he confidently puffs out his chest and licks his front paws has given me the fast impression that he's a no-nonsense type of cat, easily offended by informalities. So, if I'm to keep a low profile, I'll have to utilise all the formalities that I'd learned from watching Wolfgang interact with neighbours: the newspaper boy, people on the phone and so on.

Pharaoh approaches me confidently and cranes his body to give me a quick sniff of the head before retracting his head saying, 'just as I suspected, you died in the same manner as I did, old age, but instead of dying peacefully in your human's bed like I had done, you had to be euthanised. You want to know how I know this? I saw the hole in which the needle was administered and because I have been here for so long, I have gained the ability to sense when an animal has passed of old age.'

'Ye-Yes, my human Wolfgang Buchenwald couldn't take the thought that I was…'

Suddenly, out of nowhere, Pharaoh dropped the formal talk, he got down on his two front paws in some sort of bow that dogs often do whenever they want to play or whenever they're excited about something and yells out happily. 'Twinsies!' I lean my head away from him, even more confused and all a little frightened by this sudden shift of personality.

'Wuh-What?' I say with a stammer. 'What happened to Pharaoh?'

'Pharaoh is right here, silly. I may be a cat, but I'm an Abyssinian, so that means I share some dog-like traits, and I can't help but go into a play bow whenever I'm excited about meeting a fellow cat who'd died in the same manner as I did and has a story to tell about their lives with their humans. I love a good story!'

I look at Pharaoh, not knowing what I should do or what I should say. The best that comes out of my mouth is to ask him if he likes hearing the sad stories of other pets dying. It honestly makes me a bit concerned because if that's the case, then why was he here if he liked hearing about the despairing tales of animals and their last moments on Earth. Because from the information that I'd gotten from Koretake, Heaven was a place for the purest of angel pets.

His eyes widened, seeming to realise his mistake and how his words might've sounded. He retreats back to his sitting position, his chest-puffing out and looking like the last royal feline prince of Egypt.

'Please, forgive an old feline for getting his words jumbled. You see when the dog part of me is activated, I tend to throw words out without careful consideration. I did not mean to come off in a way that I greatly enjoy hearing about the heartbreaking deaths of other animals,' he confesses awkwardly. 'I'm really sorry that you were on the front line of seeing me in one of my embarrassing dog modes.'

'It's fine, I guess,' I say awkwardly.

'Uhm... Pharaoh?' I ask.

Pharaoh looks right into my yellow and blue eyes, 'Yes, Tiger?'

'While you were in "dog mode", you mentioned that you love a good story. Is that a fact?'

Pharaoh stares at me intently and nods slowly. 'I'm always interested in hearing about the stories of the animals of this day–and–age since my human Samir was a renowned Egyptian archaeologist in charge of looking for ancient tombs and buried treasure for the local museums in Cairo and Luxor,' he looks away slightly, 'Even if I had no idea what they were about, I loved sitting on Samir's shoulder and listening to the stories anyway.'

'Do you... well... want to hear about my human Wolfgang Buchenwald and how before he'd adopted me back in 1999, he contemplated suicide because his family had left him?' I ask him, and Pharaoh's yellow eyes light up with such anticipation that he almost doesn't give me an actual worded answer.

'Yu-You would be willing to talk about that even though you're a newly born angel? Most new angels prefer not to speak about their past lives until later on?'

'Since I'm not leaving here anytime soon and I'll need to learn to cope with it one way or another, I figured this would be a good time to talk about it since you're a cat that seems keen to hear it.'

Pharaoh stares at me with an expression and bright eyes that wants to tell me that I'm brave for wanting to take the plunge and to be so open as to reveal what had gone on during my life with my loving human. But like I'd said to him, I'm not going anywhere anytime soon. Like most pets like me, I'll have to get used to living here in Heaven without Wolfgang. As much as I hate the very thought of leaving my owner alone, I know that this is going to be my new life now and that there's nothing else I can do because I'm dead and in Heaven. But at least Heaven opens many windows for the adventurous felines. I can make friends with the other angel pets here, and if I become more acquainted here, I might reach the stage where I'll be able to tell my story without any issues, like Pharaoh can.

Pharaoh stands up and perks his tail. 'Thank you, Tiger. I commend you and your bravery. Perhaps we should discuss this elsewhere since the Catnip bar is for cats who want to get silly. Want to go to the Milkbar and meet up with Koretake and Tux? I'm sure they will also like to hear it.'

I join him in standing; my tail perks up, although not wholly straight like Pharaoh's; mine has a slight friendly curl at the tip. 'Yeah, that sounds nice. Are you going to escort me there?' I ask.

'Of course, Tiger, what kind of cat do you take me for? I'm not the kind of feline to just abandon a newly born angel upon first meeting. Please follow me.'

With that said, Pharaoh leads, beginning to walk in front of me. I follow close behind him, tail up and curled, ears perked and body straight as he leads me over to the Milkbar where Koretake and Iris are hopefully waiting patiently for us.

-Lilly-

OH MY I can't believe what I'm seeing: balls... tennis balls... lots of them... everywhere!

The entirety of this outdoor area is just balls, lots, and lots of balls. It looks like it's covered with at least over ten dog parks in one, and just one dog park is already big enough as it is, so this is like a whole town fitted just for dogs and tennis balls. It really is a doggie wonderland—the fun looks endless!

I used to have dreams about a place like this; a place that's nothing but fun and laughter and never-ending joy. Just standing here, I'm loving every moment, watching in awe at all these green tennis balls. Some are different colours, but most of them are green and not only that, I can hear the sound of other dogs playing—their squeaking and jovial barking at the sheer wonder of this place.

There are just so many tennis balls! Choosing just one of these magical balls of joy is going to be a real challenge; they all look terrific and full of bounce. I step forward and look around, seeing nothing but green, nothing but lovely, wondrous green.

'Wow,' I mumble aloud. I'm sure my eyes are wide and sparkling with joy as my legs begin to carry me through the field of tennis balls; each one I glance at makes my tail wag harder with delight like they did before when cousin Jackie and uncle Jacob would visit Mummy Paula and me and stay for dinner, and either one of them would give me a treat and play with me.

My only wish is that Mummy was here to see this magical place with me, because knowing my mummy, she'd be able to pick out the right ball for me to play with because she'd bought a lot of the right balls for me. In the land of the living when Mummy had chosen the right one for me, she'd wave it in front of my face. I wouldn't be able to contain the fizzing feeling inside me; my tail would go crazy, and I'd bounce up and down with excitement from the mere sight of the little green ball in her hand.

When Mummy could see that I was hyped up, she'd tease me with it, saying in a cheerful, playful voice, ' You want the ball? You want the ball? ' And I'd bounce up and down, running around in circles with a strong surge of energy; my tail going to town, and I'd pant like I'd just run around the neighbourhood dog park 100 times barking out, ' YES! YES, I DO WANT THE BALL! ' in response. Then Mummy would reach her arm back and say, 'Then go... FETCH!' and she'd throw the ball as far as she could. I'd immediately zoom after it, wanting nothing more than the ball inside my jaws.

'Paradise,' I say to myself. But suddenly I jump back, startled.

'Oh, sorry, I didn't mean to startle you,' says a familiar-sounding voice. I look to my side and see Ember standing beside me with her tail lightly wagging. I glance at her and ask how long she's been standing there. Another female voice from my other side replies, 'Only two minutes.'

I look at this other dog, and for some reason, I get a weird sense of... what do humans call the thing when they feel like they'd seen someone or something before? Oh! That's right, Dayjar Vu! I stare at this other dog, wondering what its name is, I try to read its collar, but it's covered by the other dog's brown fur.

'Oh, forgive my manners, Lilly,' Ember says as she glances at the other dog, prompting me to do so. 'This is my sister Chelsea. *Chelsea? Chelsea? Where have I seen that name before?* We weren't from the same litter but shared the same owners.'

'You look familiar. I think I remember seeing you at the vet with your owner during the day of my...' she pauses for a moment before saying, 'euthanasia. You probably don't remember,' says Ember, tilting her head to the side.

'Hold on!' I bark, 'You were the dog I'd seen with the two crying ladies? The dog that had Chelsea on the collar?' Now I could recall where I'd seen her name and where she was from; she was there when Mummy took me for a car ride to the vet, and Beth was the one to take me inside. But unlike me, Chelsea didn't have to stay at the vet for a few days because she was to be put down on that exact day, which just made me feel sympathy for her. I wanted to comfort her.

Now I understand the purpose behind those two ladies that were crying; they knew they weren't going to go home with their beloved dog. They knew that Chelsea was going to be put down right there. Oh my, I couldn't imagine just how those two ladies were feeling; not only had they lost Ember, but they'd lost Chelsea too. Both of their dogs were gone, but yet again, I know that Mummy and Beth had three other dogs before me, they'd often talk about how they'd missed them.

I didn't want to think of how Beth and Mummy were feeling knowing that I wasn't with them. I wish I could see them again, but Alexia made it abundantly clear that I was never going to see my owners again and that I'd just have to make do here in Heaven, making friends with other dogs here and perhaps getting a chance to meet those sisters whom I'd heard so much about, Mindy, Molly, and Chloe. I had heard so much about them, maybe they were here and I could meet them at some point?

I look down, forgetting that I'm in Tennis Ball Paradise, and think about the family I'd left behind. I miss my mummy and Beth so much. I miss everyone that I've had the pleasure of meeting, and I'd have done anything for them, anything to make their lives happy.

I feel Chelsea and Ember's tails stop wagging. Chelsea looks at the green grass. 'Yeah, that was me,' she says. My owners were crying because they knew I was dying and it would be best for me if they took me to the vet so I could be peacefully put to rest and so I could reunite with my sister Ember.'

I stare at Chelsea sadly. I can't come close to imagining how Chelsea must have felt, knowing that she was about to be put down, leaving her depressed owners behind to mourn her.

'Oh, my goodness, that means you've been here a few days before me?' I say with a gloomy tone, trying not to think back to the image of those two crying females.

'Yes, like I said, the day we saw each other was when I was due to be put down. As much as I didn't want to leave my two owners behind because they were lovely people, I also knew that I didn't want to live a life of constant pain, so I completely understood why they had booked me in for the final appointment at the vet. But the good thing about being here is that I got to see Ember again because even though we came from completely different litters, we love each other like sisters and would do everything together. We're a bonded pair,' Chelsea says.

I lean over to Chelsea to comfort her.

'I can't imagine how you must have felt when Ember died before you,' I say to her, and Chelsea looks away from me, making me want to lean my body more on her, wanting to comfort her more than ever as if she was from my own litter, even though I had just properly met her.

'I don't think Chelsea wants to be reminded of the day of my death, and I can't really blame her,' Ember says from my other side. I look over at her for a split second before turning my attention back to Chelsea, seemingly forgetting all about the magical sight of all the tennis balls around us. Chelsea turns to look back at me. She stands up, and I look over and see her tail beginning to wag and beat against my back. I watch as Chelsea pokes her tongue out and begins to pant happily. I watch Chelsea closely as she walks ahead of Ember and me, venturing further into Tennis Ball Paradise, where I watch her pick up one of the many green balls in her mouth.

I watch as Chelsea starts tossing the ball around, where she proceeds to run after it and fetch it back up in her mouth before she throws it again. Like before, she chases after it, catching it back into her chops.

Seeing her behave like this reminds me of my puppy days when I had first discovered the joy of tennis balls and how much fun it was to chase after them whenever Mummy or someone else in the family had thrown them for me. Those were the moments of my life that I will forever cherish; all those good times I had spent with my family, all those playtimes revolving around a tennis ball were bliss.

Even those baths Beth or Jackie would give me were terrific. Heck, I even loved those times when Mummy and Beth would leave me in the care of Jackie, where she'd stick these small, thin black things on my head above the eyes, something that she called "fake eyebrows" which always made her laugh.

Even though Mummy didn't really like the fake eyebrows, I couldn't complain about them—as itchy as they were—because they made cousin Jackie laugh, and I couldn't ask for anything more than to make each family member smile. Nothing filled my heart more than seeing the beaming faces of my family members. Like any other dog, I loved my human family to pieces and would do anything to make them smile.

***

EMBER! LILLY! COME! and play with me! I can't play with all 100 billion-plus balls by myself!' Chelsea's playful voice shouts from further in the field that I've come to know as Tennis Ball Paradise.

I can feel my tail thumping at the ground like a bunny I once saw on the rectangular thing with moving pictures, something Mummy and Beth often sit in front of and watch. I glance over at Ember with my tail madly thumping at the ground. I need some clarification on what Chelsea had just said. 'D-Did she say that there's…?'

Ember winks at me and says. 'Over 100 billion-plus balls? Yep! There most certainly is. I don't think anyone has ever come close to a correct estimate of how many tennis balls are here because they've all gotten distracted by the green, fuzzy surfaces; as soon as they pick one up, BOOM! They forget that they were counting them in the first place! Because once you start playing, you find yourself unable to stop!'

I knew that feeling all too well. As soon as I noticed a ball in someone's hand, I was at their feet in less than a second, sitting on my hind legs, front paws up and begging, tongue panting, waiting for them to throw it so I could happily fetch it.

'What's keeping you two?' Chelsea shouts.

'We'll be right over, Sis, just give Lilly and me and few seconds,' Ember barks back in reply. I look and can only see Chelsea's feet dancing in the air; she's on her back, and I suspect she'll begin rolling around.

'I did say it was paradise, didn't I, Lil,' Ember says to me as I fix my eyes on Chelsea, watching her happily roll around on her back as if she hadn't just told me that she'd died a few days before me.

My tail's beating like crazy, and it will take some effort to calm down. Without looking at her, I tell Ember that she isn't wrong and that it doesn't take much to get me excited. One tennis ball is already enough to send me into a frenzy, so to come here with Ember and see ten dog parks worth of balls; I expect my heart to leap out of my chest and my tail to fall off and fly away.

It's almost too much for me to handle but here I am, standing in the middle of Tennis Ball Paradise with Ember at my side and Chelsea calling me to join her.

'Huh? Oh yeah, it sure is paradise. Sorry, I just got distracted by Chelsea acting like a goofball,' I say. I keep my eyes ahead of me, still unable to stare away from Ember's sister, rolling around the field, making a fool of herself while surrounded by nothing but small green balls.

'Then why don't you join her? Bury her in tennis balls; she'd love that. Heck, when she's done, we might even bury you in them.' Gah! Why does she have to tempt me like this? It's hard enough already keeping my eyes off them as Chelsea plays with them, but now Ember is making it ten times harder, and I don't know which ball to pick up first!

This place is well and truly a dog's dream come true. I know because I used to dream about being here many times when I used to sleep in either Mummy or Beth's beds at night, (but mostly Mummy's).

'I know this will sound silly, but I don't know which one to pick up first. Don't these balls have separate dogs that they belong to?' I manage to say looking down and noticing she has one of her front paws on top of one of the many green tennis balls.

Ember gives me a strange look and flicks the ball away with the heel of her paw as if agreeing that my recent question is indeed silly.

'Uh, no... what makes you think that?'

'I-I don't know, I guess because I've never seen so many balls in one place and because of the number of dogs and cats and other animals here, I suppose each ball is for a certain dog? You know just so other dogs don't get greedy and hog them all for themselves,' I shyly respond. Ember then changes her strange look to one of agreement, saying I have a good point.

Ember pants out her tongue and smiles at me, nudging me with her nose. 'You can rest assured that each one of these balls doesn't belong to anyone because we dogs learn to cope and get along with each other. In other words, they belong to everyone!'

Well, that's great to hear, I think. *Thank you, Ember, for being patient in answering an old Jack Russell's silly questions.*

But I still have another question that's nagging at the back of my head as if a mean bird is pecking it with its beak. I look in front of me again and mumble to myself, 'Which one do I pick up and play with? I really wish Mummy could be here to pick one out for me.'

'Why don't you play with the one right before you?' says Ember.

'What one?' I ask before I look down and see a green tennis ball with a paw print on it. If I had hands like a human, I'd be using them to cover my mouth in shock because these paw-printed balls were the types of balls Mummy used to buy for my birthday and whenever I would wreck my other ones. I wanted to cry out of sheer happiness. I never would have thought that I'd see the paw-print tennis balls again after I'd died. But here they are right before me.

To save me from the lingering temptation of choosing which ball to play with, I do as Ember suggests, bowing down and picking up the paw-print ball with my mouth. That's when I feel my body stiffen, my eyes open as wide as they can go, and my tail stops as if my entire body has become frozen.

I can feel the ball clutched in my mouth; the feeling of the ball's fuzzy material has sent me digging back through the tunnel of memory lane because this ball even feels like the balls that I loved playing with when I was alive and living the best life a dog could ask for. Barks and howls alike could not even come close to the immense satisfaction I'm feeling right now from having this single tennis ball with the paw-print on it in my mouth.

I can hear Ember faintly laughing at me as she says, 'You seem to be having one of your moments, ha-ha, not the first dog to do that when picking up one of Heaven's tennis balls. Whenever you're finished, come join Chelsea and me.'

Although my eyes are open and staring ahead of me, I can't see Ember leave my side to join her sister. My eyes are seeing a vast array of bright colours crashing into each other like the waves on a beach. I savour this moment with grace, securing the ball in my mouth.

***

I finally regain control of my body and close my eyes to try and imagine my previous life: when I'd run around the backyard chasing after balls that Uncle Jacob or Cousin Jackie would throw for me. Gosh, I loved those moments just as much as I loved each second. I got to spend time with my family, and each time, I made a new human friend.

If Heaven could make me feel as happy as I'd been when I was alive, I could learn to love it here just like Ember and Chelsea had; they seemed to embrace it and prosper here. As long as Mummy, Beth, Cousin Jackie and Uncle Jacob were doing okay and still able to smile and have fun without me being present to see those wonderful smiles of joy, that was more than acceptable.

If Ember and Chelsea continue to stick by my side as my best friends, I'll very much like that. I never got the chance to meet my sisters when I was alive because they'd all died before I was born. So, with any luck, I might finally have the chance to meet them here in Heaven. I'd very much love that, too. But right now, my main concern is my family. But like Alexia had said before, I will always miss them, and they will always miss me, but they will remain in my heart as I will in theirs. As long as this remains true, I suppose I can live with that.

I'll will never forget my family: the people that taught me how to love and cherish everything that came my way.

***

The dreamy sight becomes too much for me to handle; I have to become a puppy again!

'Hey, wait for me!' I shout out with a muffled voice, and before long, my feet start to run, carrying me over to Chelsea and Ember where I then propel myself upon Chelsea's belly as the three of us start playing together like a bunch of puppies. At that moment, I feel a deep sense of belonging, as if I've always been a part of this joyous play. It's a feeling of inclusion and acceptance that warms my heart and makes me forget all my worries.

-Mittens-

NOIR LOOKS AT me, her tail curled around her as she asks me if I'd like to tag along with her again to meet a "sarrogant mother": someone to look after and care for me during my time here, in this lovely place called "Heaven".

Noir has carefully explained to me that this is going to be my new home and that if I'm to properly get used to what goes on around here, I'll need a mother figure who's patient and fitting for someone as young and "naïve" as me. Noir also tells me that because I'm still so young, having departed from the Land of the Living at not even a year old—I'll forever remain a kitten here in Heaven. I wouldn't have a real chance to grow up and experience the world as an adult cat like her and the other cats that I've seen and run into during the time that I've been following closely behind Noir. But despite that, Noir did say this shouldn't cast any gloom over my usual, cheery "wanting–to–make–friends" attitude because she believes being a kitten has so many "benefits." She even said she'd love to go back in time and live out her kitten days again.

As we're walking, I ask Noir why she doesn't go back in time and relive her kitten days. Still walking in front of me, she gives me a funny look, shaking her head before turning her head back in front of her. I continue to trot behind her and Noir's tail is still up high, meaning she's still happy.

This is grand.

'Sadly, that's not how things work, Mittens, dear, I wish it was a thing where we could go back and live our young lives again and correct past mistakes, but that sadly just isn't how things work,' Noir says.

I want to ask why, but I think that it isn't polite to keep asking questions that Noir doesn't know the answer to, so I keep my mouth shut and only ask a question that I believe has a response, such as, 'Is there a moving picture show? Something that we can use to see our families with?'

'A what now?'

'A moving picture show! You know, like those things hooman's use; they sit in front of this big box thing and watch things that move on it,' I try to explain. I recall that Marian would sometimes sit with her parents and watch the box thing; their faces a bizarre mishmash of facial emotions that I couldn't really understand because I was still relatively new to the family. I didn't know how hooman faces worked.

'A TV?' Noir asks.

'Is that what they call it?'

'Apparently so. I used to see my humans sit in front of those things; they called them TVs. They always seemed so fixated on them; I could never understand why. But that's a human thing, not a cat thing.

'Oh, okay, hoomans are funny and silly,' I state.

'Indeed, they are,' Noir says, dropping the confused tone in her voice.

'But we love them because they feed us,' I say, thinking back to all the times when I'd sit in front of the kitchen doorway, mewing loudly, begging for food, and one of the three Kushners would come to my pleadings, bring out a can of wet food and serve it up into my fish-shaped bowl. Those moments were wonderful. Hoomans are fantastic, but at the same time, they're weird.

'Indeed,' Noir agrees.

Noir comes to a stop, making me also stop before I bump into her butt. 'Well, anyway, before we get to your new surrogate mother, tell me more about this TV thing you're curious about.' Now, I have to think about an excellent way to ask my question that won't confuse her by sounding like I'm a kitten who's babbling about silly things that don't make sense.

'Well... does this place have like one of those TV things that can play things like... like... memories? Or at least show what your hooman is doing right now? Like how when you look out a window and see birds playing in the yard or in the birdbath.' This is the best way I can describe it. 'Do you understand what I'm trying to say?' I'm unsure if I've explained it the right way, but I try my best to. Like Noir has often pointed out, I'm still a kitten, so I don't know much about things and I'm not the best at getting my point across.

Noir gives me another funny look, as if telling me that she does understand me, but at the same time, she doesn't. She looks up into the never-ending sky as if considering my question and is giving it some well-paced thought, closing and opening her eyes until she peers back down to look at me, seeming to have an answer.

'Yes, yes, I do believe that there's one here. But I wouldn't exactly know because I sure haven't seen one during my time here, might have to ask your new surrogate mother about that. She might be the right cat to give you a good answer because, sadly, my mind is blank.'

'Noir?' I ask. Noir looks down at my small fuzzy face as I say her name in a timid voice. 'Can I ask you something else?' Noir tilts her head to the side before bowing her head in a nod, as if allowing me to ask her another question and one that she'd actually be able to answer.

'Please do,' Noir answers gently before walking ahead of me again. She tilts her head to the side, asking me to follow her again. I do, trotting alongside her like I had often done with my hooman Marian. Whenever she walked about the house, I'd follow her because I was interested in what she did in her day-to-day activities.

'May I ask, what's the name of my new Mummy?'

'Mae-Li, she's from Guangzhou in China but doesn't mind being called Millie as she understands that some might have trouble pronouncing her name. So, feel free to call her Millie; she'd really like that.'

My eyes widen with joy. I love that name! It's a name that sounds friendly, a name I could trust. I pick up the pace, so my front paws are now in line with Noir's.

'Wow! That's a pretty name!' I chirp like a birdie. I am now more than eager to meet my new Mummy if her name is Millie. Going by the name alone, she seems like someone who'll understand me, someone I can cheerfully mew to, someone to comfort me whenever I feel sad, someone to cuddle me whenever I feel cold and lonely and when I miss my family.

'Not far now, just inside the bamboo forest, and you can finally meet Millie, your new mother,' Noir tells me. She leads me into this open grassy area, and the sight before me causes my body to become tense. A forest of enormous thin trees stands before us with small green leaves that look sharp as knives.

I don't like the look of this bamboo forest; it gives me a scary feeling that I've seen it somewhere before, but I can't pinpoint where precisely. Those large, thin, green trees and sharp-looking leaves frighten me, and I can't quite understand why, so instead of following behind the pretty and nice Noir, I step backwards, acting purely on instinct and a feeling of heavy distrust.

I can feel my tail start to fizz, the hairs on my back rise, and my ears fold back. I continue to step backwards, away from Noir and the bamboo forest. Then, for the first time ever, I can hear a faint, strange, high-pitched rumbling noise coming from my own throat. I'm growling! I guess that Noir can hear it too, because she stops to glance back at me. She's lowered her tail, and her face has that strange, confused look on it that I should be used to by now; she's been making that face a lot. But this time,

Noir doesn't come over to reassure me like she has done before. Instead, she just stands there at the entrance of the bamboo forest, staring at me as if I've suddenly gone bonkers.

'Mittens, what's the matter? Why aren't you coming? Millie's just through here. You do want to meet her, don't you?' Noir calls me, asking me to rejoin her and meet my new Mummy. I want to press on with Noir and meet Millie but it's as if something about that forest is holding me back, like something terrible is hiding inside that only I know about. It's as if Marian has her hands around me and is trying to pick me up and keep me away from the bamboo forest

'Mittens?' Noir calls out my name again, this time sounding a bit more concerned.

'Y-Yes, I really, really want to meet new Mummy Millie, but... it's just... this forest... it... it scares me,' I call back to Noir with a frightened voice—like when I'd tried calling out to my real Mummy because I was hungry and couldn't find her; when I was very young and couldn't see yet.

Then I remember where I'd seen this similar sight from. It was one of the last things I'd seen before going to sleep and waking up here in front of Noir. It was also in that scary dream I'd had earlier today, the dream that Noir wanted me to have so that she could see the things that I'd dreamt about. 'It reminds me of the forest from that horrible dream, the one I'd seen before that thing came at me and made the dream stop,' I cry. 'What if that thing comes for me again as if I'm a mouse? What if that thing wants to hurt me again?'

Noir continues to stare at me, only this time, she lowers her tail and speaks to me in a motherly voice that soothes my heart and makes my fur feel some warmth, a much-desired change from the chilling fear that the forest has given me. Noir does her best to explain that Heaven is a safe place and that nothing will try to hurt me again because everyone is a friend in

Heaven and that my new mummy Millie will always be around to protect me as if I am one of her own kittens.

'That's why we're going to meet Mae-Li or Mother Millie; she's big and strong, so she'll be able to protect you from any dangers you find yourself in such as getting lost or wandering around the big animals like the elephants or giraffes that may not see you.

If you happen to wander astray, Mae-Li will be sure to find you and bring you back. She'll be like your forever shadow. She'll always be around whenever you need her. So, you don't need to worry about this thing attacking you because, in Heaven, we're all friends; no one harms anyone here because Heaven is a place of peace and harmony,'

'You sure?' I ask nervously, taking one tiny step forward followed by another, still not trusting her entirely because, from all I know, she could be trying to lead me into a scarier place than the entrance of this forest. My curiosity has gotten the better of me once, I don't want to let it get the better of me this time (I've learnt my lesson about wandering away from home). I stop upon those two steps and want to move closer towards the forest because I can't deny that I'm still eager to meet Millie and see if Noir is, as a matter of fact, telling the truth about Millie being big and strong enough to protect someone small and full of energy like me.

'Yes, I am one hundred per cent sure. You can trust me, Mittens, because I never lie. Lying isn't in my blood, anyway. Now would you please come with me? Millie's busy right now looking after other foster kittens, such as yourself, who have also died like you, so therefore, she can't come out and meet you directly. We have to go to her.'

I stay still, timidly glancing around to see if anything mean is eyeing me for its dinner with my ears pricked up so I can hear too. So far, all I can see are other animals playing, fighting, and chasing each other playfully as if they've been friends for the longest time. It's nice to see animals being friendly towards each other. But at the same time, it just makes me feel even more frightened because that mean animal from before could actually be hiding behind those happy-sounding animals, stalking me like a big cat on those TV things the hoomans of the house watched, waiting for the right moment to strike, and hurt me badly.

But there's nothing. I widen my eyes so I can see things better, but there's still nothing that seems to be watching me with a hungry look on its face. Everyone looks so happy.

'Mittens... no one is going to hurt you, you're completely safe here. Now I won't tell you again, Mittens. Would you please follow me to meet your new Mummy? She wants to meet you,' Noir says in a demanding tone that reminds me of the many times Marian would come home from what her mummy and daddy would call "school" and she'd call out my name, asking for cuddles or if she'd made food ready in the fish-shaped bowl for me. If she wanted something from me, she'd use that voice, so when Noir used it on me, I knew I had no choice but to tail behind her again and follow her so I could meet Millie in this spooky bamboo forest. Because if someone used the "demanding hooman" voice on me, I knew that I was either in trouble or would have to do what I was told—and Noir was demanding for me to follow her.

'O-okay... I'm co-coming!' I stammer, forcing my little legs to trot up to where Noir is. Her tail goes back up as soon as I join her by her side.

Not wanting to do what I'd done before by letting my curiosity get the better of me, I keep close to Noir as she leads me through this forest of tall, thin trees with sharp-looking leaves.

I take this moment to think about what my new Mummy Millie looks like and how she might act around tiny kittens with a basket load of questions. 'Uhm, Noir?' I ask in a small voice as my little legs struggle to keep up with Noirs. We walk around trees and over grassy hills covered in heaps of those sharp bamboo leaves.

'Hmm?' Noir answers as we continue to walk further into the bamboo forest, which just makes me much more nervous.

'What's Millie like? What does she look like?'

'You know what Tigers are?'

'No... What's a tiger?' I have never seen or heard of things called tigers. So the only thing I can do is follow Noir's footsteps. Sooner rather than later, I'll have my first encounter with a tiger.

'That Mittens,' Noir comes to a stop. She lifts one of her front paws and points in front of her to a massive cat with orange fur and black stripes, laying on those sharp bamboo leaves. From what I can see, the big cat has four other smaller-looking house cats that look around the same size as me, lazing around it, suckling on the giant cat's belly, and kneading on the big cat's tummy. The sight reminds me of when I was even smaller than I already am, before I met Marian, Edith and Zack Kushner, when I was with my real Mummy and when I used to suckle the milk from of her tummy. So, seeing this large cat letting these tiny kittens suckle and knead on her belly reminds me of my real Mummy, and it honestly fills me with both a sense of sadness and comfort.

'...Is a tiger,' Noir tells me. She then looks over to the tiger and happily calls out, 'Hi Mae-Li!'

This is Mummy Millie? I think to myself as the giant tiger lifts her big head—with round instead of pointed ears—to stare at us!

'EEP!' I cry and dash behind Noir, not wanting the giant cat to see me. Noir mentioned that Millie was big and strong, but I wasn't expecting Millie to be the most giant cat that I've ever seen in my life! The other four kittens continue to suckle and knead.

'Hello Noir, fancy seeing you in the Bamboo Forest,' The tiger named Millie says to Noir while I try my best to keep out of sight, but it doesn't work as Millie can see that I'm hiding; she can see my fuzzy white and brown fur peeking out from Noir's smooth, short black coat. 'Oh, and who is the fuzzy little creme puff behind you?'

'This is your new foster kitten, her name's Mittens, she's a new angel pet, so she's very timid and bewildered about the things happening around here. Also, she's not seen a tiger before, ain't that right, Mittens?'

I say nothing and continue to try and hide away from Millie's large body, even though I know it's pointless because Millie's already revealed to Noir that she's seen me. I still try my best to keep myself hidden. Millie then bursts into a roaring fit of laughter that still doesn't disturb the four kittens, who are still busy kneading and suckling on Millie's milk.

'Oh, such adorableness! Reminds me of these four when they first came to meet me. They were all timid and wary of me because they'd never seen a tiger before. Now, look at them: going to town on my tummy like there's no tomorrow. Just proves to you that I'm harmless and just want to mother any new angel kittens and babies,' Millie says.

Noir moves to the side so that Millie can get a good glimpse of me before I let out another 'eep' and dart behind her again.

'Oh my, what a little cutie. It's understandable that you'd want to hide from someone as big as me. Humans are sometimes scared of us tigers too. As I'm sure Noir has already told you, my name is Mae-Li, but everyone knows me as Millie. I'm a female Sumatran tiger born and bred in the Guangzhou Zoo. I died in the zoo due to old age.

'This here is Peter, a little boy ' —he's a tabby kitten like me, only he's all brown and no white. 'This is Milo, another little boy' —a ginger cat. 'This one's Yuki, a little girl '—a white cat. 'And here's Princess, another little girl ' —another white girl cat with a black tail, Millie says

And you are little Mittens. Come, come, meet your new brothers and sisters! I may be an enormous tiger, but you'll quickly find that I'm very gentle and caring towards the kittens in my care, so you have nothing to be afraid of,' says Millie in a welcoming but strong voice that's full of power. She sounds like she could easily win a fight without even trying. She also sounds like she could kill someone with kindness. Was that even a thing? I guess I was about to find out.

'See, Mittens, there's nothing to be scared of; Millie may be a huge, powerful tiger, but like everyone here, she's friendly and is one of the best foster mums Heaven has to offer.'

Noir comforts me, which has resulted in me having the guts to peek my head out from behind Noir and look Millie in the eyes. I haven't wholly shown myself to Millie yet, but at least I've gained enough courage to show my face to her and mew, even if my words are in shy stutters, which isn't like me as I'm known to be full of bubbling joy and to love everyone on first meeting.

'H-hi Mm-mm-Mummy Mil-Millie. M-My name is Mi-Mi-Mit-te-tens.'

Millie winks at me as if to say that she likes me. I gulp back in response. 'I think you and I will get along just fine. It might take some time to get used to someone of my size, but sooner or later, you'll be joining these four here on my tummy. Besides, you called me Mummy Millie, I like that very much,' Millie tells me.

I take a small step out from behind Noir as I can feel my tail starting to perk up. It will be pretty neat to have someone as big and strong as Millie as my Mummy, and it will feel nice to have other kittens like me to play with.

It looks like this is how Heaven is meant to be: other kittens and puppies that die come here, they meet new friends and parental figures, and sooner or later, their lives become whole again. And I suppose it's now my turn to become whole again.

Part Four – Turning Points
-Colin Trembley

ACCORDING TO MY bedside clock, it's 10:15am. I get out of bed and head into the kitchen to make myself a honey sandwich for breakfast. It's a day off so I think my parents are still asleep.

I sit at the dining table with my just-made honey sandwich and a clean plate I'd taken from the dishrack. I feel empty, incomplete; like a large chunk of my heart has been forcibly stolen from my chest.

As I sit in my chair in the kitchen, I can't help but stare absently at my sandwich. I made it and it was ready to eat in front of me, but now as I stare at the sandwich, that I realise I'm not hungry—like my appetite had died in my sleep, leaving me with this empty hole in my belly. I can hear my stomach making those stupid, hungry, growling noises, and I know that I want to eat this sandwich in front of me, but my hands just won't move to pick up the sandwich and bring it to my mouth. Instead, I feel my fingers clutching at the fabric of my pyjamas as my eyes continue to stare blankly at the sandwich spilling with honey.

I feel my shoulders tense up, and my body starts to feel an unnerving chill. I turn my head to peek into the living room, hoping to see a familiar form lying asleep with a blue and green pull rope clenched in its teeth.

But no... Atlas's body is gone, along with the zentangle elephant carpet he'd been lying on during the moments that had happened last night. I suspect the carpet has been put in the washing machine to be cleaned from the blood or was hanging on the clothesline to dry. As for Atlas's body... I have no idea. For all I know, my parents could've buried him while I'd been crying in my sleep, tossing and turning from the nightmares, or they've moved his body outside so I won't be able to see it; if that's the case, I thank them because I know I won't have the courage to face his dead body again. I'm grateful that my parents had moved his body away from my sight for the time being, at least until they figure out what to do with him.

Speaking of my parents, they enter the room quietly and without looking at each other as if they're strangers. I watch them from the corner of my eye as Mom makes a cup of coffee and Dad gets himself some cereal. They both join me at the table soon after, sitting on opposite sides of me.

We're stuck in silence for about five straight minutes, the only sounds being of Dad eating cereal and Mom taking small sips of her coffee. Meanwhile, my honey sandwich continues to remain unbitten. Finally, Mom breaks the silence, giving out a solid but depressing sigh, putting the now empty coffee cup on the table and staring at me and my untouched sandwich.

'Colin... we've spoken to your school, and they've allowed you the week off because we mentioned that Atlas was more than just a dog: he was your best friend, he was family,' she pauses briefly before saying, 'So you can relax knowing that you don't have to go to school at all this week.'

I nod sadly in response, and once again, there's more silence for another five minutes. This time, Dad breaks it. I hear the slow ting as he put his spoon on the table.

'We need to talk, Col...' he draws out a long sigh that tells me that this is serious. I can tell that he's looking at me, even though my eyes remain on the honey sandwich, which continues to ooze honey. He doesn't need to say anything, as Dad's tone hints at what he wants to talk about: what they'll do with Atlas's lifeless body. I feel like swiftly excusing myself from the table to retreat up to my room, so I can hide under my covers and cry. I don't even want to talk or think about Atlas or about anything that happened that night. I just want to be left alone.

But I don't leave; I keep myself at the table as it would seem rude to just up and leave the table without so much as a word. My shoulders are clenched, and my eyes start to tear up. I sniffle, blink, and feel a single tear from my bottom eyelash where it hits the black and white checkerboard tablecloth. There's a lump in my throat that makes me feel dizzy and sick, and my body tenses up, I start to feel cold... so cold that I can feel goose pimples begin to form on my skin. I expect cold wafts of breath to be visible from my mouth because of how chilled I feel.

'Your dad's right, Son; this is a topic that we must get out of the way,' Mom says.

'I know but I don't want to talk about it right now. I blubber in a voice that sounds broken and constricted as if an invisible boa constrictor had started to choke me. I wipe my eyes, feeling the wetness of tears on my fingers. I then force my eyes to glance up at my parents, slowly darting my eyes from Mom to Dad, Dad to Mom and so on, waiting patiently for one of them to talk and to say what needs to be said.

It's Dad, 'Now, I'm sure you're probably wondering where his body is since it's not in the lounge room?' He asks in a caring, gentle voice.

'N-No... not re-really, I don't want to discuss this. Can you just leave me alone, please?' I say again in that strangled tone as more tears fall from my eyes.

'Well... your Mom and I have moved him outside and put the rug covered with his blood over him. We can wash it later after his body's been dealt with.'

Stop... stop talking.

'And we're also considering making an appointment with the Paws to Remember pet crematorium in Ontario to have him cremated. But we aren't going to do that without your permission since Atlas was mostly your dog,' Dad adds.

I know what I want for my dog. I know that I don't want the duty of burying him or knowing that he's buried somewhere in our backyard or at a nearby cemetery for pets. But I also don't like the idea of my dead dog's body being burned in a crematorium and his ashes put into an urn, or a small fancy-looking bag with a small card around some rope that had his picture, birth date, and the date of his death, which had been last night at around 10pm, making the date of his death June 20, 2019. I'm not a fan of either option because I want Atlas to be with me every step of the way; he still had so much to live for and so many friends to make. I want Atlas to wake up and run into the house to smother my face with happy licks and slobber. I just want him back.

But if I have to choose the fate of my dog's corpse, I'd have to choose... *Why am I even considering this?* For some reason, I can't contain a strong emotion that I feel bubbling inside of me, its anger; anger at my parents and anger at myself for feeling this way.

'Cremation, okay?!' I suddenly shout, slamming my palms on the table. 'Christ, can we not talk about this! Ju-Just leave me alone,' I yell at them before feeling bad and apologising and saying that I want Atlas to be cremated like Uncle Fred was.

My parents just look at me as if they understand why I'm angry. 'Are you sure Colin? Do you really think you could live with a bag containing Atlas' ashes?' My Dad asks, bringing me back into the now instead of thinking of the past and when Uncle Freddie died.

'Mason, honey, please don't say it like that; the boy's still badly hurting. Like he said, we should stop talking about this, it's upsetting him,' Mom says.

'I know that, Tori, but won't it be more straightforward for him if we have Atlas buried instead of cremated?

'I want him cremated,' I say simply, focusing my eyes on Dad, who's staring at me with uncertainty. He's biting his lip and is darting his glance from Mom to me as if he isn't sure that my decision is the best and believes that sending Atlas' body over to be buried is the best option for me and my mental state. I mean, it probably is the best choice but in this current situation, I don't know what I'm mentally capable of.

The only thing that matters is my dog; I want to be in his presence, even just his ashes. My only wish for Atlas is that my boy is happy wherever he is and that he's playing with other dogs like him who have died similarly to him (murdered by a nasty person). And I hope that he's playing with all the pull-ropes that he could possibly imagine.

'I know what I want for my dog, and that's for his body to be cremated. I want something of him to hug. Even if he's not going to be here with me anymore, at least I can go to the bag of ashes and hug them. They might not hug me back in return, but at least I can find some comfort in knowing that I'm holding his remains, his... what do smart people call it? E... ess...'

'Essence?' Dad suggests.

'Yes! That's the word: essence! Thanks, Dad.'

I look up as Dad gives me a sign of defeat before nodding at me. He then turns to look at Mom and opens his mouth to say, 'Tori, can you make an appointment with the Paws to Remember Crematorium so we can opt to get Atlas cremated ASAP.'

Mom sighs, blinks sadly at him before saying, 'Yes, yes, I can do that now if you like.' She turns back to me. 'What do you think, Colin?'

'Yes, please, I would really like that. Thanks, Mom,' I say and slowly nod, finally putting my fingers around my untouched honey sandwich and picking it up.

***

After our late breakfast, I leave the table to go into the lounge room, where I sit on one of the couches. Hunched over, hands cupped and thinking sadly to myself, I stare at the floor that's missing the bloodied carpet that Atlas had passed away on. I feel drained, both in my mind and in my body. Once again, the depressing thought of Uncle Fred's funeral comes back to me.

I sit still on the couch and wipe my eyes with the back of my hand as tears start to fall out of them. Seeing Uncle Fred's coffin being dipped into the ground and the disturbed Earth shovelled onto his coffin painted a horrible image in my head. If I'd chosen the same thing for Atlas's body, would Atlas have been placed inside a coffin that was fit for a dog of his size? Or would he be buried without one? I didn't like the thought of either one of those, but if he was buried without a coffin, I suppose that would be even harder.

To see my best friend's lifeless body being gently placed into a small, freshly dug-up hole made for him, only to then have dirt tossed upon him, while my family and friends—who knew Atlas as the good boy he was—gathered around and watched him get buried right before their eyes, their faces becoming wetter with each shovelful of dirt tossed onto my rottweiler's dead body; his tombstone a homemade wooden T-shaped marker above it with his name scribbled on it with black paint. To make it worse, the tombstone would have a framed photo of him leaning in front of it: one of the pictures of him smiling playfully at the camera.

I don't think, no, I *know* that I wouldn't be able to cope with seeing that in real life. Just imagining it playing out is hard enough. I think something like that would cause me to want a month off school instead of a week because I'd be a sobbing mess, shutting myself away in my room (only coming out for the toilet and to eat), pillow over my face, crying heavily into it. My mind would be replaying the same image of Atlas's lifeless body disappearing under the Earth and the smiling photo staring up at me.

I'm not ready to say 'Goodbye' to my dog. His fur hadn't even started showing the first signs of aging. I remember hearing from one of Dad's friends, Stacy Mclaughlin, who had a black Pug named Mug that had died back in 2005. Stacy told me that Mug passed away peacefully of old age at fourteen. Stacey said Mug's short, trimmed black coat had started turning grey, very much like an old person.

Atlas was only nine years old.

I continue to sit; the only sound being my own faint sobbing. Dad comes into the room and sits down beside me. He doesn't need to say anything when it comes to asking how I am. I guess he can already tell how I'm feeling just by looking into my face and seeing my shoulders and the rest of my body shake. I peer up at him. I can feel my own mouth trembling. I throw my arms around Dad's chest and hug him, not wanting to let him go. Dad places his arms around me and rubs my back in a way that's comforting and meant to give me some ease over the horrible thing that happened last night—an event that will stick with me forever. June 20, 2019: the night my dog Atlas was murdered. The night my best friend was snatched from me.

'It's okay, Col. It's okay to cry. Don't feel ashamed about crying; I don't blame you, and neither should anyone else. Last night, we lost a very special boy.'

'Why did that man have to come and kill my dog? Breaking into someone's house is bad enough, but why did he kill Atlas? Why did he have to kill my boy?' I cry into his chest. My arms wrapped tightly around him, and I can't control the tears as they wet Dad's morning clothes.

'I don't know what made him want to kill Atlas; maybe it was out of defence because Atlas was attacking him, and it's normal for people to attack back at their attacker, which sadly happened to be Atlas. But Atlas was attacking him for a reason. He was a good boy who did his duty and strived to protect his family, and he ended up paying the price for his heroism. Which is why it's better to sometimes not play the hero and just let things slide,' Dad paused.

I glance up at him, my eyesight briefly fuzzy from my tears, but Dad wipes them away for me with his thumb. He then cups my chin and gently lifts it so that I'm staring right into his dark but friendly eyes that look a little pink. I think Dad's also been crying. I guess that Mom also has pink eyes too as she loved Atlas to pieces, and we were all experiencing a kind of shared sadness and loss for the Rottweiler who had sacrificed himself for his family's money and safety.

'But that's not the important thing to think about, my boy. The important thing to remember is all the good memories we had with him and that wherever he is right now in doggy Heaven, he's living peacefully and happily,' Dad says.

My jaw trembles, and I wipe my eyes with my black and green dinosaur pyjama sleeve. 'But do you suppose that he's thinking of us?' I really didn't know why I asked something so silly if I already know the answer. But I guess that's the thing about being sad and by what Mrs Sandy Dennison, the librarian at school calls "mourning." (I asked her when Freddie died since Mrs Dennison claimed to have had six siblings but five died due to various circumstances.) She said when someone close to you dies you feel an overwhelming amount of sadness, knowing that loved one is dead, and they aren't going to come back.

'Of course, he's thinking of us, Col. I don't think that there's a single second that he doesn't think of us, the family that raised and loved him. It's a dog's natural instinct to think and miss their owners if they don't see them. That's why whenever we arrived home, Atlas would be at the front door, bouncing around with joy because dogs love attention and their owners, even in death,' Dad pulls me closer to him and rubs my hair with his hand.

'Do you suppose that Atlas will meet Uncle Freddie up in heaven?' I ask him, considering it to be a possible thing that could happen up.

'Perhaps they've already met or are going to meet. I can't say, Col, but like I said, the important thing is to remember the good times with him and keep him in here,' Dad gently pulls me away, putting his finger above my chest and pointing to where my heart is. 'Uncle Fred's in there, and so is Atlas, and so will your Mom and I when it's our time to go.'

I think about his words in silence. I glance down at my hands as I lap them over each other and place them on the area where my heart is for a few seconds before I fling myself into his chest again. I'm glad that he and Mom understand how I had felt and are doing everything in their power to help me, and I love them for it.

'I love you, Dad. Thanks for understanding,' I cry into his chest.

'I love you too, Son. And it's my job,' He replies, rubbing my back and hair.

After Dad and I spent around ten minutes hugging, I pull away from him to see Mom standing in the doorway patiently. Her hands are cupped low, and she appears to be clutching a small lilac-coloured hanky. She has a face of mourning, the exact same look that all of us have. She's looking at us while giving out the occasional sniff, bringing that lilac hanky up to her eyes and rubbing them. But I can tell that she's trying to keep her tears at bay, for my sake. Because Mom knows that if I see her cry, I'll start crying, too. Mom and I have a strange connection like that: where we share sadness. Mom feels sad whenever I'm sad, and I cry whenever she cries.

'And? What did they say?' Dad asks her as he turns around on the couch and sees her in the doorway.

June 23 is when they're going to cremate him, and tomorrow, we're going to have to drive Atlas up to the crematorium. As for his ashes, the vet said they should be ready to collect a week later, but hopefully, it will be earlier than that.' I watch as she covers her eyes with the hanky, which looks moist with her tears. I want to cry from seeing them, but I hold them back as hard as I can.

'Okay, we'll do that first thing as soon as they open tomorrow,' Dad then looks down at me again. 'Are you okay with staying home alone for about an hour or two while your Mom and I sort the things out at the crematorium?'

I nod slowly in response. My mind shuts itself off from reality at that moment. Mom and Dad talk amongst each other as my mind trails back to the idea of Atlas in Heaven, what he's doing up there, and if he's happy. Is he playing with a lifetime supply of pull-ropes with other Rottweilers or other dog breeds, or was he being a piggy and stuffing his face with all-you-can-eat food? Whatever he's doing in Heaven, I hope he's happy, and his tail's wagging, and his tongue is panting.

I say aloud quietly, 'I hope you're happy wherever you are, Atlas, I hope you're well looked after over there in Doggy Heaven. I love you so much, Atlas. You'll always be my good boy.'

-Wolfgang Buchenwald-

I'VE HAD THE week off work and while it will be good to not have any more stress put on me, not having something to do around the house or someone I can talk to and express my grief with translated to a week of never-ending loneliness and depression.

My best friend and only loving companion is no longer with me, and there's nothing I can possibly do to ease the sorrows that I've carried on my back like a ton of bricks, weighing me down and keeping me from rising up.

I have no one to turn to. My remaining family members want nothing to do with a silly old fool such as myself. Ever since my wife left me, my daughters became more loyal to their mother, who was more into change and the new things the world brought. She wasn't a Luddite like me, and I don't exactly have any friends outside of work aside from Erwin and I can't ring him and wallow to him while he has an important job to carry out, being a management analyst. I'm just a foolish old man who happened to lose his pet cat. Therefore, the only thing I can think of that will hopefully be enough to ease the burden I carry is to do my daily chores, such as cleaning and maintaining house duties, getting them out of the way before deciding on the next chapter to write in my life's book.

But I suppose there's nothing else to write in the book; I have nothing to live for since Tiger is gone. So, because Tiger has gone perhaps I should too… I think no one will think twice about missing me or even acknowledging that I'm gone in the first place, because that's how it's always been in the sad, lonely life of Wolfgang Buchenwald: a man so overwhelmed with loneliness after his cat's death that he can't take it anymore and kills himself.

I have some sleeping pills in the bathroom, maybe I could overdose? Yes, suicide doesn't seem like a terrible option at this point. No one will come asking for me, and I'd be the last person my two daughters would contact. Why should I continue to live underneath the shadows of everyone else? Why should I continue to live a life that has no meaning anymore? Why do I insist on trying to write myself into other people's scripts? Caring and providing for Tiger was my meaning, and now that he had to be put down because he was too sick... I... I don't know what I'm supposed to do now.

As I sit on one of the kitchen chairs, I look up and see the framed photograph of the first picture I took of kitten Tiger staring up at me with his wide, curious yellow and blue eyes. The photo is almost torturous to gaze upon. Still, I can't remove my sights from it, and the more I keep my eyes fixed upon those big beading eyes, the waterier mine become.

I close my eyes and try as hard as I can to remember back fourteen years ago when I adopted him in 1999 from the kind Kiefer family in Mannheim. I remember that I'd taken him home and let him down on the living room floor, where I watched him wander about curiously, approaching various furniture and sniffing them with his little nose. I thought the occurrence of kitten Tiger sniffing random things was too adorable not to capture so, I quickly went into the spare room (Carina and Dorothea's old room), took out my old Kodak camera stored in one of the drawers, and returned to the living room where I snapped the photo.

This is the photo I now find myself holding with trembling fingers and hurting eyes as I stare into those playful tiny beady eyes. The more I stare at the photograph, the more I miss him and the more I want to be with him the more the idea of suicide doesn't seem that ba... No! enough with that kind of talk, I have to remain strong! Tiger would want me to remain strong. Tiger. 'Oh Tiger…' I moaned.

It's a struggle, and I don't want to do it, but I have to for the sake of my sanity. I manage to put the photo down on its face and slid it a few centimetres away from me. I sit in silence, thinking about how my life has turned out this way and why everything seems to go wrong for me. I take my hands off the table and hide them underneath as I place my head down on the polished wood.

My house is large and silent: the only sound I hear is the sound of my own crying and the traffic going past outside. I don't try to fight back the biting tears or do anything to make them stop. I just let them take their course to dry up on their own.

I can't take this grief. I leave the room, go into the bathroom, and start going through the cupboards until I find a jar of sleeping pills. I'm supposed to take one at night before bed because I suffer from a mild case of insomnia. I open the jar to spill its contents into my hand when the image of Tiger sleeping beside me in bed flashes before my eyes.

'Oh, my boy, my precious little boy. Why did it have to be your time?' I sniffle to myself as I try to think of something else. Then, the idea of Heaven comes into my mind, and I try to focus and think about that and what it would be like to walk among angels with my own set of wings and a halo made of gold that sits above the head. Was Heaven really as good as they tell you? Was it really a place of peace and prosperity?

'What's Heaven like up there, Tiger? Is it as good as they tell you in school? If so, consider giving me an early pass so I can be with you again.'

I take a pill from the jar and look at it closely before throwing it back into the jar and screwing the lid back on. 'Come on, Wolfgang, you old drink, quit wallowing in your own grief!' I chastise myself as I stand up from the bath. I lightly smack myself with the back of my hand. 'You were considering doing some housework to put your mind at ease, the toilet and tub still need cleaning, so do that.' I smack myself in the face once more to let the idea of housework sink in. I stand up straight and decide to clean the house and do my daily chores before deciding on anything else.

    I venture into the laundry, pick up the clothes basket and pour them into the washing machine, when I faintly hear the sound of my phone ringing from the kitchen where I'd left it sitting on the table. It probably isn't necessary; it could be one of those scam calls or those people that ring to try and sell stuff. Whatever it is, I pay no attention to it as I close the washing machine's lid and press the ON button on the washing machine, hearing the activation bleep.

    Upon leaving the laundry to go into one of the storage cabinets to get the old 1981 Hoover vacuum cleaner out, I hear my phone ring again from the kitchen, but I ignore it again. Instead, I take the 80's Hoover out of its spot and direct it into the living room, its lead dragging behind it. My breathing is shuttering as I vacuum the living room floor, going over the carpet that still has pieces of loose fabric coming off it from all the times Tiger used to play with it. Then the thought comes to me that if Tiger had fur, I'd be sucking up those tufts of hair into the vacuum, where they'd get thrown about with other bits of mess that the Hoover had picked up. Sucking up those elements of a cat that was once full of life and had a tendency to rub his tail and head across my face whenever he could sense that I was feeling down and needed some extra support. Oh dear, my heart is aching at the very thought of my old cat and all the things he'd do whenever I was sad: like the memories of my ex-wife coming at me with divorce papers, or whenever I sat brooding about Carina and Dorothea going to leave Germany to live out their lives with their partners, saying I lived in the past and was too foolish to be a part of their new life chapters, cutting ties with me as if I was never a part of their lives to begin with.

I never could quite understand why my family wanted to distance themselves from me, but there was nothing that I could do; those was their lives, and if they didn't want me to be a part of them, I had to respect that. But even if my family had wanted nothing to do with me, I could always rest assured that Tiger would be around to sense the pain I was going through and comfort me during my times of need. He'd meow to alert me that he was coming to me right before he'd come out from wherever he was hiding or sleeping. Tiger would stare at me for a brief moment before meowing again. He'd trot over to wherever I sat, jump up on my lap and rub his head against my chin. And if I was crying, he'd rub his tail across my eyes as if to wipe the tears away, turning his tail into some kind of makeshift tissue.

I loved those moments when he did that (I just loved him altogether). He was always around whenever I needed him, and knowing that he was around and never ran away filled my heart with joy. The feeling of his leathery pink skin, the sharp prickle of his claws when he kneaded on me, and the gentle vibrations of his purr had never once failed to put a smile on my face. I'd do anything for him, even trade my own life for his. But that sadly isn't how things work. Tiger's dead, and there's no amount of bargaining that I can do to bring my little boy back.

When I turn off the Hoover and unplug it from the power board, I hear my phone ring again.

I'm getting frustrated with the constant ringing of the damn phone and those damn telemarketers, but I swallow up my anger and sigh. 'Okay, Okay, I'm coming.' I say to no one, leaving the Hoover in the living room. I enter the kitchen, pick up my phone, and see five missed calls from... Dorothea!? What could she possibly be ringing me for? Personally, I don't really care what she wants; she's picked an awful time to ring me to brag about her perfect little life.

Then Dorothea rings again for the sixth time, and this time, I answer it, though I don't sound happy to hear my eldest daughter's voice in over ten years, because like her mother and sister, she'd disowned me and I wasn't going to let that slide.

'Dad? You there?' I could tell by her voice that Dorothea sounded ten years older, possibly around her forties, and much wiser; she sounded like her mother when I last saw her in '96. While it was nice to hear my daughter's voice again, I still wasn't going to forget when she'd said I was just a simple-minded old fart who lived in the past and couldn't keep up with today's standards. That had been the day my heart split in two.

'Hello, Dorothea?' I say with a strangled voice.

'Oh, thank goodness I have the right number. Hey Dad. I've been trying to reach you for the past hour and a half.'

'Well, you've reached me now... what do you want, Dorothea? This really isn't a good time to be calling me,' I say, feeling the tears wanting to push themselves out of my eyes.

'Yes, I know, I get that,' she pauses vaguely for a moment. I can hear her make a sighing noise before her voice comes back. 'Look, I understand that Carina, Ma and I haven't exactly been the best to you during these past ten years with not texting or keeping in contact with you because, well... Ma asked us not to but your boss Stefan Gunner rang saying that Tiger passed away. And look, Dad, I just... we just want to say that we're really sorry. We know how much Tiger meant to you. You have our condolences.'

I'm shocked and slightly offended. Was this all it took for them to even consider contacting me again? My beloved cat being put down? Was Tiger's death all that was needed for them to ring me again or even acknowledge me as a part of their lives? If they think that saying sorry is going to be enough to make me forgive them for all the things they'd said about me right before cutting the strings that held our relationship together, they're gravely mistaken.

The only one that was ever truly there to ease my sorrows was Tiger, and now that he's with the angels, they finally decide to ring me again after ten years of forgetting that I even exist in the first place. They've finally decided to check up on me and see if I'm doing okay. If you ask me, it's a callous thing for a daughter to do to her old mourning father.

I almost have a mind to finger the red telephone icon and end the call as I don't want to hear any more, but I'm not the type of man to abruptly hang up calls. Even if the conversation drags on and is getting nowhere. I always allow people the opportunity to express themselves because it's polite. It would be improper if I hang up Dorothea's call for the first time in ten years.

'Dad?' Dorothea says.

The tears come now, flowing out with such velocity that I can't control them. As much as I try to, they won't stop. They just kept pouring out.

'Dad, Dad, Are you okay?'

'Is this all it took for you to ring me? My cat dying? Were you and Carina waiting for Tiger to die just so you could contact me again? Is that it? Were you just waiting for this sad old man to get even sadder?' I blubber without restraint, letting my mouth do the talking instead of my brain.

'N-no, it's nothing like that! Honest! We just...'

'Then what is it, Dorothea? It's been ten years! TEN since you and Carina left me. My cat has died, and ironically you want to ring me again? Do you have any remote idea just how much my heart aches whenever I think of that day? I did everything for you and Carina, and that was how you repaid me? By telling me that I wasn't good enough, by leaving with your mother. By saying that I'm too much of a stupid old goat that's living in the past to continue being a part of your lives?'

'Dad, please... you don't understand. Just hear me out for five seconds.'

I can't stop. 'I thought about you, your sister, and your mother every bloody day and the more the years went on, the more I thought about that day in 2004 and the more painful it became to the point that I couldn't think of my once little girls anymore without feeling hurt and betrayed.

'The pair of you went ten years without so much as texting me to ask if I was okay! And let me tell you something, Dorothea, if I didn't have Tiger here to help me through those difficult times, I would've-'

'DAD! STOP IT! JUST LISTEN TO ME!'

'COMMITTED SUICIDE!!' I scream into the phone in a voice that doesn't feel like mine.

Dorothea is silent after that, the only sound being her deep, shuddering breathing for a few seconds. I think she's going to hang up, but to my surprise, she stays on the line. With what I needed to say out of the way, but feeling bad about it, I calm down, take some deep breaths. As I wipe my eyes and apologise for venting in such a negative way before expressing how I'd felt without my daughters.

'You, Carina, and your mother Irene have no idea how lonely it's been without you three to check up on me, but that was the good thing about Tiger; he was here to heal my wounds, and he'd stopped me for contemplating ending it all. Look, I'm sorry for yelling like that, but like I said before, this really isn't a good time to talk to me.'

'I see that now... I've caught you in a bad time. I'm sorry too, we all are. I've been thinking about you but never had the courage to contact you.

None of us meant to cause you this much harm, and I realise that I'm the last person you would want to talk to because of all the things we said to you all those years ago, which now we all regret and wish we could take back. But during those busy ten years, there wasn't a moment that we didn't at least think of you because you're our dad, and we love you. So, will you please forgive Ma, Carina, and me for the things we did all those years ago and accept our condolences for Tiger? We know how much you loved that little hairless feline.' Dorothea speaks in a gentle tone that begs for forgiveness. With a nasty thought in my head, I want to tell her to get religion if she wants forgiveness but I dismiss the idea because it's improper and as hurtful as that day in 2004 was, and as much as I brood on it whenever things get me down in the dumps, I can't allow myself to keep a grudge against them; Dorothea and Carina are still my children, my daughters whom I love.

As long as they come clean with me and admit their mistakes. Even if it was ten years of nothing from them at least Dorothea has finally made an effort, on behalf of Carina and herself, to apologise for what she and her sister had said all those years ago. I open my mouth and say, 'Thank you, Dorothea Can I perhaps speak with Carina if she's around?'

'Sadly, no, Carina is somewhere in Stockholm with her fiancé Bruno Strickland. I'm still in Venice with my Italian fiancé Lorenzo Ricci.
'There's actually something I've meant to ask you,' Dorothea says.

Oh dear, here it comes, she's going to say that Carina is due to be married and that I'm sadly not invited. Where are the tissues when I need them? After this humble discussion with my eldest daughter, I'm quickly going to be forgotten again, left to wallow in the puddles of my own grief. This is how it's always been, so why would this be any different?

I take a deep, hardened breath, cross my heart, and prepare myself for what Dorothea is going to ask.

'Carina is due to be married on the sixth of December this year, and she was wondering if you would come? She says she and her fiancé Bruno will go halves on airfares if you decide to attend because Bruno wants to meet you. In other words, she's inviting you to her wedding. Will you come?'

My jaw hangs low, my eyes widen, my hands shake and feel sweaty, the phone almost slips from my hand.

I never thought I'd hear this from Dorothea or Carina! Is Carina actually inviting me to her wedding? I want to believe this, but it's Dorothea disclosing it, not Carina herself.

'Is this some kind of joke?' I say, wiping my eyes with my wrist.

'No! No joke, I'm dead serious. The reason Carina didn't tell you herself is because she's swamped,' Dorothea explains to me.

While it would be nice to see my daughters again for the first time in ten years, I can't just forget about the knife that remains pierced in my heart. I can't forget about the times I'd spent with Tiger and all the times he'd been there for me when Irene and my daughters weren't, and now that he was gone, I'd been invited to Carina's wedding in Stockholm. I know that I can't just stop these tears from flowing; Tiger's death is still so incredibly raw, and I propose that I'll be like this for a while. So, the best answer I can give my eldest daughter is that I'd think about it because the passing of my cat is still so fresh, and I need time to mourn his death.

'Yeah, okay, Dad, take all the time you need, just be sure to send Carina or me a text when you've made up your mind, okay? If you don't have Carina's new number, I'll forward it to you.'

'Yes,' I say simply, the thoughts of Tiger racing back to my head.

'I love you, Dad.'

'I love you too, Dorothea., Goodbye for now,' I say. When she says 'goodbye,' I press the red phone icon and end the call.

I then head back into the living room where the Hoover still sit where I left it. I sit on the couch and stare at the rug that Tiger loved playing with as a kitten, while thinking about that phone call and how out of the blue it was.

'Carina's getting married and invited me?' I mumble to myself as I stare at the flakes of fabric springing out from the sides of the rug and silently think to myself as if I'm talking directly with Tiger.

While your death is still so fresh in my mind, I'll be crying for a while and forever missing you, Tiger, because you were my little boy. But I think things are starting to turn out for the better, I can say that I won't be as lonely anymore as there's been a turning point in my life. My family has started to own up to their past mistakes and contacted me, and Carina even invited me to her wedding. But even during the wedding, I'll still be thinking of you, Tiger, because while you were a cat without fur, you were my cat without fur, and I loved everything about you, right down to every wrinkle you had. I miss you so much, Tiger. I hope you're being treated like the king that you are up there in Heaven.

With those thoughts out of the way, I stand up, go over to the Hoover. I turn it on and resume the vacuuming. My troubled mind feels a little less bothered now, knowing that after ten years of loneliness and being alienated from my family, I've finally been contacted and not only that, I've been invited to my youngest daughter's wedding.

-Paula Lahey-

IT'S THE MORNING after Lilly's passing and it's playing out exactly how I'd expected it: gruelling. My head is a never-ending jungle of disjointed thoughts and memories of the times Beth and I spent with our endearing little Jack Russell. I remember when Beth and I adopted her—from that lovely Glosser family in Bagdad in 2009, right up until she was taken to the vet a few days ago to see Elliot Prendergast so he could find out what was wrong with her, the reason she wasn't eating and just didn't have the energy she was known throughout the neighbourhood for.

I don't feel like getting out of bed, but I know I have to. I can't allow myself to stay in bed and do nothing. I need to eat something. And as impossible as that task seems right now, I can't avoid it. Humans and animals alike need to eat. A bowl of cornflakes will do for now; thoughts of lunch and dinner can wait until later in the day.

I pull the doona off my legs, strain to lift my unnaturally heavy body off the bed, and let my legs spill out. I sit on the bed and stare at the carpet below me, brooding about why Lilly had to leave us so soon, especially when she still had so much to live for. Eventually, I get myself out of bed and put on my dressing gown. I didn't feel like getting dressed today. I'm not planning on going anywhere. If I see someone walking their dog along the street, I might break down at the memory of walking Lilly and of Beth putting on Lilly's pink harness to take her out for her daily walkies. So, for the well-being of my mental health, I'll spend today at home, doing some knitting or watching the news on the TV.

I go into the kitchen, where Beth reads the paper at the dining table. I open the cupboard above the stove and take out a box of cornflakes. I kneel, despite the strain in my back, and take out a small bowl from the lower cupboard place it on the counter near the carton of milk Beth's used for her bowl of cereal, which sits in front of her as she flicks through the pages of the daily newspaper. I go join her shortly after getting my breakfast as if there's nothing amiss.

'Nothing of interest this time if that's what you're going to ask aside from silently grieving,' Beth says without so much as a glance as she flicks through the last page of the paper for the next few seconds before she closes it, folds it from top to bottom, leaving it on the table and heading into the lounge room, leaving me to deal with her empty bowl.

I say nothing as I eat my bowl of cereal as soundlessly as I can. The only person I can talk to is Beth, but she's grieving in her own way—which is pretending that everything's normal. When I finish, I continue to sit, staring at my empty cereal bowl for about a minute before I turn my head to look at the framed photographs hanging up on the wall. They're photos of my three children: - Michelle, Elizabeth, and Jacob, along with my grandchildren: Scott, Nina, and Tyson, who are Michelle's children, and Jackie, who's Jacob's daughter.

I turn my head and look to my right, where I see the hanging photographs of all three dogs that I've previously owned; Lilly was up there too, making it four; only this photo of Lilly was when she was still just a puppy—about eight months old. At this moment, as I look at the picture of Lilly staring curiously into the camera, it dawns on me that Lilly's passing's been the most impactful of the four dogs I've owned. Why? I can't answer this; maybe it's because of Jackie and Jacob—the impact she'd had on their lives as well as my own. Jackie told me yesterday about Lilly now being my guardian angel. I close my eyes and imagine a silly image of Lilly sitting on a cloud, angel wings coming out of her back, her tail wagging pleasantly and a halo resting above her head, wearing it like some kind of levitating crown. I think back to yesterday when Elliot Prendergast called in to give us the heart-shattering news about what had happened to Lilly, and the difficult task of ringing Jacob and telling him about Lilly's passing. I know Jacob and his only daughter Jackie absolutely loved Lilly, especially Jackie, who used to dog sit her. And I can't blame them; Lilly was a sweet little girl who stole the hearts of everyone. I believe Lilly's motto was, 'I don't care who you are or what you've done; I love you! '

    She'll be greatly missed by everyone who had the pleasure of meeting her in person. When it boils down to it, Beth and I will miss her the most since she was our dog and one of the best ones at that, with her placid and endearing nature that was almost impossible not to love. Her ability to make people fall in love with her at first glance was commendable, and she needs to know just how extraordinary she was. And yet, I wonder why her death is breaking me this way... I should be used to this, considering I had lost three other dogs before her. What was it that made Lilly better? Was it the impact that she had towards those around her? Was it her never-ending love towards her family? Or was it because she brought out the best in people?

    'Do you think Lilly's happy where she is?' I randomly ask Beth without looking at her; my eyes still fixed on the picture of Lilly and the three other dogs that had come before her trying to puzzle out what made Lilly more special.

    'Sorry? I didn't quite catch that?' Beth calls from the lounge room. I don't recall seeing or hearing her move.

    'I said do you think Lilly is happy where she is?' I ask again. I look at her this time, seeing that she holds the framed pencil drawing Jackie had done of Lilly: tongue panting and just being the happy little dog she was known for. I can faintly see a tear creeping down Beth's cheek as she caresses the photos with her fingers, sliding them wanly down the glass casing that protects the drawing.

'I don't know,' she says as she places the picture down on the couch next to her. 'Maybe, but I really can't say, Mum,' she adds. I nod back in reply. I can understand what she's getting at because the existence of Heaven after someone dies has often been a topic of debate. But even if I don't believe in Heaven myself, I do wish that Lilly is happy up there wherever she is. Even if it isn't Heaven, I hope she's happy regardless, and I do hope that she's making more dog friends and that there are so many tennis balls to play with she doesn't know what to do with them.

I let out a deep breath and finish up the rest of the cornflakes in my bowl before stacking it inside Beth's bowl. Straining only slightly, I take both empty cereal bowls to the sink and place them in the dish rack to be washed later.

***

'OH MY GOODNESS!' I cry as happy thoughts of Lilly wash over me like a tidal wave crashing into a cliff. Those memories and the inconceivable truth that Lilly's no longer with us makes me want to go back into my room to cry into my pillow until I have no more tears left. My hands are shaking, and my vision starts to blur, clouded by tears that fog and stain my glasses. The memories—oh, all the sweet memories—of someone who's no longer here to comfort me when I needed her so desperately, especially when I think back to the car accident that had nearly killed Beth and I. Lilly had an incredible gift and was a master of comforting simply by just being around, spreading and bringing joy to everyone she came across.

I collapse.

'MUM!' Beth shouts from the lounge room, stopping what she's doing and running over to help me up.

'I can't believe she's gone, really gone,' I blubber, feeling Beth take me in her hands, where she proceeds to tug me up to my feet. The first thing I do as soon as I'm standing once more is wrap my arms around Beth and hug her as tightly as my weak arms can manage.

I'm in such a state of distress. I need as many hugs as someone can give me. Even if they're brief, they're soothing. I just need someone to be here, to share their love with me and to offer the kind of comfort Lilly had given when she was alive

She was there; she'd sense when someone was feeling down, offering extra comfort that could only come from a friendly canine friend. This was no different... I need Lilly here with me to feel the warmth of her tongue as she licked my hands or the cool touch of her wet nose. But this is the hardest part because Lilly is...

Beth tugs at the lilac cord of my nightgown, ushering me over to her. 'I think you need to sit down. I can do the dishes, ring Michelle, and let her know about Lilly. If someone else rings when I'm talking to Michelle or working on the dishes, do you think you'd be able to talk to them?' she questions me as she leads me into the living room and gently beckons me to sit on one of the couches. I do so without hesitation or question, sitting on the couch. The old, weakened muscles in my body are trembling. I can feel my lips wavering, and my eyes become blurry again from all the tears trapped inside.

'Just sit there. I'll sort things out, okay?' Beth says.

'O-okay,' I rasp out. I hover my arms in front of me as if I'm holding something that only I can see. One hand is near my shoulder, and the other hangs low. It's as if I'm trying to hold a residue of Lilly.

Beth's voice emerges in the background, talking with someone I presume is Michelle, though she could just as easily be talking to her daughter, Nina.

Still holding the invisible Lilly. I begin to rock back and forth, thinking of nothing but images of Lilly and the faces she'd make when she was happy, her tail wagging so furiously, Beth and I would often joke about it falling off from the speed of all that motion.

I feel tears flush down my cheeks. I take off my glasses and place them on the arm of the couch beside me. Then I resume holding the invisible Lilly-shaped thing, teetering as I sob like there's no tomorrow. I know that Lilly's passing would be difficult, but I didn't expect it to be this hard: her death is like losing all my four brothers and three sisters all over again. Losing them one at a time was very hard, and I don't know how I managed to cope and still be here to tell their story and what it was like to be the last remaining member of the Letruc's.

My eldest brother George had been lucky to survive World War 11 in Austria, only to later die from a brain haemorrhage after falling down some steps during a holiday in Bangkok, Thailand in 1951. My second brother, Eric suffered a stroke just two days after his 61st birthday and died of cardiac arrest in 2016. Gene, my third brother, was a heavy smoker. As expected, the damage to his lungs caught up with him. He died of emphysema at just thirty-two years old, one year and four months after George passed.

My youngest brother, Ben made it to ninety years old. He died in his nursing home room in 2018. His death was the most recent.

My eldest sister, Rachel, a year older than Eric, had been a leukemia sufferer since she was 10. It took her in 1948 when she was only twenty-three years old. My second sister, Linda, struggled after losing her husband, Deacon, to malaria in 1964. Three months later, spiralling out of control she took her own life with a sturdy knitted noose.

Finally, my youngest sister, Leslie, just five months younger than me passed away from heart disease in 1978.

I am the only living member of my family now. At eighty-six I know it won't be long before it will be my time to join my brothers and sisters, parents, and the four dogs I've shared my life with dogs I loved, like my own children, with four legs, tail and fur.

Oh, the thought of those furry faces had come back to me. The very sight of those four dogs in the mornings was a blessing (dogs will always be man's best friend). Seeing their wagging tails, happy eyes, and panting tongues had always filled me with a certain kind of joy that I don't think any person could replicate a special kind of joy unique to dogs.

Every morning all four dogs did the same thing, they'd jump onto my bed, waiting eagerly for me to rub my eyes and wake up. Their happy faces, panting with excitement, were always the first thing I saw in the morning when I opened my eyes. There was something uniquely special about how Lilly went that extra step to make my mornings the best any grandma could have. When her jumping on my bed didn't wake me up, Lilly, instead of waited patiently for me to open my eyes, she'd move to the side of the bed and lick me on the cheek. Her tail beat would thump against my chest, as if saying, 'Wake up Mummy! Wake up! It's time for breakfast! ' I had no choice but to wake up.

'Alright, alright, I'm awake; you can stop licking me now, ' I'd mutter in a tired voice, patting her head. This would send Lilly bounding around the bed. She'd race ahead of me into the kitchen, the sound of her joyful running on the carpet was always a welcome sound.

Living with Lilly really was the best thing I could ever ask for. She made every day such a splendour, even when she was naughty, making a mess of the stuffed toys we bought her and leaving the lounge room a sea of fluff. I'd call her out for being a "naughty little girl."

Despite her mischief, I couldn't help but feel a sense of wonderment around her. Even when she wasn't doing what she was told half the time, giving people puppy eyes to get more food despite having food in her bowl I knew she was a good girl all the way through. She wasn't spiteful, never hurt anyone, never growled. She had a golden heart, loved everyone she met and just had an uncanny ability to make everyone fawn over her like a newborn baby. Lilly just had to look at someone, and bam, she had a new friend!

The same was true when she was naughty. She'd had to look me at with those magical eyes, and I couldn't stay mad at her for long. I'd let her off the hook about a minute after telling her off.

Lilly's impact on our family was big. My brother Ben, who got to know her nine years ago before moving to Lane's Home for the Elderly back in early 2016, adored her. She was indeed a one-of-a-kind dog that would always fill people's heart with something that no one could ever replace.

My thoughts return to the real world at the sound of dishes cluttering and water dripping into a sink, meaning that Beth is in the middle of washing the dishes from this morning. I glance over to her and open my mouth to ask how Michelle and Nina are upon hearing the news of Lilly's passing, but I hesitate. Instead, I ask if Beth needs any help, two pairs of hands are always better than one.

'No, I'm fine, nearly finished anyway,' she answers.

'Oh...' I mumble pathetically, noticing that my hands are now in my lap and no longer holding the invisible Lilly. I clench the silk fabric of my dressing gown, my heart growing heavier with each passing second as I think about Lilly and her absence from the house.

'Michelle says that she's sorry and that she encourages us to stay strong,' Beth says, prompting me to ask more about my eldest daughter and granddaughter, who live up in Sydney and have done so for the past couple of years. Michelle only really comes down to Tasmania for my birthday or for special family gatherings, so Beth, Jacob, Jackie, and I, don't get to see her much. As for Nina, she's a very busy woman and rarely has the time to visit us in Hobart. But I can't really complain. Nina rings me here and there to see how Beth and I are going, and that's a good thing. It makes up for not being able to see her face-to-face.

'How are Michelle and Nina?' I ask.

'Nina is working somewhere in the city. Michelle said she'll ring her when she can. Michelle says she always loved hearing about us, how Lilly is, and whether she's destroyed anymore tennis balls. Michelle says she's hurting at our loss, but like I said before, she urges us to push through this and stay strong.'

'Did you say thank you?' I ask, not really knowing why because I already know her answer. Of course, Beth would say thank you; anyone would say thank you to someone who gave their condolences for having someone who lost someone dear, whether it be a family member or a pet.

'Yes. She also said that she'll let Daniel know about Lilly too,' Beth says. Daniel, Michelle's husband, was highly fond of Lilly and of animals in general. From the many phone conversations I've had with him, he often talked about spending his time watching nature documentaries with Michelle. So, no doubt that Daniel will be just as shattered as we all are at the passing of a certain Lilly Lahey.

I get off the chair and wander into the kitchen where Beth is still in the cleaning process. I stand by the dining table, watching her clean the last pieces of cutlery before placing them in the dishrack to dry. Beth puts her hand into the water and pulls out the plug, draining it. When she's done, she comes over to where I am, and I open my arms out and pull her in for a hug. I can feel her chin on my shoulder and hear the sound of her sniffling.

'What are we going to do, Mum? Things just don't feel right anymore. The house feels so lifeless and empty without Lilly running around,' she says in a morose voice, putting her arms around me and hugging me also.

'I don't know, we'll just have to wait and see,' I reply trying but failing to sound brave and in control. I think Beth can tell that I'm trying to appear strong for her, from the way I struggle to not to stammer and keep my lips from not trembling. Still, she also knows it isn't really working in the way I'd hoped. She buries her face into my shoulder, and that's when I hear the heavy sound of her crying, feeling her tears seep through my lilac dressing gown. Usually, when someone close to me, like Beth or Jacob (on rare occasions) or Michelle, starts crying, I can't help but cry too. So, it comes as no surprise to Beth or me when the tears start falling from my eyes, despite my best to wipe them away with the sleeve of my dressing gown.

'I really miss her, Mum.'

'I know, my sweet Elizabeth,' I tell her softly, soothingly. 'I miss her too, but there isn't much we can do now. Just stay at home and mourn her death just like we did before when the other three before her had passed away.' I'm looking at Jackie's drawing of Lilly, then at the photo of puppy Lilly on the dining room wall, the one that shared the same frame as the dogs we'd before her: Mindy, Molly and Chloe. All wonderful girls with lovely dispositions. But as beautiful as they were, none of them could compete with Lilly or her unique gift of making anyone she met fall in love with her; of turning strangers into friends. I sigh, briefly thinking that there will never be another Mindy, Molly, or Chloe and almost certainly never another Lilly. She'd embedded herself too deeply into people's hearts for anyone to ever fully let her go. Her memory will stay there for a long time…forever.

Beth glances at me, using the palms of her hands to wipe her eyes.

She sniffles before asking, 'Are we going to have her cremated like the rest?' I can't quite understand why she asks, though, she already knows that cremation had always been our first and only choice whenever we lost a dog. It had become a sort of tradition within the Lahey household that whenever a pet passed away, they were cremated, and their ashes kept safe in the house. That way it felt like they were still with us, even if they weren't running around and causing trouble.

'Of course, we're going to get her cremated. Why wouldn't we? Mindy, Molly, and Chloe have been cremated; we have their ashes. It wouldn't feel right if Lilly wasn't cremated like her sisters,' I explain. The thought of those small bags containing the ashes of our three little angels comes to me, and the concept of receiving one of those little bags containing Lilly finds its way into my mind, forcing me to heave out a breath at the very idea of it, and knowing that it will one day become true.

'Yeah, I suppose that's true,' says Beth, a little late on the reply as she stares at the floor below her as if thinking about Lilly's cremation for herself and placing Lilly's ashes next to Mindy, Molly, and Chloe's bags. Sniffling myself, I pull away from my oldest daughter and lean on the polished wooden coffee table behind me, which holds my many bags of knitting wool, needles, and booklets. I grab a box of tissues, pull two for Beth and two for me.

'Thank you,' says Beth as she takes the tissues from me and wipes her face with them.

I do the same before disposing of them in the bin under the coffee table.

I sit in my chair again and Beth joins me a few seconds later, settling onto the couch across me, near the coffee table. I glance at her, and she looks up at me, her face washed with sorrow and grief.

'I'll call Elliot after my shower. I'll ask him to call the crematorium and make an appointment to get Lilly cremated.'

Beth nods slowly, returning to staring at the ground, hands cupped and thinking.

I feel a sharp sense of oppression tugging at me as I take one of the knitting bags off the table, holding it in front of me without really thinking about what I was going to do with it, what I was going to knit, or if there was something I'd started that I needed to continue with. I stare into the bag, seeing the knitting tools inside, thinking about the piece of my heart that's now missing. Oh, the many happy faces Lilly made when either Jacob or Jackie visited, the many times she'd the play bow in front of Jackie, the many toys, and balls she destroyed. She'd always wake either Beth, Jackie (when they'd stayed over for the night), or me in the morning. All the times she'd snuggle up to me in bed, and... 'Oh,' I mumble to myself. I can still see her all the time, sitting there, staring into my eyes with an expression that says, 'I love you, Mummy. I love you so much because I'm your dog. I'm you're Lilly! '

Yes, it's true: there will never be another Jack Russell like Lilly Lahey ever, and nothing will ever change that. Lilly will always remain in my heart and in the hearts of everyone that she considered a friend. The best thing we can do is stay strong for her. No one said that grief is easy to handle; everyone deals with it differently. But if things are going to get better, I'll need to turn myself around and remember that Lilly will always be in my heart—and that piece of her will never fade.

I..., no, we , all of us—, will miss you, Lilly... so... much.

-Marian Kushner-

EVERYTHING FEELS WRONG. I feel cold... really cold. My arms are covered in goose pimples and I can't stop my body from trembling. The house feels empty, as if it's missing something important. Things just don't feel right anymore.

My parents and our kindly neighbour Angus Caterwaul (who's the one who discovered Mittens' body) have suggested that Mittens was possibly attacked and killed by a feral animal while she was out exploring beyond the backyard. My parents and I still can't quite understand how she got out in the first place since we have a strong fence that keeps out the neighbouring pests such as squirrels, chipmunks, and feral cats and dogs.

Still, Mr Caterwaul suggested that Mittens might've gotten out through a hole or dodgy plank in the wooden fence. He said she could've seen an opening in the wooden boards and decided to squeeze her way through them as, 'You know how young kittens are; they love any opportunity to see the world around them and explore new territory.' Which was something he'd mentioned when I visited him and told him the news about Mitten's joining our family.

I think Mr Caterwaul is a lovely man. He has white hair and a moustache, and he loves talking with the neighbours and hearing their stories. He always waves and smiles when he sees me. Not to mention he was always patient with me, even when I'd brag about my best friend Sheila's new bicycle or her two-week holiday in Spain with her parents.

I watch nervously through teary eyes as Dad gets off the couch and stands up. He glances at Mum, who's sitting next to me. Her arm still around my shoulder in a comforting way.

'Zack?' Mum asks him, wanting to know what's on his mind because Dad has a habit of standing up whenever he has an idea. I curl my arms around myself. I still feel so cold.

'I'm going to search the fence, see how she got out, and then I'm going to see about fixing it so we can prevent something like this from ever happening again especially if we decide to get another kitten or even a puppy.' 'What do you mean *if*? We *are* going to get another one, right?' I ask.

'We're not sure yet, Marian; the impact of Mittens' death is still too raw. We'll need some time to mourn her before we decide to get another pet. You understand, Marian?

I glance at Dad and Mum. I can't see the details off their faces because my eyes are blurred, full of my own tears, and the more I think about getting another pet, the more I cry. But I don't need to see my parents to know they're hurting as much as I am. And deep down I know they only want the best for me because they're my parents and they love me. They understand how hard this is for me and know it's best not to rush things, letting them take their course. So, I totally understand what they mean about not hurrying to get another pet. Just seeing a kitten or puppy would make me sadder and miss Mittens even more.

'I understand,' I reply sadly, my head and voice low. Dad leaves the room to go outside to check the fence. I turn and hug Mum. I want as much of her love as she can give me. I feel Mum rubbing my back and hair, telling me that everything is going to be okay; that wherever Mittens is, she isn't suffering anymore.

That's when I realise that I don't want her to leave me, scared that if she stops hugging me, she'd leave me, just like Mittens had. I don't want to be alone.

'You know what happens to those of the purest of hearts that die?' She asks me.

I look up at her, wiping my eyes with my fingers. 'N-No. What happens?' I sniffle curiously.

'They grow a set of angel wings,' she says.

I close my eyes and try to imagine my Mittens growing some white feathery wings. Mum continues, 'Then a golden ring expands around their heads like a royal crown that hovers about an inch above their heads. That becomes a halo.'

I imagine this too, seeing Mittens gaze upward as a gold ring grows above her head where it humbly sits. I also picture Mittens flicking at the halo with her tiny paws, watching it fall over each time, as if it were some kind of flying ring toy teasing her just like the sparrows outside used to do whenever she sat by the bird fountain, watching them clean and pecked at their feathers.

Mum pulls me close, and my ear presses against her as she tells the final parts of her story. 'And after they have their wings and halo, they fly away, up into the sky, into the clouds where they meet other angels like them. Do you know what that place is mostly known as?'

'Heaven,' I say, remembering that I'd heard others use the word, often when someone they know and loved has died.

'Yes, and I bet that's where Mittens is, making new feline friends and doing all the exploring she can possibly want,' Mum says.

'Are you sure?' I ask, wanting to believe her because I don't like the idea of Mittens in pain or feeling lonely without us caring for her. After all, she isn't even a year old. So, she'll need a better understanding of the world around her. Everything was new to Mittens; even our house, which had become Mittens' home, was strange and unusual, and she was still exploring everything the house had to offer, right down to every nook and cranny.

Thinking about Mittens exploring reminds me of the day Dad and I picked up Mittens from the Thomson household. I remember she was trying to hide inside her mother's fur. She looked to be the runt of the litter.

Mrs Thomson held out the kittens so I could get a better look. When I'd decided she was the kitten I wanted, Mr Thomson disappeared into the house for about two minutes. He came back with a teal-coloured pet carrier that had in it a small bag of dry Whiskas kitten food, and a small pink and orange pet blanket with black paws on it. Mr Thomson handed the carrier over to Dad.

I was mesmerised by the tiny kitten's adorable features, her soft white and tabby fur, her cute little face and fuzzy tail, right down to her small paws with those equally cutesy pink and black toe beans. . She looked around as if she was trying to work out what was happening.

'What do you think, my little princess? ' Dad asked me. I remember the feeling of him placing a hand on my shoulder and leaning over to see the kitten's beauty with me. I remember glancing up at his face with the biggest smile on mine as if this was my very first and best Christmas.

'I love her! ' I said, and Dad leaned in more to smack a kiss on my cheek as a sign to tell me he was glad.

'Yep, we'll take that one, ' Dad had said to Mr and Mrs Thomson, confirming that the kitten would be coming home with us.

I returned the kitten to Mrs Thomson, who gently took her while Dad fumbled in his wallet for the one hundred pounds the Thomsons were asking for. He found it and handed it to Mr Thomson, who took it with a friendly smile and a warm 'Thank you'. I glanced back as Dad opened the latch of the pet carrier, took the packet of dry kitten food out and handed it to me. He then picked it up by the handle and held it up for Mrs Thomson to carefully place the curious little kitten inside before he closed it.

'Oh! Before you go, make sure you give her the best home. Here, this was one of her favourite toys, ' Mrs Thomson said, then disappeared into the house, she returned with a small pink plush toy in the shape of a foot, it had a cartoon smiley face on it and the words My BFF. I took the pink foot toy from her and squeezed it into the carrier door for the kitten to play with on the car ride back home. After that, Dad and I thanked the Thomsons, who wished us luck. Mr Thomson quickly asked me what I was going to name her. I didn't need to think hard about it, so I happily stated, 'Her name is Mittens.' To which he replied, 'That's a lovely name for her. It suits her.'

The Thomsons wished us good luck once more. Dad and I thanked them in return and we headed back to the car. I remember being so excited; I couldn't wait to show Mum the surprise; however, I later found out that she knew all along about us getting a kitten because both she and Dad had been planning it in secret.

The sad thing is that Mittens could never explore fully like she probably wanted to. she couldn't even explore the rest of the back and front yards anymore because, as Mr Caterwaul had said, her curiosity had gotten the best of her. Mittens had ended up in an area she shouldn't have been, and that led to her being attacked and killed by a feral animal. Mittens would never grow up to live the life of an ordinary house cat; she wouldn't be able to pig out on food and get fat, and she wouldn't spend most of her days sleeping on the couch or windowsill. But the thing that she'd never get to do that made me the saddest was grow up, and she'd never be able to snuggle up to Mum, Dad or me) She wouldn't be able to do any of those things... now that she's... dead

I hear footsteps enter the house, getting closer with each step. Dad pokes his head into the doorway, his face is white as a ghost.

'What did you find?' Mum asks him.

I realise my fists are clenched and shaking with impatience. I want to know how Mittens had escaped and if he could fix it.

'One of the boards is crooked and poking a few inches out from where it should've been; she must've squeezed through that.

I'll get another plank tomorrow and fix it in case the next pet finds it,' he tells us.

While it's correct that Mittens had only been with us for a short time and was still in the process of settling into her forever home, she was a baby... my fur baby. She was a kitten I could cuddle whenever I was feeling sad. She was someone I could play with, especially since I was an only child, and just seeing the curious look on her little fuzzy face, those tiny beans on her little tootsies, her soft white and tabby fur, and her bushy tail—was enough to make me smile. What was not to love about her? She was just a really, really cute kitten, and she would've grown up to become an equally beautiful cat... If only that nasty feral animal hadn't attacked and taken her away from us.

'What are we going to do until then?' I ask them both. Wiping my eyes for what felt like the hundredth time.

'Sorry?' Dad asks, as if he hasn't heard me.

'What are we going to do until then?' I repeat. I watch with clearer eyes as Dad glances at Mum before returning his eyes back to me.

'Suppose we'll just have to do what any other family would do in this situation, and that is to get along with our daily lives,' Mum says. She gives out another sigh then turns over to look at me. Her face is distraught, and she appears to be holding back her tears.

'Marian, I understand you want to stay and hear this, but this might be too much for you. There's a reason I don't talk about Auntie Robin's friend Roslyn: because it's painful.'

'I don't care,' I say. I want to hear it because then I can comfort you while you both comfort me.'

Mum tears up, wipes her eyes with her wrist and throws her arms out to me. I wriggle into them. She hugs me, whispering, 'Thank you,' in a shaky, torn voice.

After Mum explained her story about Roslyn's bunny Charlie—how he'd been discovered lying motionless in the backyard, his body covered in blood and bite marks—, I feel sick just imagining it. But I'm even more disgusted when I think about how Roslyn Timberton must've felt, upon finding her bunny like that. I hear Dad whisper the word, 'Damn.' At the same time, I hug Mum tighter knowing she needs it. Mum gently pulls me away, sniffling, and places a tender hand on my shoulder. Dad looks at me, and I at him. He opens his mouth to say, 'Okay, Marian, I think you've heard enough, would you please…' but I interrupt him, speaking to Mum.

'Do you think we could talk with Robin after we get another pet and arrange a surprise for Roslyn if she's still friends with Auntie Robin?'

Mum stares at me with a strange look as if she thinks I've either gone silly or is considering my idea. She gives me a forced smile, as if hoping it will make me feel at least a bit better about this whole thing, and while I can't lie that Mum's smiles are a highlight in my life, same with Dads, I really do want to smile back at her, the hurt of losing Mittens is still too fresh in my mind. The best thing that I can do is to temporarily stop crying and try to think about what Mum would be thinking in reply to my idea.

'That sounds like a lovely idea. But I'm unsure if Robin's still friends with Roslyn; I'll have to call her but it won't be today, maybe in a week.'

'Why a week?' I ask. I can feel my eyes starting to water each time I blink, so I wipe them.

'So, we can have time to mourn Mittens,' Dad says from the couch near the doorway. 'Remember, Marian, it's best not to rush these things. We need to take our time,' he tells me in a patient voice, knowing death is still relatively new to me.

I know that it happens to everyone; I learned this in school. I remember when Scott McDenvers told us his uncle Joe's best friend passing away due to this cancer called Leukemia. Scott explained that his uncle Joe had been going through a tough time and that his parents would pick him up at lunchtime so they could go to Joe's and support him. So, while I understand about death, I've never actually experienced anyone I know dying. Mittens was the first, and her death makes it all the more challenging for me.

'Oh... right, I thought maybe it could help take our minds off being sad,' I say.

'Yes, we know, darling, and it isn't a bad thought, but we should wait before we decide to do anything else. Besides, Roslyn might already have a new pet,' Dad says as he glances over at Mum and asks her the year when Robin's friend lost her rabbit again.

'I was eight, Robin was eleven, so .... 1982, I think,' Mum replies before turning her attention back to me. She tenderly touches my cheek and wipes away the tears I've missed. 'But my sister's friend isn't the focus right now, Marian; the focus is you and how this is all affecting you. We need to focus on helping you through this, since it's the first time you've experienced death and what it's like to be in mourning?'

'Yes... and I already hate it,' I say with a soft sniffle, lowering my head to stare at the hands on my lap that are shaking again as I think more about Mittens. I shut my eyes tightly and feel my teeth grind as images of Mittens playing with her toys, chasing butterflies and staring at me before running off come into my head like an unwanted house guest.

I start crying again. Only this time, I can't control the tears or do anything to hold them back; they just spill out of my eyes like a waterfall. I can't do anything to stop them, only let them fall as images of Mittens flood my mind, a mix of happy memories and the haunting thought of what her lifeless body must look like.

'Why?' I cry, clapping my hands on my face and crying into them. 'Why did that horrible animal have to take my Mittens from me? She was still a baby! She wasn't even one yet. Why did Mittens have to escape and get herself killed? Why couldn't she just stay inside where she was safe. Why did she have to die too quickly? Wasn't I a good mummy to her?' I blubber out without really thinking about what I'm saying. I just say things from the top of my head, and even if they aren't true, it doesn't matter I can't think straight.

'Marian. Stop,' Mum cries. I feel her hands hold my cheeks and Dad orders me to stop, but I can't... even if I want to, I can't keep the images of Mittens's dead body away from my mind, try as I may, they won't go away!

'IS THAT WHY SHE ESCAPED? DID SHE WANT TO GET AWAY FROM ME?' I scream.

'No, Marian!' I hear Dad yell and feel Mum grab my arms, pull them away from my face, and ask me to look up at her. 'I can't,' I tell her, shaking my head, 'They won't go away, the pictures, they won't leave me alone!'

'What pictures?' Dad asks. His voice sounds closer, and I can feel another hand grasp my shoulder and lightly shake it, meaning that Dad must've come over and kneeled on the floor beside me.

'Mittens! Her body!' I cry before shooting my eyes open and seeing both my parent's broad-eyed, concerned faces staring at me. I'm breathing heavily as I gaze from one to the other, letting out a small gulp. I ask them through teary eyes and a hurtful tone.

'Did Mittens hate me?'

My parents hug me as soon as I say that, and they both start to overwhelm my ears with 'no and 'of course she didn't.'

'Then why did she escape?' I ask hoping one of them can give me a reasonable answer.

'Because that's what cats do,' says Dad. 'They can't help but get curious about the world, and they love to explore things, even if it does get them into trouble.'

It's like that saying that I often hear in school: 'Curiosity killed the cat. But I never liked to think it was true. I always thought it was a silly saying to make cat people paranoid about letting their cats go outside. But I suppose in this sense, it was true. We had left the back door open for Mittens to get out and play around the garden in the backyard while my parents and I went to take Sheila back home.

I wipe my eyes, sniffle for a second and look at Dad. 'Dad?'

'Yes, darling?'

'Tomorrow, could you and Mum ring the Leidy's and ask them to drop Sheila down? I feel like I need to see her and tell her about Mittens.'

Dad looks down at me with a sad look. He blinks at me slowly, like he's considering it. I expect him to disagree, since he might not think it's right to tell Sheila about Mittens' death. But perhaps he realises it will benefit me.

'Okay, Marian, we'll ring Amanda and Tim tomorrow around lunchtime. Just promise us that you'll stay strong.'

'I'll try,' This is all I can say, even though I can't promise.

'Good girl,' he pauses for a moment before asking me if I'm hungry. I shake my head timidly and simply ask for a cup of banana milk. Banana milk always helps calm my nerves, or whenever I'm sad. I cup my hands together. Dad leaves the room, and Mum put her hand on my shoulder. I close my eyes and think to myself, *I hope we get another pet soon; I don't like feeling this way. Oh, why did you have to leave me so soon, Mittens?*

Part five: Wings

-Atlas-

2021

I'VE BEEN HERE for a while now. I can't tell how many days (that's if days even exist here). I can't deny that it's nice, even lovely here in this place called Heaven, I feel like I've been here for at about five months, and in that time, I've come to see this place as my new home.

I've made friends here, too: Colonel, a French husky; Otavius, an Irish Wolfhound; Smudge, the cat, and Perry the green budgie. We all play tug-o-war together. Even though we've been playing for what feels like countless days, the others sometimes beat me by snatching the pull-ropes from my teeth, which Smudge and Perry always find hilarious, and prompts Smudge to meow in a joking way, 'Aw, come on, what was that? You're allowing them to win! '

It's a nice thing to do: to lose here and there. One time, I even lost to an English Bulldog half my size named Frank; that had felt good. But winning and taking the pull rope for myself always felt more powerful——like the way I used to with my owner. And when I did win, my friends would always cheer me on and offer to take me to the Boneyard, so I could find the largest bone. We'd all take turns in having a bite on it, of course, since we're dogs. But Octavius tends to be a little greedy, often tries to keep the bone all to himself, so we have to remind him to share. He always apologises and lets the next dog have their turn.

So, while I've learnt to face the fact that I'm dead and that I might never see my owners again, I have my friends here, helping and guiding me through the tough times. But I certainly can't deny that I miss Master Mason and Mistress Victoria and their quant little house in Quebec in Canada. Nothing will ever make me forget them. Even with all the times my tail wagged, or my tongue panted, playing with my new Heaven friends, I'll never forget the humans that raised me from puppyhood all the way up to adulthood. And I also couldn't possibly allow myself to forget the most important person in my life: my daddy: the young boy named Colin. There's no way I could forget him. I'll miss him every day. Even when he grows as old as the Master, I'll miss and love him and think about him daily. That little boy was the entire reason I lived the most incredible and happy life.

Without a doubt, I feel honoured to have been a part of the Trembley family. They've given me so much, and I couldn't possibly have asked for more. They welcomed me into their home and raised me to be a good boy. What more could a dog want than to be called a good boy? And my family had made sure to remind me every day that I was with them, that I was a good boy, that I was their dog and that I was Atlas Trembley, the family Rottweiler!

I'm lying on my back on the soft green grass, paws in the air, my eyes staring at the blue sky, and its puffy white clouds. Birds are tweeting happily as they flutter around in the sky. There's a soft, warm breeze that blows gently through my short, silky coat. It feels lovely to just find myself lying here. I blink, and a thought comes to my mind, an idea that I soon dismiss, knowing it would never happen: the idea of seeing my family again. But I know that isn't possible. I know I'll never get to see my family again, not until they pass away themselves.

But whenever I'm alone, this thought comes back. With the thought in my head, I turn and look at the first thing I see: the Birdcage, a giant golden dome-shaped structure. It's suspended on some clouds off in the distance. Birds like Perry, of all shapes and sizes, go there when they want to relax or sleep. Underneath the Birdcage is where other animals sleep, relax, or play.

It's always a pleasant sight to see animals playing and being friendly. But at the same time, it makes me sad when I catch glimpses of kittens and puppies here, meaning that they've died before getting a chance to have their masters celebrate their first birthday and shower them with treats and new toys to play with.

This thought of puppies and kittens reminds me of the time I came across a tiny Golden Retriever puppy named Chip. He was only a month old, lying by himself on the open field near the induction clouds and softly whimpering, whoever he'd come down with must've wandered off and left him there.

I felt sorry for the pup; he was such a small defenceless baby, so, I decided to try what Shelby had done for me and help him because I expected it would feel good to be able to help someone new. I approached, sat by him and asked him what was wrong. He looked up at me with little brown eyes and said in a small voice that he was lonely and scared because he didn't know what was happening around him. He told me that a black and tan dog had brought him then he went to look for someone else but hadn't returned, leaving him scared, confused and alone.

I laid next to him and explained that I'd felt the same when I had arrived and that most other animals felt that way, too. I didn't ask him how he died or tell him he was in Heaven because he'd died. But I did ask Chip about his owners, and when he answered that didn't have any owners it shocked me enough that I jumped backwards. Chip told me he was a stray, born to an abandoned mother who was on the run from the scary place (I had assumed he was talking about the pound).

Chip then explained the last thing he saw before waking up in Heaven. Chip said he went to go looking for his mama when he came across a rugged area that didn't have grass on it.

He said there were massive, fast-moving metal monsters raced across it. Chip didn't need to tell me anymore as I leant down and licked him on the head and behind his soft little ears, I could imagine what Chip saw during his final minutes, and it frightened me probably as much as it had scared him.

Little Chip had been run over.

I comforted Chip for a while; soothed the little puppy until he asked me if I'd be his friend. I smiled and told him I'd would and added that I could offer him more than just a friendship of an adult rottweiler—I could introduce him to other friends his age: kittens, puppies, foals, and chicks. His little beady eyes lit up.

'Rwelly? he asked me in his tiny puppy voice. I nodded and Chip got to his feet, licking me on one side of my face. His little tongue was so soft that it stirred memories of when I was a young puppy myself, nursing from my birth Mum. I felt my tail start to wag.

'Thank you, big doggie!' he said with a cheerful little yap.

Big Doggie? Why would he call me that? At first, I had wondered. But then I thought about it and supposed it was okay for the little Golden Retriever to call me that. After all, I hadn't even told him what my name was, which I decided to do at that precise moment.

'My name's Atlas, but you can call me Big Al if you like,' I said introducing myself. Chip bounded up and down on the spot and spun excitedly around in circles, which was a lovely sight to see. This made my tail wag some more.

My name's Chip! Mama name me and my bwothers and sistas after hooman snacks. She said a nice hooman girl fed her some doggie biscuits as well as crackers and chippies.'

'Is that so? Well, maybe we might be able to find your mum here if we look hard enough. Who knows, perhaps she's taking care of your future buddies? Because I've come to know that this place can make anything your heart desires a reality. So, if you want to see your mum, she might be here,' I say, starting to feel like a big brother to Chip, and that I'd do anything for the little puppy.

Chip's eyes lit up again with the sunlight that gleamed off his fuzzy golden fur 'RWELLY?!' he yapped cheerfully (there was that funny word again). His tail wagged frantically; it reminds me of a female Jack Russell I'd seen around here; she was playing with two other dogs in Tennis Ball Paradise. Her tail wagged so much it threatened to fall off. Seeing Chip's tail wag that hard reminded me of her.

After I'd gotten Chip all worked up about the possibility of seeing his mum and making new friends, I told him to follow me.

It didn't take us long to get to the Nursery: a large, welcoming building in the shape of a house that almost resembled the home where I'd grown up most of my life with the Trembley's. The Nursey also had a giant milk bottle with the word: "NURSERY" beside it out the front. Again, it reminded me of that place where cats go for a drink or two. Chip and I entered the building, and the first thing we saw was that it was full of surrogate mothers and babies of all animal species (who'd had the misfortune to die too young, much like tiny Chip next to me).

I looked around, seeing mother dogs with puppies and even kittens. I even saw a dog that looked like Chip. I was about to wander over to her when Chip stopped me, saying. 'There are many doggies and kitties here, isn't there, Big Al?' But I didn't respond because I was taking in the beauty of the Nursey and staring at that mother dog with the golden coat.

I'd never been inside the Nursery before; I'd only walked past it. It was indeed a sight to behold because it was full of mothers and baby animals and matched the warmth that I'd felt back in the Trembley house, back with the Master and Mistress and Daddy Colin. I stared at the bright yellow walls that made me think of the Master and Mistress's bedroom. Sometimes Colin and I would go into their bedroom because Colin would have a bad dream and needed the comfort of not just his loyal dog but his parents too. I couldn't blame him. And it didn't matter that he wasn't cuddling up to me, as long as my humans were safe and I was in the same room with Colin, that's all that mattered.

'Atlas!' I remember shooting my head around much to the confused puppy next to me, as I thought I'd heard my Daddy's voice; the voice of the little boy who'd raised me from puppyhood. But I soon realised this was my imagination, and I sighed with mild disappointment.

'Big Al?' Chip asked.

'It's nothing; I'm okay,' I'd said with a swift shake of my head. 'Let's see about getting you some friends!' I said to the little puppy, trying my best to sound strong. I only managed to take one step forward when I heard another voice again. This time, it was female, and it wasn't just me who'd heard it: Chip did too. Chip and I looked around to see where the voice had come from, and it was Chip who noticed her first. She was similar to the big dog with the golden fur I'd seen moments before, but this one's fur was longer, making me think that the other dog mother I saw earlier was a Labrador. This one who called out was a big dog with fluffy golden fur. She walked towards us, trailed by five puppies of different breeds; only one of the five looked like Chip. She saw Chip and boy, did her tail wag!

'Chip? Is that you, Chippie?' She spoke to the little puppy at my feet, and I peered down and watched him take a small, timid step towards the mother dog, followed by the five tiny puppies.

'Mama?' he asked before I saw his little tail wag frantically as it had when I had first proposed the idea of meeting new friends to him. 'Mama!' cried Chip as he bounded towards the mother dog, who Chip had recognised as his Mommy.

It made my tail wag. To see a mother reunite with her lost puppy was a wonderful thing.

'Chip! Oh, my beautiful little baby Chippie boy!' cried the mother as she pulled her son close with her paw and showered him with licks. The puppies that followed her gathered around Chip, and the one that looked most like Chip seemed to recognise him, too.

'Chippie!' The other puppy yapped, showering Chip with licks much like his mother was doing, and that was when I realised that Chip was smaller than the other puppy of his breed.

'Yes, Biscuit, this is your brother Chip!' spoke the mother, and the five puppies gathered around Chip and smothered him with their love. It was almost too hard not to join in the cuddles myself. But it wasn't my place, and to the mother, it would seem strange for a random Rottweiler join with the licking and cuddling. So, knowing that my job was done, I turned my back and made my way out of the Nursery when I heard the voice of Chip's mum calling out to me.

'Hey, excuse me, Mr Rottweiler!'

I turned to her as she trotted a few feet over to my side. 'My name's Bella, and your name's Atlas, right?' she asked me. I guessed it was common for complete strangers to know one another's names here, as I suppose word gets passed down, probably by the cats and the birds, as I figured they'd be the types to love gossip.

'Yes, that's my name,' I told her before I said, 'You don't have to thank me if that's what you plan on doing. I simply acted out of impulse when I found him lying alone outside.'

Bella insisted, 'But I do have to thank you. You may not understand how much seeing Chip here means to me—it means a lot. After I died from being run over while looking for some food to give back to my puppies, I was terrified by the thought of my babies growing up without a mother to feed them, especially Chip, since he was the runt.

'Then when I woke up in Heaven, I was so surprised to find Biscuit, one of my little girls who'd passed away due to the horrible conditions we were living in and because I couldn't find enough food. So, I quickly reunited with her here in the Nursery upon seeing her, and soon after that, I became a foster mother to these orphaned puppies you see around me. Then, it just so happens that you show up with my youngest puppy by your side, the one I'd been most worried about because he's so small and young.

'So, while I'll miss Cookie (girl), Oreo (boy), and Popcorn (girl) because they're alone and without their family, I hope that kind human girl, Summer, who used to leave food out for me, finds them and can give them a forever home and keep them safe from the terrors of the road... the thing I failed to do as a mother.'

I heard Bella make a faint whimper. Chip, his sister Biscuit and the other puppies cuddled up to her. She gave them each a grateful lick on the head before turning her gaze back up to me. Her eyes were wide.

'So again, I must thank you, Atlas, for reuniting me with my youngest son. My puppies each mean the world to me, and to see them looked after and living happy lives is the best thing for me. Thank you for comforting Chip and bringing him here.'

After that, I left the Nursery in good spirits, knowing that I'd made a mother and a young puppy's day, even though they'd died and the other three puppies were still in the Land of the Living.

***

NOW, AS I lie on the grass staring out at the animals playing around me, I close my eyes and wonder if I return to the Land of the Living to see my daddy again in person, will he already have a new puppy or dog to play with? A dog to comfort him during his time of mourning, or would he be visiting my grave?

IN LOVING MEMORY.
ATLAS. 2010-2019.
A gentle soul that will be missed by his family and friends.

I hope it's the first two and not the latter. I can't comprehend the sight of seeing Colin sad, or worse, sitting on his knees in front of my grave, crying at the picture on my grave with one of my favourite pull rope toys gripped tightly in his hands. I hoped that if I got the chance, Colin would smile as a tiny puppy ran around him, high on zoomies, playing tug-o-war or fetching sticks. Even if this new strange puppy was playing with my owner, I wouldn't have it in me to get all defensive and growl at the pup and tell it to stay away from my daddy. I know that the puppy will now be Colin's new best friend, and as long as the puppy is doing its job well and making Colin and the Master and Mistress smile and giving them good memories, that's all that matters. As long as the Trembley's can still smile... even without me... I'm more than pleased with that. As long as they're happy, I'm happy.

'Yo! Atlas!' I turn my head to see Octavius, the Wolfhound, coming in my direction, along with Rudolph, the Husky.

'There you are!' barks Rudolph. I get up from my laying position, and with a big stretch, I stand up and wander over to meet my new heavenly friends.

'Hi, my fellow canines,' I say to them. Rudolph comes to my side and puts one of his front paws on my back, and Octavius nears my face. I can see biscuit crumbs around his mouth; an obvious sign that he's been at The Munchies Parlour (where animals of all species go to have a wide variety of snacks—one of

Octavius's favourite places in Heaven. He touches my nose with his nose… a funny gesture, I think to myself.

'Smudge taught me that, Octavius says. She calls it a "boop," and it's a common thing that cats do. Why I have no idea,' he says.

Rudolph glances at him, 'Because she's a cat. All cats are weird. Genevieve—my owner before I passed away due to eating rat poison, mistaking it for treats—used to always say that. At first, I never understood why, but now I'm inclined to believe her.'

'Speaking of Smudge. Where is she, the Colonel and Perry?' I ask, looking between them.

Rudolph opens his mouth to speak, but it's Octavius was who answers the question for me. He tells me that Smudge is at the Milkbar with this hairless cat named Tigger - or something like that. Colonel Barkins is having a nap outside somewhere, and Perry is hanging out in the Birdcage, doing bird stuff.

'Oh, well, that's nice that she's socialising with other cats, even if the cat's unfortunate enough to be hairless,' I say.

'Yeah, I wonder how hairless cats go when it's bath time since I know that cats HATE water and just being wet in general. And from what Genevieve told me, hairless cats have to be bathed daily because they sweat because they don't have fur.'

'Bathed daily!' barked Octavius, who seems to shiver at that thought. 'One bath is enough for me! Yikes, now that makes me feel bad for the Xolos and the hairless cats.'

Rudolph looks at the Irish Wolfhound again, examining his scruffy coat, which appears to not have bathed for a few years, at least. 'Otto, when was the last time you even had a bath? Have you *ever* had a bath?'

Because of his pampered lifestyle, Rudolph often brags about how freshly groomed his coat looks. He also gets embarrassed when speaking about his death - caused by mistaking rat poison for treats.

As for Octavius, he didn't ever like talking about his past, or his death. He only said that he was raised on a farm in Dingle, Ireland, and had a middle-aged Master named Brian Doherty. Perry was the one who told me about Octavius's death because he'd eavesdropped on him, mumbling in his sleep. Perry mentioned that Octavius had ended up falling into a ditch of water while he was out hunting for some wild pigs. He'd slowly drowned. It's perfectly understandable that he doesn't want to talk about his death; I can't imagine dying alone and slowly.

I can still hear him and Rudolph bickering in the back, so I decide to defend my Irish buddy by speaking up about something on the "bath" topic, but in a way that doesn't tease Octavius about his scruffy coat.

'You know, not all cats hate water. I used to sit with Mason Trembley to watch wild animals on the square thing that humans call a TV. We'd watch tigers happily jump into rivers to catch fish or swim like they were kittens,' I say, remembering a pleasant memory of sitting with the Master on the couch while the Mistress helped Daddy with his "homework" in the kitchen. I didn't fully understand TV the way my family did, but I liked watching it because my family did. Sometimes, when a squirrel or chipmunk appeared on the screen, I'd sit right in front of it and bark at it, making the Master laugh while also trying to tell me to stop barking.

'Huh! Interesting. I wonder if Millie or Tambo do that. Next time I see one of the tigers, I'll be sure to ask,' Rudolph says as he stares up at the sky as if in deep thought. 'Okay, you do that. Meanwhile, I want to stay here for a little longer,' I say as I lie back down on the spot.

'Any reason, Atlas?' asks Octavius, pawing the grass once with his front paw. I look at him, and my tail wags slightly. 'Nah, not really, just kinda want to do what Colonel Barkins is doing and have a nap myself since there's no bedtime here in Heaven, and we can do whatever we want and sleep whenever we want.'

While part of this is the truth, and I am feeling a little tired, I want some time to myself, some time to lie down and think about the world I left behind and all the sweet memories I'd had with my family.

'You do that, Rudolph and I will be at the Tennis Ball Paradise when you're done, and if we ain't there, we'll be around,' Octavius says, leaning down and giving me a tiny lick around the ear. He never liked being alone, so he often went where the French husky went.

'Thanks,' I say with a nod, and after that, both Octavius and Rudolph walk away.

I want some time to think about all those happy times when I'd lie on the floor as my belly would be rubbed by my family. My foot kicked out in the air. All those beautiful moments when Colin would take my favourite pull rope out of the "ATLAS' TOYS" box and would tease me with it. His face would light up as he darted the pull rope from side to side, getting me excited before he led me into the backyard, where he'd throw it as far as he could and watch me happily pant after it. I want to think about those moments again, to understand that I had one of the best lives a dog could possibly have. It was all thanks to the Trembley's who opened their hearts to me, raised me to be a good boy and stayed with me right up until I repaid their kindness by saving them from that bad man with the L-shaped object. I allowed myself to get shot five times. Still, in the end, the bad man was captured and taken away according to Shelby who'd seen it somewhere in the induction cloud, and I'd saved my family and their money, but I wasn't able to stay awake long enough to see the next day, and I'd died in my daddy's arms.

If I could, I would do anything to see him again.

-Tiger-

THE RAGDOLL NAMED Smudge kept trying to sniff my butt as if she was a dog or had at least been raised by them.

'What are you doing?' I ask. She tells me that she wants to get used to my smell so that if she sees me again, she'll be able to tell me apart from any other Sphynx cats here. She also mentions that she enjoys my company.

'Well, do you think perhaps there's another way of getting used to my scent that doesn't revolve you getting your nose in my buttocks? Because it's kind of awkward with other cats watching. Besides, shouldn't my eyes give me away?' I ask her, prompting Smudge to give me a look by tilting her head to the side, telling me that she's confused and doesn't really understand what I'm trying to get at.

Smudge stares into my eyes, studying them like a human studies a book's words. 'Huh!'' she says as her tail flicks up into a happy gesture. 'Well, I'll be—one yellow eye, and one blue eye, just like a Turkish Angora and a Devon Rex, I don't think I've seen a Sphynx with different coloured eyes before.'

'Really? I heard it's quite common for my breed,' I respond.

Smudge gives out a slight chuckle. 'I haven't met a lot of Sphynx cats. There's a lot of animals here, but you'd have to be like only the second hairless cat I've seen here. Anyway, I'll see you soon, Tiger. I'm gonna go look for my canine friends Atlas and Barkins, buh-bye!' And with that, the overly fluffy Smudge leaves the Milkbar with her tail up in the air.

Smudge is an odd cat: she's friends with dogs that are ten times bigger than her, and she sniffed my butt just like one of them. But I can't hold that against her; this is Heaven, after all. You can become friends with any animal because violence doesn't exist here; it never happens whatsoever, and everything that the heart desires becomes a reality— except when it comes to seeing our human owners.

In Heaven——an animal wonderland——everything relies on making friends and hanging out at places made for all the different kinds of animals that come here. So the idea of a cat befriending a dog is strange to me, but in Heaven it's the norm.

I'd made friends with Koretake, the Persian Chinchilla; Pharoah, the Abyssinian who acts like a dog at times; a wild barn owl from Australia named Sorell—who had died from stress after getting her wings tangled in some barbed wire—, and a teen elephant (yes, an elephant) named Mumbo who was sadly killed by poachers for his tusks. But I don't often see Mumbo because he hangs out with the other large animals in a place called The Mountain.

I haven't been to The Mountain personally, but I've heard things about it. It isn't actually a tremendous mountain; it's really just a vast open space that Sorell said is surrounded by trees, hills and ponds that never empty (which sounds so peaceful). The name Mountain just implies that it's mainly for the big animals such as elephants, giraffes, hippos, gorillas and so on: animals that one would find in the wild like in Asia and Africa.

It's lovely here in Heaven. I can't deny that obvious factor, mainly because everything lives in harmony and fighting never crosses anyone's mind. It's a place where you can do whatever you want, whenever you want, without being judged. Making friends is a guarantee here; even if you've just arrived in Heaven, you're bound to make at least one friend or two.

I finish drinking my share of one of the never-emptying bowls of milk. I then make my exit out of the Milkbar and notice Sorell standing in front of the entrance, preening her wings as if she's been waiting all this time for me. She wasn't perched or anything, just standing in the grass in the middle of the most famous feline hangout. I admire her bravery—going to these areas without so much as a care in the world where potentially dangerous animals are, such as crocodiles, poisonous snakes, and bears.

'Oh, hello, Sorell,' I say to her.

'Hello Tiger, you filled up?'

'Sorry?'

'Milk. Has it filled you up?' she says, rephrasing.

'Oh, yes, yes it has. Where did you just come from?' I ask as she turns to her side and points one of her wings straight ahead. I can just faintly make out the neck of a giraffe. Sorell has come from the Mountain.

'Oh ho,' I chuckle, 'How is Mumbo and all that?'

'Mumbo is as right as the rain that sometimes falls. He and Bob the Hippo (Bob is one of Mumbo's best friends) are fostering an orphaned Bear who got separated from her mum and siblings and ended up dying of starvation only a few hours ago. They've comically named her Bee … since, you know, Bee's make honey and bears love honey.'

'Well, that's lovely that Mumbo and Bob are comforting a bear cub. I remember hearing from Mumbo that if he'd been able to grow up to be a full-sized African elephant, he would've liked to have a legacy of being a father to his own child,' I say.

Sorell nods her head in agreement and says, 'Mumbo is a gentle soul who didn't deserve the passing he got because of those poachers,' Sorell says and pauses for a second. I can tell that she's thinking about Mumbo and the pain he must've felt when he was shot again and again by bad humans, had his ivory removed and left for dead, and the fact that he wasn't fully grown yet just made it even sadder.

But then, Sorell spreads her wings, kicks the ground, ascends into the sky, where she hovers there for a bit, staring down at me.

'So, whereabouts were you heading before you found me?' she asks.

I don't know how to answer Sorell's question as I didn't have a precise place where I needed to be. I think about this and consider telling her that I was planning on heading out to look for Koretake or Iris at the Catnip Bar— where the three of us could roll around like pigs in some mud and act like we're dogs instead of cats. But I quickly reconsidered the thought because while Iris and Pharoah will definitely be there, Koretake, on the other hand, might not be—because like most cats, I've come to know—he's a bit of a wanderer. One minute, he's with me and the other cats having a pleasant time rolling around in a hill of catnip, having a friendly conversation about all the times he's got zonked on the stuff, the next, he's gone… poof! Almost like how a chameleon camouflages itself with the environment around it.

So, finding Koretake will be tricky as he likes to do disappearing acts on those who aren't watching him. Either that or he's in the clouds introducing another confused, and frightened cat who's recently died. I remember him telling me that he gets a sense of satisfaction showing new angels the ropes of Heaven.

My tail whips to the side once on its own before it sits up straight like it always does when I'm contented with something. But I was mainly content whenever I was around my old human, Wolfgang Buchenwald. I still miss him greatly and think about him because he'd given me everything a hairless cat with a blue and yellow eye like me could possibly want. When I was alive and living with him in his lovely home in Frankfurt Wolfgang had well and truly made me feel like I was the luckiest cat in Germany. There just wasn't a foul bone in his body.

Because of the welcoming nature of Heaven, where everyone lives together in peace, going about their lives as if nothing wrong could possibly go wrong, I'd come to terms with being dead.

I've made some good friends, even if I never thought it possible for a cat to become friends with an owl or a big teenage African elephant, of all things. I'd come to terms with the idea that Wolfgang needs another companion to help ease his loneliness. He could search those local newspapers (as humans call them) and look for a family nearby that have cats or maybe dogs up for adoption. But if Wolfgang can't find one close to Frankfurt, he could go to a cat or dog home and find a pet there that would be a perfect fit for him, just as I'd been. It wouldn't matter if he got a dog, cat, bird, or a damn hamster, as long as he felt the same joy he did whenever I'd sleep on his lap, that would be all that would matter.

'Hey, Helloooo? Sorell to Tiger. Do you hear me?' I hear Sorell hooting in my ears. I shake my head to get myself back into the real world in front of me and glance up at her hovering above me, her feathery wings flapping up and down.

'I'm sorry, Sorell, I'm having one of my moments,' I say to her as I feel the tip of my tail curl in a friendly, almost playful gesture.

'Fair dinkum, what kind of moment would that be? Reminiscing about that man, Buccenwalt Wolfgang, right?' I always found it slightly amusing that Sorell was a species of bird known for being wise. Yet she could never pronounce the last name of my human correctly. It didn't matter how often Iris, Pharoah, Koretake, Mumbo, and I would correct her. She'd never get it right and would always say Buctwall or Buccenwalt, much to the amusement of the five of us.

I shake my head in amusement and confirm that I'm indeed thinking of my old human. I'm about to ask her if we could go somewhere, perhaps on the grass and just relax and talk about our past lives when I hear a familiar voice calling out to us.

'Yo Sorell. Tigger—could only be one cat— hi!' I immediately recognise the voice and the mention of "Tigger". It's none other than Koretake, the Persian Chinchilla male with the luscious coat. He who often disappears on us.

'It's Tiger. I say irritably. 'I look and sound nothing like that bouncing tiger from those books humans love.' It still annoys me whenever Koretake refers to me as that bouncing tiger. That tiger has fur, and I don't. To me, it feels mocking, but I can't really hold it against him. Koretake is a good cat that means well, so I suppose I can let him get away with calling me Tigger. It isn't like he's calling me Baldy or Pinkie, *that* would be insulting and embarrassing to me and my breed.

I shake off my irritation and watch in silence as Sorell lowers one of her wings down. Koretake leaps with one paw out and smacks her outstretched wing, a movement that's meant to replicate a human's handshake. It's a classic move between the two. Personally, I don't understand it, and I doubt I ever will. I guess it's one of those Koretake and Sorell things.

'Sup me, amigos and amigas! Iris taught me some basic Portuguese! That's where I've been – with Iris, in case you were wondering,' he chirps.

Sometimes I'm convinced that Koretake has spent too much time with the dogs here. Because he certainly acts like one and is always happy to see the others and me, his tail is basically always held straight up. Despite being dead like every other animal here. He's a very optimistic cat indeed. He was having the time of his life.

'I can see that,' I say simply, not really knowing what else I'm meant to say in response. One thing that Heaven's taught me is that I can improve at having conversations with different species of animals. I never thought that would be possible.

'Amigo means the same thing in Spanish,' Sorell says.

Koretake's eyes widen as if he's heard the 'catnip' word. 'Darn, owls, really are smart'.

'You flatter me, Koretake, but I wasn't saying that to sound smart. It's just a common fact. It's basic Spanish to humans that don't even speak the language. I should know; I encountered a few human tourists out camping near my tree when I used to go out hunting for field mice at night. Hoot, I do miss the good old days of hunting in the dark, but the seeds at the Birdcage work just as well, I guess.'

Sorell lowers herself to the ground, where she lands. Her head is low, staring sadly at the grass billowing at her talons. I can tell she's having one of those recollection moments that I have all the time, and I know that many other animals here have them too—like Koretake, Mumbo, Pharaoh, and Iris.

Sorell remembers the moments when she was alive and free to fly the country of Australia, long before, she'd flown into that fence, where she'd flapped around in a frantic panic for what she described as hours, maybe even days until the inevitable happened. She died from the stress of being stuck and alone, with no kind humans finding or helping her so she could continue to live as a free bird.

'I know how you feel, Sorell,' I speak, walking over to her and putting a paw gently on her back. 'As I've mentioned many times before, I still miss my human greatly, and I would love a chance to see him again and to know what he's been up to.'

'Everyone here has felt the same, even me, despite not showing it and always trying to put on a happy face for my friends and for the newly born angels. Sometimes, I can't even help but have a moment when I miss being alive and wonder how Rita and the rest of the Paewai family are doing.

'Have they managed to make enough money to get themselves a decent house rather than living in a deplorable neighbourhood house on the poor side of Auckland like they previously lived in when they were in Warkworth with me? These are questions I often ask myself whenever I'm alone,'

Koretake adds as he sits curling his big, bushy tail around the rest of his bushy body. Sorell glances at the fluffy Persian and asks, 'You were abandoned, right?' Koretake leans back a bit as if a little scared himself.

'I would prefer not to say that I was abandoned. Rather, my family couldn't afford to take me to Auckland with them, and as a result, I wasn't pampered or fed on a regular daily basis like I would've liked. Heck, I only recently found out from a Boxer, named Hemi, from the Bay of Islands that my name actually means "failure" and Pupuhi means fluffy. How about that?'

I watch with sympathy as Koretake lowers his head. Sorell puts a wing over his back to comfort him. But he quickly dismisses it and looks back at Sorell and me seeming to not want to sour the conversation.

'But hey, I guess Rita thought my name meant fluffy since she was still fairly young, and she perhaps thought that Koretake suits me more than Pupuhi. Yet again, I guess being called failure in Māori was partly why they didn't take me to Auckland with them. And because they didn't take me, I passed on due to the loneliness I felt at the time—there weren't a lot of cats around that part of the neighbourhood, mostly dogs, ones that didn't take too kindly to cats like myself and Tiger here. I try to mask the sadness from my fellow angels by putting on a happy face because if new angels arrive, they need someone positive to show them the way.'

'Time sure does fly. Do you know what year it was when you two passed on? For me, it was 1996,' Sorell suddenly asks Koretake and I. Before Koretake and I get the chance to say anything, Sorell goes on to say that Mumbo was killed in 1974 and is still quite sensitive when it comes to talking about those poachers who frightened him away from his herd and lured him into a trap where they shot him multiple times, until he could no longer take it. Scared and in pain, he died...

I ask Sorell what brought this up. She says that Koretake's abandonment reminds her of how Mumbo and Bob ended up here. She also mentions that Bob the Hippo died in the same year. But, unlike the elephant's best friend, Bob died shortly after losing a fight with a rival hippo.

'Oh, hoot! Seems I got ahead of myself there talking about Bob and Mumbo. What were you two felines going to say?' Sorell says.

Sorell could really talk, but despite times when she didn't know when to shut up, she did know how to control herself and could tell from the expression on the other animals' faces that they wanted to have their say.

'Wow, hard to believe that it was 2007 when I passed away. What year is it now?'

'2021. At least, I think it is. It's hard to tell here,' Sorell answers him simply.

It's easy to forget what year it is here since days pass by like seconds. I think about it. That's when my eyes widen because I realise how long it's been since I'd departed from the Land of the Living.

***

It's been eight years since I was put down. It had felt like only yesterday when I arrived here in Heaven and met Koretake, Iris, Pharaoh, Sorell, and Mumbo!

'What about you, Tiger? Do you remember the year of your passing?' I hear Koretake ask me, bringing me back to now instead of then.

'I can't believe it's been eight years since I first arrived here, and you were the one to brief me on my situation,' I say, and once again—like it often does—my mind races back to Wolfgang Buchenwald.

Goodness, he'd be at least eighty-seven now! He was seventy-nine when I was put down. I hope Wolfgang has done himself a favour in those eight years and adopted another cat. Perhaps a therapy cat: to help him out whenever he feels down or is in desperate need of someone to warm his lap and heart. Even better, I hope his family has had the right thought to contact him, asking if he was okay and that they wished him well, after so many years of separation without any kind of communication from them. That would be one of the best things that could happen to him during those eight years of my death.

'You died in 2013, and it's already 2021? Well, dice up me some tuna and dish it in a bowl! I still remember fondly when we first met. You were a lost and frightened sphynx cat waking up on the Induction Cloud, wondering where the heck he was and what the heck was going on before you saw a fluffy, yet handsome cat, with a luscious white and grey coat,' Koretake says.

'Cut to the chase, will you please, Koretake?' Sorell interrupts, placing her wing on his back, making him jolt, cry out and arch his back up as if someone had come up from behind him and deliberately tried to scare him. Sorell quickly pulls her wing away, to avoid it getting damaged or losing any feathers.

'RAOOW! Don't do that, Sorell! You know how that startles me,' shrieks Koretake.

'So, sue me,' says Sorell.

'Huh?' Koretake responds.

'It was a thing I used to hear humans say when I was alive,' Sorell says. 'Oh, okay, well, can you please not touch and interrupt me so suddenly like that with your screechy owl voice so close to my ears,' Koretake says, putting his back down and relaxing his fluff.

'It's okay. I understand what you mean. Do you guys remember when you first arrived in Heaven after death?' I ask this question in a small, gentle voice to try to not startle any of them.

'Yes,' both Koretake and Sorell say in unison. 'The arrival is one of the fondest memories you have here,' states Koretake. 'It never goes away, no matter how many memories you create here, combined with the ones you had when you were alive. It's an important memory as it's the start of your eternal life, a life of peace and harmony. The arrival in Heaven always remains a strong one. Just as strong as the happiest moments in your life.

'For me, it was taking my first flight out of my parent's tree when I was still a fairly young chickling,' Sorell adds.

Both she and Koretake regard each other for a moment before Koretake opens his mouth to say. 'But when it comes down to it, the passing is always the strongest and most intricate memory to forget. Because it's the revelation that you've officially left your life in the Land of the Living behind, have spread your wings, and ascended to the skies to join other animals whose lives have ended— whether it be natural or sudden.'

Both Sorell and Koretake are silent for several seconds. Finally, the barn owl, Sorell, breaks the silence by saying something wise.

'Words spoken like the humble Great Gray who sits perched on his tree and recites the ways of the wind to his disciples,' Sorell often prefers to only invoke wisdom if it is indispensable or if she feels like she's in the mood to deliver some to those around her. Either way, it's usually sound knowledge that we all thank her for.

'Well, I might fly off and see how Mumbo and Bob are going with that orphaned bear cub, named Bee,' Sorell says, spreading her wings and lifting herself off the ground with delicate motion. 'What are you two felines going to do?'

'Me? I might go look for Iris and take her out to get some catnip and maybe Pharaoh if he's in the mood,' answers Koretake as he stands up (Koretake has a habit of annoying Pharoah with silly questions and rubbing his tail over his face because he claims he wants to bring out the dog side of him).

My tail springs into the air as I say, 'As for me, I might go to Tennis Ball Paradise and watch those silly dogs behave like puppies, especially that female Jack Russell Terrier, who has an upside-down heart mark on her side. She's most entertaining to watch.'

Koretake laughs, and Sorell says goodbye to us. We say goodbye back before Sorell flies off toward The Mountain to meet up with Bob and Mumbo.

'Those dogs are silly animals. If you're still there in an hour or two, I might bring Iris over. Dinner and a show,' Koretake says.

'You know what, Koretake? I'd like that a lot,' I tell him as my tail shoots up into the air, nice and straight, making Koretake's tail excitedly quiver in the air.

'Done! I'll see you at Tennis Ball Paradise later! Bye, Tigger!' he chirps. He happily darts in the other direction as I yell 'Bye, to him.

'I'll let you off the hook this time, Fluffy,' I chuckle as I walk straight ahead to Tennis Ball Paradise, looking to see if that upside-down love-heart Jack Russell is there.

-Lilly-

TENNIS BALL PARADISE has become one of my favourite places to visit and play in. It's the ultimate doggy playground where dogs such as Chelsea, Ember, and sometimes Alexia (because she's often in the Induction Cloud) get to muck around and just be dogs.

Anything that a dog could want is here, and there's nothing more satisfying than picking up a little green ball with your teeth, pulling the fluff off it, and just tossing it around like you're playing fetch with yourself.

There are lots of other dogs here to play with, sometimes I approach them and ask if they want to play with me. The dogs that love tennis balls as much as I do, almost always say yes in the most cheerful of voices, that often remind me of when I was a puppy.

I remember that I was a completely different dog throughout my puppy days. I was a shy little puppy who didn't know much about my surroundings or really anything at the time. I didn't know that the family that had adopted me would very quickly become the best people in my life, the ones that would give me everything that a happy little Jack Russell such as me could ever ask for. I couldn't have asked for anything more from them because every second I was with them made me happy. The only real thing that I wanted more was the opportunity for them to take me to the local dog parks to socialise with other dogs and make even more friends. And, of course, to visit the rest of the family (don't get me wrong. I loved Jacob and Jackie to bits, but it would've been nice to see the whole family).

One thing that I often noticed and wondered about was why I'd rarely see Michelle. Beth's older sister, who, from what I frequently heard from the other family members: Jacob, Jackie, and Mummy, Michelle, lived in a place with a funny name.

Sydney, I think it was called. I always thought it sounded like a beach.

We never got to visit them, and they never got to see us, and I was left to ponder why that was. Was it because Michelle didn't like dogs and preferred cats? Absolutely not! Michelle loved dogs! I heard Mummy say. Michelle even had a pet Blue Heeler named Schatzi, which I think is German for Sweetheart. So, if that was the case, why didn't I meet Schatzi or Michelle's kids, Scott, Tyson, and Nina? Was Sydney too far away from where we lived? Supposedly, that was the reason behind it. If it was true. That was fine, I wouldn't hold it against Mummy and Beth; they were my owners, and they were the ones that made me happiest. I know I shouldn't dwell on the past, especially since I now have everything I could possibly want.

However, I can't stop myself from thinking about the family I'd left behind if they still think about me. It's a silly question because my friends here have told me that, like the rest of them, I, of course, am going to be thought of and remembered for being a truly wonderful and beloved family dog.

Suddenly, I hear a noise, my ears perk, and my tail bolts upright as if I'd heard the familiar sound of those dark circle-shaped things rolling down the driveway, which always meant Mummy was coming home from this place she called "bowls". A place that I always imagined was a building covered in dog and cat bowls, a place that, back then, had sounded fun.

I look around and see one of Ember's paws on me (Chelsea's somewhere in the Fields).

'Hey, Lilly,' Ember says. 'Have you ever noticed that hairless cat watching you?'

'Cat? What cat?' I ask her, and Ember points to one of the entrances of Tennis Ball Paradise. I follow the direction her paw is pointing to, and there's this cat.; it's hairless, pink, and wrinkly, sitting on the ground patiently as if waiting for someone.

Maybe the cat is friends with one of the dogs that frequently comes here to play to re-enact its days of Puppyhood? If so, that isn't really a surprise to me. I've come to get used to seeing former enemies in life become the best of buds here. I'm friends with Chelsea, Ember, and Shelby (who I remember had been the dog of one of Jackie's friends), as well as a three-legged wolf named Vill, and a white rabbit named Flower. I speak to Alexia whenever I see her, but she always seems preoccupied with things in another part of Heaven, so I rarely see her.

Flower spends most of her time in the Field or Farmyard with the animals that humans mostly see on farms, such as horses, cows, chickens, ducks, rabbits, pigs, and so on. On the other hand, Vill likes to hang out in the Bamboo Forest, acting as a foster father to kittens, puppies and other baby animals or practising his howls at the Mountain. Vill is very active and tends to never stay in one place long enough for a long conversation, not when he has things to do. But despite that, Vill is friendly enough, but, back to the cat that's looking at me, stretching its paws out across the grass.

'Looks like you have a secret admirer. I mean, who couldn't love that upside-down heart marking on your side? You have "love" written all over you,' Ember barked cheerfully, which was meant to sound like she was trying to be funny.

'Really? Because I heard that Vill has a crush on you,' Lilly says.

'Vill has a crush on any female dog he sees,' Chelsea responds.

My tail starts wagging as I turn around to look at the hairless cat watching us for reasons I can't and don't understand. *Do the cats here like watching dogs behave in silly ways?* I think to myself. Only this time, another cat has joined the furless one. I can't deny the beautiful look of this white Persian cat's coat, and I expect that its coat would feel just as lovely as it looks. I almost want to stop playing with my new friends, walk up to the two cats watching us, and ask the fluffy one if I can feel what its fur feels like. But I decide against the idea.

I think that the fluffy white Persian might feel a little awkward with a seemingly random dog approaching it and asking if she can pat it like a human would, like how my human friends used to pet me all the time while I was still alive, when I used to play fetch with anyone who picked up one of the tennis balls around me. Those were some good memories that I miss a lot.

Suddenly I hear a loud echoing howl, which makes me flinch and come back into the now, or as some of the intelligent dogs, such as the Border Collies, like to call it, "the present". Ember, next to me, heard the howl and the two cats sitting and watching us did too, because they both bolt their heads up at the same time and look around in the sky as if trying to pinpoint where the howl has come from.

But very quickly, the paranoia of the cry being something terrible disappears as soon as it started because I remember that nothing wrong ever happens here; it's only Vill doing his usual hourly howls. The sound reaches Tennis Ball Paradise and is heard by anyone near it, like the two cats sitting at the entrance. Considering the Mountain is reasonably far away, Vill's howls always seem to carry across the Fields.

I hear footsteps approaching, followed by the voice of Shelby. Shelby always picks her words carefully and know what to say in any situation; a trait that I honestly think is terrific. Shelby always has some sort of story to tell.

'That Vill... he always has to make his presence known to everyone by howling,' Shelby says.

I look over and notice that Shelby's being followed by another dog, whom I recognise all too well as being Ember's sister, Chelsea. Since I'd heard from Ember that Chelsea was previously in the Fields somewhere, I figured Shelby must've found her there and asked her to tag along to the doggy playground.

'Like we know that you're still here in Heaven, you don't have to hourly let everyone in Heaven know,' Chelsea barks in a funny way.

I think about what Shelby said about Vill wanting to make his presence known by howling. It makes me think of something... something that I know wouldn't be true, but the way Chelsea said it made me think differently. So, I walk over to her, completely forgetting that I'm in Tennis Ball Paradise and completely forgetting about Shelby, the other dogs here and the two cats watching us.

'Hey, Chelsea. Uhm...' I start, not really knowing how to precisely get the words out.

Chelsea looks at me, and her face lights up. I'm happy to say that I've recovered my unique ability to make those around me happy whenever they see me. It's always worked like a charm around humans and works just as well with dogs. Maybe it was the upside-down heart marking on my side.

'Hi, Lilly!' Chelsea barks happily as her tail starts to wag, an obvious sign that my extraordinary power is still as strong as ever, even here in Heaven.

'How are you feeling today? Guess what? Shelby found me playing chasings with some Yorkies and Chihuahuas. She thought I was teasing them because of how small they are, so she asked me to leave the small dogs alone and come here to meet you and Ember to focus on playing with the tennis balls and be more productive. Hey, are you feeling alright? You look as if you accidentally ate a bee.'

Chelsea puts a paw on my head, then lifts my chin to look at her. I can tell that she sees my troubled face as I notice her tail has stopped wagging; a clear sign that she's concerned about me, like the good friend she is. She offers to take me to the Fields where we can have a private talk about what's on my mind. I agree, and Chelsea leads the way out of Tennis Ball Paradise.

Chelsea walks me a few paces to one of the large hills spanning the Fields, where we both sit and look up at the blue sky, seeing many birds and fish flying and swimming above us without so much as a care in the world. Yes: the fish swim in the sky and the neighbouring cats and bears do nothing to catch them, they just let them swim by. Again, Chelsea asks me what's on my mind, and this time, I tell her without much hesitation: That there's something about the sound of Vill's howling that makes me question something about the laws and how things work here in Heaven. Maybe Vill's gone somewhere I don't think is possible, and his howling is expressing something about this experience.

'It's about what you said about Vill, about how he likes to make his presence known by doing his usual howls,' I say in a particularly sad tone that I never like using because I don't like being sad. Being sad makes others feel the same sadness, and I don't like it when those I care about feel morose just because I feel that way. I'm meant to be a happy dog, not a sad dog.

'Yes? What about what I said about Vill? I don't quite understand what you're trying to get at Lilly,' Chelsea says sadly.

'Think about it, Chelsea: Making his presence known. Could this mean that Vill has been to the Land of the Living? Maybe to see how his pack is going on without him, or perhaps we've gotten it wrong about him. Maybe he's actually not making his presence known... maybe him howling is how he expresses his feelings and how he expresses that he gravely misses being alive and that he wants to see his pack members again, even if they aren't able to see him? What if his howling is his way of telling anyone who'll listen that there's a chance? If Heaven knows we really miss our owners, could we actually get the chance to visit them again? Like maybe we can see them, even if they aren't able to see us, maybe we can see them and see how they've been coping with our deaths. Perhaps Vill has a mate back in the Land of the Living that he really misses; that's why he howls a lot, because he misses her and wishes to see her again. Think about it... if we get the chance, we could see our beloved Masters again!'

Chelsea is looking at me, but her eyes don't meet mine, like she's deep in thought. I can tell that my speech has gotten to her and she's considering the possibilities of what could happen if she and Ember are able to revisit their owners again as ghosts. Thinking of all the things they could do to ensure their owners know they're okay and that they're living a great life up here in Heaven.

'I... I haven't thought about that before Ember, and I have been here for quite some time. We have yet to even consider something like that,' she says, turning her gaze back at the sky focusing on a particular school of fishes. I follow her gaze, seeing the clouds slowly drift past and the birds fluttering playfully in and out of them like they're playing peekaboo with each other.

'Ember and I always thought that once you die and your soul leaves for Heaven, that was it; you can't ever return and see your family ever again. I mean, you can see them if you ask for it, I mean, really ask for it, but not in the Land of the Living. I've heard stories of, some of the many clouds granting requests and floating down from the sky to sit in front of you. It doesn't even matter where you are in Heaven; they find you and project a kind of clear image that's like looking into your own reflection in the water of a bath. The image lets you see your owner and what they're currently doing. I should know because when I was taken to the same vet that you passed away at, where I was humanely put down, I arrived here, Ember greeted me with a sea of kisses and tail wags.'

'Was Ember the one that greeted you when you first woke up on the Induction Cloud? Like how I woke up to Alexia?' I interrupt her in a gentle voice, genuinely curious about how Chelsea must've felt when she was put down a few days before I was. I remember seeing her with her two female owners. I recall the owners looking heartbroken, like they both knew that they weren't going to leave the vet with their dog by their side. Only instead of being put down on the spot like Chelsea, I stayed there for a few more days while they did strange things to me and put this needle thing in my paw that always made me go to sleep. Then they'd wake me up sometime later and put me back in the cage until they took me out for one final time, where they put that needle into my paw for the very last time.

'Yes, she was, ' Chelsea says. 'When she led me down into the Fields, she explained that she saw me on one of the clouds and knew that my time was coming to an end. Ember said she rushed up to the Induction Cloud to sit patiently for my arrival, and shortly after, there I was. Ember couldn't contain her excitement and her sorrow, knowing that I'd died like her and that our owners—Heidi and Irene McLeod's were their names, by the way—were all alone. They just had each other... no other pet to help them with their grief,' Chelsea says, looking down. I hear her start to cry at the thought of her owners suffering without her and Ember. I shuffle over to her and put a paw on her as if to say it's okay, everything will be alright. Chelsea leans in and licks me on the head. My tail wags in response.

'Now you can let Ember know what I told you and how there might be a way for us angels with tails to visit our owners in ghost form if we ask and show that we really miss them. I believe it's something to do with how much we miss our old lives and if Heaven sees that we miss them in our hearts, maybe it'll grant us permission to see our owners,' I tell her. Chelsea shows me her gratitude by giving me another lick on the head around the ears.

'Thank you, Lilly. Thank you so much! You've made me think of things differently. All because of something I'd said about Vill,' I lick her on the side that I was leaning on and tell her she's welcome. I then ask her what she plans to do now, and being no real surprise, she says she wants to tell Ember and every other pet she knows about my theory. She says that every animal who's had a loving owner deserves at least one chance to see them again, even if it's for the very last time. Being granted that one opportunity to see how they've coped and see if they can still smile is more than enough for them. I know it would be to me. I would love the chance to play with one of the tennis balls at home. I would die all over again for a chance to see the smile on Paula Lahey's face again.

I get up just as soon as Chelsea does and was going to head in the direction she was because I don't really have anywhere else to be. I stare up at the clouds for a moment before looking down when I hear the voice of Flower, the bunny.

'Oh! Hello Flower,' Chelsea greets her playfully. She and I glance down at the small white ball of fluff on the grass, looking up at us with big, curious, dark eyes.

'Good morning, Chelsea and Lilly, or is it afternoon or evening? I can never tell here,' Flower says, standing up on her hind legs, staring into the sky. 'It seems to always be nice and sunny here,' she continues.

'Yeah, I've noticed that too. It's seldom night here in Heaven; I wonder why that is?' I say out loud.

'I think it's because of the prey and animals that would usually be hunted at night by predators,' Chelseas adds.
The three of us look over to see Shelby walking with Ember across the Fields to meet us and join our little talk. My tail's wagging as they came over and say hello to us. Ember has even brought a white flower called a rose around for Flower because, Flower loves flowers and grazing in the grass.

'Oh, gracious. Thank you, Ember!' exclaims Flower. 'I do love roses, especially white ones!' she squeals, hopping over to Ember and rubbing herself on one of Ember's paws. Ember laughs at the feeling of the rabbit's fur against her own.

Shelby continues. 'So, to ensure that everyone is happy and safe, it never gets dark. The prey animals don't have to worry about being hunted at night, and dogs can play around all day without needing to worry about their humans telling them to stop playing and go to bed. That's what I think.'

'Hey, Shelby,' A random male Rottweiler walking behind Ember and Shelby says.

'Oh, Hello Atlas. Nice to see you again.' Shelby responds to the male Rottweiler as he passed by to join another group of animals on the Field, a German Shepherd, a cat, an Irish Wolfhound, and a Husky.

'Who was that, Shelby?' I ask. 'I don't think I've seen that dog before.

'That was Atlas Trembley. He's one of the dogs I met in the Induction Cloud. He died a hero.'

'Oooooo,' We all say in response.

'I feel like this is a conversation for dogs, so I might hop off to the Patch and eat some carrots. Goodbye, friends.' We say goodbye to Flower. She hops away to meet with her fellow rabbits in Vegetable Patch, the go-to place for rabbits and other animals that love green food.

Shelby continues again with her story of how she met this supposed hero dog. 'Yes, when I met him, he was convinced that he was a bad dog because he wasn't with his owners, but I convinced him that he indeed was because Atlas got shot five times to save his family from being robbed or, worse, killed.'

'Wow!' gasp Chelsea and Ember together, expressing their surprise and marvel.

Meanwhile, my wonderment is on the inside, which I can't help for some weird reason. It makes me feel quite horrible about myself... because I know I could never do anything like that for my family; the only thing I can do is play fetch with my owners and make them smile. I certainly wouldn't be able to save them like that dog Atlas, or be like that tiger nicknamed Millie and welcome and care for orphaned babies of entirely different species.

I could never do anything exceptional such as being a mother figure. I'm just a simple Jack Russell with the ability to make friends and humans smile. I'll return to the thought of seeing Paula again another time, right now it seems like there is an animal that could do with some cheering up, and I love it whenever I can make animals and humans happy. I'd like to be known as the little dog that can brighten anyone's day just by looking at them. So, I guess that honour is better than nothing. Some animals don't even get the privileges of a good reputation, such as when a cat's curiosity gets them into big trouble. It makes me sad that some animals don't have that. I always feel the urge to find those animals and make sure they feel good about themselves. Now that I think of it...

'Hey, do you mind if I head off to the Bamboo Forest for a bit?' I say.

Shelby stops talking once again to look at me, along with Ember and Chelsea, who both have the same confused tilt of the head. Ember is the one who steps forward, her head still tilting to the side in confusion. Her tail perks up with an alert gesture.

'The Bamboo Forest? Why would you want to go there? That's where the big cats and bears hang out, like a mini version of the Mountain.'

'I feel like making someone's day with my irresistible charm; and some of the babies in Fa and Millie's care could use some cheering up.'

'I think that's a lovely idea, Lilly. Cassandra always said that Jackie spoke very fondly of you because you could always make her and everyone around you smile,' Shelby says.

My tail begins wagging again when she mentions Jackie's name (I miss you, Jackie). I sometimes have to remind myself that Shelby belongs to Jackie's friend Cassandra, and the other dog Cassandra has is Eddie, who's still alive and who Shelby sometimes says she misses.

'Will we see you again?' Chelsea asks me with pleading eyes as if she doesn't want me to go alone or at all. Ember bumps into her side, making her stagger. She stares at her sister, wondering why she'd pushed her.

'Of course, we will, Sis, don't be silly,' Ember says. 'Lilly's just going to the Bamboo Forest to make some smiles, and when she's done, she'll be right back here or Tennis Ball Paradise to meet us again. You're making it sound like she's going to get eaten or something like that.'

'She might,' Chelsea says, obviously joking, and Ember bumps her side again and tells her to shush.

After saying goodbye to the three of them, I head in the direction of the Bamboo Forest, with the idea of possibly being able to return to my old home to see Mummy Paula again. Nothing would make mine or any Angel dog feel better than to be given a chance to see their owners again; even if our owners wouldn't be able to see us, they'd at least feel our presence and know that we're happy in Heaven and that we still love them as our owners. Always and forever in our little doggy hearts.

-Mittens-

'MITTENS! COME PLAY with us!' Milo calls out to me.

'Let's play chasings with Zoila!' Yuki shouts out to Peter and Princess.

I look up at Mummy Millie with big, curious eyes, asking her what I should do because I'm still not sure that I belong among the other kittens my age. Mummy Millie is big, strong, and very kind to me. She reminds me of the taller female hooman at home. I wonder how she, the tall male hooman, and Marian are doing without me. Have they befriended Mr Bird, who'd sit and wait on the birdie fountain for me? Have they caught that scary animal that sent me here? I wonder how old is Marian now?

'Hey, Mittens! You coming?' Milo calls out my name again, his voice sounding like a mouse I saw once. This time, I quickly look over at him, seeing Peter, Yuki, and Princess playing with the baby cheetah Zoila and a leopard named Bakari, who'd been trying to sleep on his foster Mummy's leg. A big animal with black and white fur and black eyes,
 that Mummy Millie says is called a giant panda. Her name is Lao-Bai.

Bakari loves to sleep most of the time with Lao-Bai, while Zoila is always on the go and loves running around, using up her energy. Then, when she's done, she wanders off to the other cheetahs, lies down and goes to sleep.

'Go on now, Mittens, dear. Young Milo is asking for you to play chasings with him, Yuki, and Zoila,' Mummy Millie says. Her gentle but powerful voice almost makes me jump. I whip around to look up at her again; I'm still unsure about joining them in their game. I still feel like I'm the odd one out, even though everyone here has been so friendly and kind to me.

'B-But Mummy Millie, I don't think Princess and Peter like me as much as Yuki and Milo because I'm still new here.

They don't really trust me as well as the other two,' I mew in a small voice, which makes Mummy Millie make that snorting noise that Yuki says is called a chuff - a noise that tigers make when they're happy. Milo says tigers can't purr like the rest of us cats.

'Oh, come now, dear Mittens, don't be so silly. You've been in my care for the last four years. I can assure you that Peter and Princess like you just as much as Yuki and Milo do. Even Zoila thinks you're great, though she's always running around to her heart's content. Asking her to slow down is out of the question. Still, but she's a good cub. Lao-Bai and Zeneri, take good care of her—you remember them, don't you?' she puts one of her giant paws above my tiny head and gently pats me with it. I'm still looking at her with my big, curious eyes.

'Are you sure?' I ask her, and she bows her head slowly and blinks.

'Absolutely. Now run along and have some fun, young Mittens,' I look over at the group of kittens and cubs playing together and think about going over and joining them trying to catch Zoila and convincing Bakari to join them when suddenly, I hear a voice that I've never heard call out.

'Hey! Hello!' The sudden voice makes me jump. I hide under Mummy Millie's enormous paws. But Mummy Millie doesn't seem bothered by the sudden voice at all! Instead, she just makes another chuff before laughing and telling me in her usual kind, gentle voice that there's nothing to be afraid of; it's just the neighbourhood therapee dog coming over for a visit.

'Therapee dog? What's that?' I wonder out loud. Mummy Millie chuffs again and asks for the small-looking dog with a short white and brown coat to come over and meet me. Meanwhile, I try my best to hide behind Mummy Millie's paw, even if I know it isn't really working.

'Hello Lilly. What brings you to the Bamboo Forest on this fine day?'

'G'day Mae-Li, I've come to brighten some days,' the weird voice belonging to Lilly says. I was confused about how Mummy Millie and this strange dog know each other so well—they talk like best friends. I don't know what to do about this situation, so I just stay by and watch.

Another chuff from Mummy Millie, 'Of course, how silly of me to ask, come, come, meet little Mittens,' she moved her paw away so the dog could see me curled up shaking. 'Don't be shy, Mittens, Lilly won't hurt you. She's the last dog that would even consider hurting anyone. Lilly's here to make you happy. She's a therapy dog; it's what she does.'

'Happy?' I look up at Mummy Millie again, then at the dog named Lilly.

'Yes, Mittens, that's what she does. She sometimes goes to different parts of Heaven and speaks with an animal that she thinks is feeling a little down, and she sits and talks with them until they start to feel good and happy again. Lilly was raised by a good family that loved her dearly, and she shows that love to others. If you ever need to talk to someone, Lilly's your dog.'

'Hi Mittens, my name is Lilly Lahey. You don't need to be shy. I'm here because I want to be your friend and make you happy!' the dog says while wagging her tail and panting her tongue.

'Happy? Friend?' I ask quietly.

I see the dog's tail wag. Did I somehow make her cross? Why did she sound so happy even though her tail's wagging? I ask Mummy Millie why her tail's wagging. She tells me that dogs do that when they're happy. So, while cats hold their tails up straight when they're happy, dogs wag theirs. I wondered why I've never seen a dog before and I realise it's because dogs don't really come to Bamboo Forest.

'If you don't mind me saying, but you're a cute little cat, aren't you?' Lilly says, making my fur fluff out and my eyes even bigger. I start to stand up and move my little legs over to her.

'You think I'm cute?' I ask her curiously. She gives me a nod with her head and her tail starts wagging faster. Does this mean that I'm making her happier? Can someone as young and small as me make a dog happy? I guess they can because I'm making Lilly happy, and I don't know how I'm doing it, but it feels good to make someone I don't know happy.

I stand right at the foot of the dog's paws. She stares down at me with friendly eyes, panting, and her tongue lolling out—another thing Yuki says dogs do when they're happy.

'That you most certainly are Mittens. My human cousin always used to say how cute cats were, especially the kittens, and I can see why she thought. You're adorable!' She then leans down licks me on the head and around the ears. Does she like me so much that she wants to clean me, even though Mummy Millie had done so a few minutes ago? I have much to learn about dogs here.

'How did this little bundle of fuzz come to you, Mae-Li?' Lilly looks away from me to the tiger looking after me.

'A cat named Noir. Have you heard or seen her around? She's a black cat,' Mummy Millie replies. I look over and see that Mummy Millie is standing up so she can stretch out her paws; she'd been laying down for quite a while.

It still amazes me, yet frightens me a little just how big Mummy Millie is. According to her, the males, like one of her brothers named Fu-Pan, are even bigger! That thought alone makes me want to fall over and pass out.

'Sorry, Mae-Li, the name doesn't ring any bells, and there are lots of black cats here,' Lilly responds.

'Oh right, silly me,' I stare at Mummy Millie as if she's in that square-shaped thing the Kushner's liked to sit in front of. She lowers her body to lie down again and talk with Lilly, the Therapee dog. I, on the other paw, decide that it's time for me to go and do what I'd been planning to do before Lilly showed up, and that was to join my friends and play chasings with them.

I wander away from Mummy Millie and Lilly and approach the five waiting for me. Bakari is far too tired to play and enjoys his naps on Lao-Bai's foot who continues to lounge around and eat sticks of bamboo, which pandas apparently love to eat. Then, as soon as Milo and Yuki see me, they bounce over to greet me. Milo seems incredibly happy with my arrival. His tail is at its straightest, and he keeps rubbing himself on me. While Milo's doing that, Yuki comes over to clean my face. She appears to be more in control of her emotions than Milo. He just can't keep his excitement inside him—he bounces around like a bunny or those weird-looking hopping animals that Zoila said are from a funny place called Australia. Kangaroos, I think she called them.

'You finally came, Mittens! You finally came!' He squeals, 'Playing with Zoila and the others isn't as fun without you! I'm so happy that you finally decided to come!'

'I told you she'd come over when she was ready, Milo. You just had to be patient,' Peter says, looking at me and nodding, Even Princess is bobbing her head at me. This nodding head movement shocks me. It means both of them are letting me into their friendship group to play games with them. I always thought that Princess and Peter didn't like me because I'm new and they don't know me as much as Yuki and Milo. But I guess Mummy Millie was right and they actually do like me. That's a nice thought to think about; that they actually want to be my friends but didn't know the right moment to approach me. Peter and Princess were both kind of shy. So, it was twice as shocking that Peter even said anything to begin with.

Milo's now bouncing around me like the Australian kangaroo and Yuki walks alongside me, as we reach Princess,

Peter and Zoila who are sitting and waiting for us. I can see that Zoila is shaking, trying very hard to keep herself from running around causing a ruckus, because that's her favourite thing to do.

'Welcome to the club, Mittens. It's good to have you here. Yuki Milo, Peter and I haven't had much of a chance to properly say hello and ask if you'd be our friend,' Princess mewed as I sit next to her. Her words leave me speechless.

Princess giggles and mews, 'I know how this must sound to you, but you don't have to worry about saying anything. I can see in your eyes that you want Peter and me to be your friends too, and we both say, 'Of course, we'll be your friends, ' Princess says. I feel as if I have butterflies in my belly; that if I wanted to, I could grow wings like the ones Mr Bird has and fly away without a care in the world! It makes me so happy to hear Peter and Princess asking me to be their friend.
'So what game are we going to play?' I ask the five of my new friends.

'CHASINGS!' shouts Zoila.

'We just played that,' says Peter.

'Let's play it again!' Zoila yells.

'No, Zoila, let's play something different,' Yuki says.

'Hey, I have an idea. Why don't we let Mittens choose the game? After all, she's here now.'

'M-Me?' my eyes widen at Peter as if he's gone bonkers. 'I-I don't know what to play! I don't even know what games there *are* to play,' I look behind me and see the dog named Lilly has gone and that Mummy Millie is looking over at me to ensure the other four of her foster babies and I are getting along.

I look back to my friends, and Milo says in his usual happy voice, 'Just say anything that comes to your head.'

'O-okay...' I look at my surroundings, trying to figure out what could make an excellent game to play. I think long and hard about what to play, and when I feel I've decided, I open my mouth to say it. But instead of my voice coming out, another voice does.

'C-can I jo-join?' a strange voice says, and the five of us look ahead and see a baby animal that looks like a mini version of Lao-Bai, only the fur is utterly brown instead of black and white. From what I've learnt here and what I can see, this animal looks like a baby bear. The bear is hiding behind a bamboo tree.

'Who are you? Aren't you a grizzly?' Zoila asks the little bear. The bear flinches and tries to hide more behind the tree.

'M-my name I-is B-Berry, a-and I can't find my m-mommy.'

I step up and walk towards the bear named Berry. Berry makes a squeaking noise and tries to hide behind the tree some more, but it's not really working, because the shape of his body makes him stick out like a sore paw.

'What does your mummy look like?' I ask Berry in a small voice. He stares at me with water dripping from his eyes. His body is shaking. He's really scared and doesn't know what's going on. I can't blame him. When I find out from Noir that that big scary animal had killed me and sent me here, I was frightened and confused too because everything was so new to me and I didn't really know how to deal with that. So, I can perfectly understand why Berry looks so terrified.

'Sh-she looks like m-me, b-but really big,' Berry says. Learning from how Noir spoke with me when I first arrived here, I ask him what he remembers from before he woke up here. He timidly looks behind him as if to ensure nothing's behind him. Then, he lets out a breath and speaks about what everyone in Heaven and I have come to know as the final moments.

'One minute, I was walking alongside her with my brothers and sister, looking for some food, when we went to a creek somewhere near a place called Yellowstone National Park. Mommy and my siblings came to this creek, and she tried teaching us to catch some fish for when we grow up. I leaned over the water as fish jumped out. I opened my mouth, hoping one would hop into it. But instead of going into my mouth like I wanted it to, the fish jumped and smacked me so hard on the side of my face that it knocked me off balance and into the rushing water.

I screamed out, "Mommy! Mommy! Help me!" as the river carried me away from her and my brothers and sister.

"Berry! Hold on, I'm coming!" cried Mommy. When I could raise my head above the rushing water, I saw her and my siblings run as fast as they could across the side of the creek to try to get to me. Then I heard the sound of running water get closer and Mommy scream, "Oh no! WATERFALL!! BERRY, LOOK OUT! SWIM, BERRY, SWIM!"

I looked and saw that I was heading straight for a waterfall! I cried as I tried to swim in the other direction, but the water was too strong for my little paws. I fell over the waterfall as I heard Mommy roar, "BERRRRRY!!"

The last things I remember are drifting further down the river. My body couldn't take it anymore, and I went underneath the water, then everything went black. Then I woke up here. And now I can't find my Mommy anywhere, nor my brothers or sister.'

I just stare at Berry. I can't speak, move, or do anything. I just stare as I realise what had happened to him. I don't need Mummy Millie or any of my friends to tell me Berry had drowned. And here I thought that my death was scary—when I saw that hungry mouth coming at me. I can only imagine how Berry must've felt when he drifted down that river, crying out for his mummy.

When I'm able to move again, my five friends and I walk behind the tree where Berry is hiding. We start to rub and clean him as he darts his head around and flinches, still very scared; not understanding what we cats are doing to make sure he feels safe. After he feels more comfortable, we'll include him in our playgroup because the more animals to play with, the better.

'Wh-What are you doing? Where am I? And where is my Mommy?' Berry asks.

'Don't worry. You're safe here, Mr Berry,' mews Milo, rubbing his tail around Berry's back.

'We're cleaning and rubbing our scent on you. It's what we cats do when we like something,' says Peter.

'This place is called Heaven,' adds Princess.

'I'm pretty sure we might be able to find your mother here somewhere if she's passed, and if not, there are plenty of foster mothers here,' says Yuki.

'Either way, Berry, you are never alone here because everyone here is friends. Why don't you come and join us? We were just about to play Hide and Seek,' Milo says, looking into Berry's frightened eyes.

Berry's lonely like I was when I arrived here, shaking my tail between my legs. He could really use a friend or two, someone to cheer him up and make him happy until his mum or siblings die, so they can reunite, be happy and continue to live their lives as they'd done before that sad incident took Berry away from them.

'So, how about it, Berry? Want to play with some cats?' asks Milo in his usual friendly, welcoming voice.

Berry nods, slowly puts down his paws, and steps out from behind the tree to meet us all correctly.

So, since I was the one who offers to talk to him first, I introduce myself to my new friend, Berry, the bear.

Milo steps up next—of course, happy Milo always jumping at the idea of making new friends—followed by Yuki, Princess, Zoila, and finally, Peter.

After the introductions are over, we lead Berry into our little friendship area, where we try to decide who should be hiding and who should be seeking. But one thing is for sure, Berry should be one of the seekers because he's big, but also because I know it would be mean for us to leave him alone to try to find us. So, we have to work out who'll be seeking with him because it's better for him if he has a friend to help him out.

'Um, excuse me?' I see Berry with one of his paws up like I remember seeing Marian do whenever she had something to say to the taller hooman's.

'Yes, Berry,' Princess says as she turns to look at him.

'This is going to sound really dumb, but what is Hide and Seek? I've never played it before? M-My siblings and I used to play Climb the Tree or Play Fight, but never this game called Hide and Seek. How do you play it? It sounds fun.'

Beating Milo to the explanation, Zoila steps forward, sits down in front of Berry, and carefully explains the idea of how to play Hide and Seek.

'Okay, there are hiders, and there are seekers. It's a bit like Predator and Prey; the hiders are the prey, and the seekers are the predators. The hiders have to hide anywhere and wait until the seeker finds them. So, the goal for the hider is to be the last one that's still hiding. Get it?' She asks Berry in her usual speedy way.

'Yes, Yes, I think so.' He says. 'The hiders go hide somewhere, and the seekers try to find them. Is that right?'

'Yep, that's basically the game. Still want to join?' asks Peter. He's cleaning one of his front paws.

'Yes, it does sound like fun. Should I be a hider or a seeker?' Berry asks.

I feel a little more confident in myself around my new friends because we're under the watchful eye of Mummy Millie.

'I think you should be a seeker, and someone can seek with you,' I say and turn to look at the others, wondering who should help Berry in seeking. 'Who would like to help Berry try to find us hiders?' I add.

I'm caught by surprise when Princess steps up instead of Milo. I'd come to know Princess as being, what was the word: royalty? Yes! Yes, that was the word; she was a kitten living with a wealthy family. Hence, she likes to speak funnily and walks in a very formal way. Mummy Millie had told me that she'd died being poisoned by eating a fly that had been sprayed with fly spray.

I also know that the deaths of my other friends: Yuki and Peter were run over, Milo died in a house fire, and Zoila was killed by a lion after wandering too far away from her parents.

After Princess walks over and stands next to the bear, it's decided that Zoila, Milo, Yuki, Peter, and I will be the hiders and Berry and Princess the seekers.

'Alright, Berry. You stick with me, and we should be able to find everyone hiding,' Princess says.

'O-okay, thank you, Princess,' Berry is sitting there, clapping his paws together in a way that shows me he's happy despite the terrifying way he'd died. He was pleased to know that he now has friends who want to play with him! And seeing those clapping paws makes me happy also. My tail flicks up straight.

'Alright, everyone! Scatter! Berry the bear and Princess the kitten will be coming for you!' shouts Princess. And with that, the five of us go in different directions around the Bamboo Forest while Princess counts to ten. We all hide in different places: Zoila's in a tree while Peter, Yuki, Milo, and I hide either behind trees or in the bushes. Then Princess shouts that she and Berry are ready and that they're coming to find us.

'Watch out, kittens! Here comes Princess and the Mighty Berry!' Berry calls out. I can't help but feel happy at how cheery

Bear's voice sounds. I just know that Berry will become one of my friends! Just like Milo, Yuki, Zoila, Peter, and Princess are.

Heaven is truly a wonderful place to make friends.

The Return

Shortly after the game of Hide and Seek with her new friend, Berry the brown bear cub, Mittens, along with her other friends, receive a rather special invitation to the Induction Cloud. The invitation is from Lilly, who was told about it by a hairless cat and a Rottweiler. At first, Mittens is a little hesitant to leave her friends behind, but seeing as Lilly insists, she decides to go along with her. When they arrive, Mittens meets the hairless cat and the big rottweiler, which were also invited. All four animals stand before a cloud in the middle of the Field. While all puzzled and a little hesitant, all hop onto it and are carried away.

Once back on the Cloud where they'd first arrived, all four animals look at each other. Some even recognised one another from the first time they arrived in Heaven.

Atlas Trembley, the Rottweiler, widens his eyes when he sees the Jack Russell with Shelby. Lilly Lahey, the Jack Russell, also widens her eyes when she sees him, along with the equally familiar sightings of the hairless cat that was watching her in Tennis Ball Paradise and the little kitten, Mittens she'd come to enlighten.

Tiger Buchenwald, the Sphynx glanced around. His blue and yellow eyes caught sight of Lilly, Atlas, and Mittens. Mittens Kushner, the White Tabby kitten, looks as frightened and awestruck as the others are, wondering what's happening and why she and these other three animals have been called here. Tiger wonders what's going to happen. Then, as the animals are just about to introduce themselves to each other, one of the many clouds formed around Induction Cloud comes down in front of them and speaks in a gentle voice that sounds neither female nor male. It's simply a soothing voice that eases the spirits of the confused four.

'Greetings,' it says. *'I welcome the four of you.'*

'Who are you?' they all ask the cloud, to which the cloud replies, *'I am the voice of Heaven itself; I have no need for names. But this isn't why I summoned the four of you here. The reason why the four of you are here is that I am offering you a chance to walk with the humans again. I've decided to grant you this opportunity after seeing and listening to your adventures here in Heaven,'* Spoke the cloud. Atlas took a few steps forward, his eyes watering and questioning.

'Yu-You mean, we get to see our owners again?'

'That is exactly what I mean, Atlas. You are very attentive, and you, too, Lilly. You were the first dog to come to the theory that pets can traverse through worlds to see their owners again. And to answer your question: yes, Vill's howling is his way of telling anyone that will listen that there is a way to traverse back into the Land of the Living.'

'Wait, so I can see Wolfgang again? Even if he might not be able to see me, I can still be with him?' Tiger askes stepping up to where Atlas is.

'Yes, that is true, Tiger; your owners will not be able to see you, but you will be able to see them in the environment you've known and personally see how they have been coping. The reason why I have picked you four is because I saw it in your hearts how much you are struggling without your owners and so I am offering you this chance for some closure and to see that they are doing okay.' There's a bittersweetness in the cloud's voice, but despite that, it still maintains its comforting tone.

Lilly is next to join Atlas and Tiger. She appears as if she's going to cry. 'Is this a one-time thing? Or can we visit our owners as much as we want? Can we play with them?'

'You can visit them as many times as you wish unless you know they are doing well without you and will always remember your legacy. You can decide if you want to return or not; it is really up to you. And yes, you can play with them by interacting

with the things you loved in life such as your old toys. Once you have attained the information that you need regarding your legacy and the impact you had on their lives, you will be qualified to move on and stay here in Heaven. Once you have moved on will you not be able to return.'

Finally, Mittens trots towards them, asking the cloud her own question. 'But what if our hooman's get another pet that they like more?'

'You know what, Mittens, just because they enjoy themselves with their new pet doesn't mean they will ever forget you because humans who love animals can never forget the impact of each pet they have owned. So, rest assured, the four of you have had some kind of impact on your owners' lives, the same as every other animal here. You all have had a story to tell. Every single Angel Pet in Heaven has a story to tell, no matter how mundane.

Now, to go into the Land of the Living and reunite with your loved owners, step into this doorway.'

***

RIGHT AFTER THE voice had finished speaking, the soft ground beneath them all pulls up and forms into the shape of a door. In the middle of the doorway is a spiralling mass of colours that beckons the four to enter it. Knowing that they're given a chance to see their owners again, they're no longer hesitant and venture forward into the doorway that calls out to them.

Atlas first, then Tiger, then Lilly and finally Mittens.

Part Six: Reunion

-Colin Trembley-

I ENJOY PLAYING with my new Doberman puppy, Buddy. Those floppy little ears, short black and tan fur, and stubby little paws remind me of Atlas as a pup, based on the pictures we have hanging on the loungeroom wall. But while I love Buddy a lot, I love Atlas more because I grew up with him and, he'd been there with me and was my best friend since I was only two years old. And it will take a while for Buddy to fill in the gaps when Atlas died. But even with those gaps filled, nothing will ever stop the massive amounts of love I have for my first dog.

Not only was Atlas my best friend, but he was also my hero. He saved mine and my parents' lives that night. My boy took five literal bullets for us so he could drive that burglar away.

It's been two years since Atlas was shot and killed. It's 2021 and I have Buddy. Things are starting to get back to normal. Even though it's been two years and I'm thirteen, that night when I saw Atlas lying in a pool of his own blood and the life slip from his eyes, still haunts me so much. Sometimes I find myself unable to sleep at night so I go into my parents' room and sleep in their bed. Sometimes, I think back to when Dad took Atlas' body in his car and took him to the crematorium while Mom stayed home with me because she knew I couldn't stay home by myself or go with Dad to deliver Atlas's body.

Then, a few days later, Dad got a call from the pet crematorium saying that Atlas's ashes were ready for pickup. I couldn't stay home this time, and I begged Dad to take me with him. When we arrived at the crematorium, Dad went up to the counter while holding my hand tightly. He told the brown-haired man at the counter that we were there to pick up Atlas Trembley. The man then spoke into an intercom on the desk he was working at, and about two minutes later, a tall, uniformed man with blonde hair came out from a room and asked us to follow him. We did without question. The entire time, I was trying my hardest not to cry so I kept sniffling and biting my bottom lip.

But then we entered into a waiting room. The tall blonde man told us to sit and wait for a few seconds. Another minute passed, and the man returned again. This time, he was holding a small blue velvet bag. As soon as I saw the bag, which I knew had Atlas' ashes inside, the tears burst out of my eyes. It didn't matter how much I wiped or sniffled; they wouldn't stop.

I saw the blurred figure of the man holding the ashes to Dad. Dad took them, and I heard him let out a few sniffles before saying 'Thank you' to the man. I then heard Dad tell the blonde-haired man that Atlas was my dog and he'd been my dog since I was two.

The man uttered a soft 'Oh and then, 'I'm really sorry that such a young boy has had to experience something such as the home invasion and how Atlas met his end'.

After that, Dad thanked the man for the final time, and we left the crematorium to go home. I sat on the passenger seat during the ride home, holding the blue velvet bag as I cried heavily onto it. I hugged and I kissed it.

I turned the bag around in my hands and looked at the tag hanging from it, unable to stop myself from crying. One side of the label showed a small photo of Atlas, and the other side were the dates:

DOB - 02/12/2010
DOD - 05/20/2019

Beneath the dates was a message that read:
HEAVEN HAS GAINED ANOTHER ANGEL.
I cried some more at this.

When we finally got home, Dad opened the door, and Mom was waiting for us. She had a box of tissues in her hand and a damp tissue in her other hand, she'd been crying while waiting for us. Then, without saying anything, I looked up at her and held the blue velvet bag with Atlas's name on it to her. She flinched back and almost dropped the tissue she was carrying. I watched Mom put the tissue hand to her mouth for a moment before she wiped it over her eyes again.

'We brought Atlas home,' I sobbed, still clutching onto the bag of ashes with my life.

Mom went into the kitchen. I followed her and watched her put the box of tissues down. I handed Atlas's ashes over to her so she could have a look. She examined the bag, read the label tied to it, and brought the tissue to her eyes again. Then, without thinking about it, I pulled a tissue out from the box and wiped my eyes and nose before deciding that I couldn't keep staring at the ashes, knowing that would just make me cry more heavily.

So, I headed into the living room and sat on the couch, but even being away from the bag of ashes wasn't enough to help ease my mind. Because everywhere I looked, I saw photos of Atlas and me.

Every time I closed my eyes, I saw him: doing his play bow, his tongue lolling out, him dropping his favourite pull rope toy in front of me, to tell me that it was playtime.

It didn't matter what I did, I couldn't get rid of the thoughts of Atlas. The more I thought about him -, his panting tongue, how his tail would wag every time he saw me. The more I missed him, the more I wanted a chance to rub his belly again, and the more I remembered how his paws felt on my shoulders when he hugged me, especially when I came home from school crying because my lunch money was stolen by Cole Waterson or he gave me a black eye.

And I knew it wouldn't matter to Cole if he found out about Atlas's death. That jerk would probably use Atlas's death as an excuse to bully me even more. I hated Cole. I wish he'd just leave me alone! I remember feeling that it was a good thing that I wouldn't be seeing Cole for a few days after Mom had called the school and told them what had happened and that it was really affecting me.

Atlas was and will always be a good dog.

***

I STILL GET emotional whenever I think about Atlas, but at least most of that emotion has disappeared because I now have my new puppy. Dad had organised the adoption for me three weeks ago. So, most of the sadness and tears have gone.

I have the chance to be happy again because of my new puppy, like having fun discovering his favourite toys: the squeaky star toys with cute cartoon faces on them. These are Buddy's favourite kind of toys: the squeakers. This is a good thing because if Buddy discovers the pull-ropes and starts playing with them, I might get emotional all over again— the pull-ropes were Atlas's favourite toys, especially his lime and grey one.

We still have some of Atlas's old toys, like the lime and grey pull-rope, stashed away in his toybox named Atlas's Toys, while the other toys he didn't really play with in life were donated to nearby dogs' homes.

We bought new toys for Buddy, which he loves to pick up, shake around, and throw, just so he can chase after them some more. In other words, he plays fetch with himself. And to watch those little puppy legs chase after those toys never fails to put a smile on my face. It's just like watching Atlas when he was a puppy and when he used to run after any toy, we'd throw for him.

I love Buddy just as much as I loved Atlas.

One night after I went to bed and was thinking about a presentation about climate change that I had to give at school the next day something strange happened; something that's never happened in the three weeks since Buddy has lived with us.

Buddy is usually quiet at night, sleeping like a log, but sometimes he dreams. I imagine he dreams of racing, his little legs kicking in a running motion. I've seen him do it in his puppy bed, which Mom and I bought for him about two weeks ago.

That day, after a long session of running around outside and practising his hole-digging skills, Buddy took a nap. Lying on his back, with his little legs in the air, he started making those funny running movements. It reminded me of a video someone showed me at school of a sleepwalking dog that ran into a wall.

But tonight feels different. Something is wrong. A noise from downstairs. What it is, I don't know but my chest tightens with fear, thinking of the worst: that Buddy will end up like Atlas. I throw myself out of bed and run into my parent's room to let them know what's happening.

'Wha…? Colin? What is it?' Mom asks as she wipes her eyes.

'Somethings wrong!' I urge her.

Now, Dad sits up, rubbing his eyes too. He looks at me with a tired expression. 'Col? What are you doing?' he asks. I'm surprised that they both don't hear the sound of barking or yapping from downstairs.

'Can't you hear Buddy barking?' I question them with alarm.

'No. Col, it's 1:30 in the morning. You have school tomorrow,' Dad says, picking up his mobile phone from the bedside table.

Then I notice that Buddy's yapping has stopped, but I'm still not going to take any chances! I'm not I going to just lay down and sleep if my Doberman puppy had been hurt, or worse...

'Just go back to sleep,' Mom yawns, about to pull the covers over her and lie down again. But I tug them away from her.

'I know I heard him barking and growling!' I cry. 'Please believe me! What if someone's broken in like when Atlas was alive? I'm not going to take any chances for my dog to be harmed,' I say. Finally Dad removes the covers off him and tells Mom he'll go with me to check on Buddy and to make sure that he's okay and that nothing's happening to him.

***

My home's exactly how I remember it. The furniture is still in the same places but the carpet where I bled out on is gone, replaced by one with a turtle design on it.

It's been two years since I was killed on this very spot. Now that I'm home again, I want to wander into Colin's room and see how he's doing. It's late, and everyone is probably sleeping, but I can't resist.

I take a moment to breathe as a tear rolls down my cheek. Being in the Trembley house, my beloved house where I'd made so many good memories, is bittersweet.

I take a step forward but suddenly I hear a yapping sound: a puppy! Then, darting out from behind the couch, comes this little dog sporting the same-coloured coat as mine. He crouches into a defensive posture, letting out a tiny little growl.

'Who are you? What are you doing in my house!' *he yaps.*

I can't help but stare at the tiny little pup, the understanding dawning on me that the Trembley's have another dog. But I'm not worried or feeling betrayed. Nope! As a matter of fact, seeing that they'd bought a puppy makes me happy because a puppy in their lives will make them happy again, especially Colin.

If Colin's happy, that's all that matters. Nothing makes a dog happier than to see his owner smile. That's the only thing that ever truly matters.

'Get out! Don't make me bite you! I will, you know! I a good boy, I protect house! Get out!'

Like a chihuahua, he continues to yap and tells me to go away, but I just can't help but wag my tail at this tiny pup's big personality. He'll grow up into a well-trained dog to protect this family with his life.

I step towards him, not scared, and sniff at his little head.

'Hey, take it, easy little fella. What's your name?' *I ask in a calm, gentle voice as I continue to sniff him before lowering myself to the ground to show that I'm not a threat.*

'Buddy! And I'm not little! I'm a Doberman!'

'That's a lovely name and something I'd expect Colin to pick for someone as cute as you,' *I say. Then Buddy stops yapping and growling. Instead, he asks me how I know Colin or, as he calls him,* 'Mastah'*.*

My tail wags and I can feel tears drip from my eyes. I sit down, and Buddy sits in front of me, tilting his little head, confused about how I know Colin and the Trembley family. I'm more than happy to tell him.

'Before you, I was Colin's best pal. I was the Trembley's loved Rottweiler. My name's Atlas. Before you were even born, I lived in this house with the Trembley's for nine years. I've grown up with Colin and he with me—since he was two years old, in fact. But sadly, on this exact spot that I'm sitting on, I died here. You see, a nasty man came by wanting to hurt the Master and Mistress. I leapt into action and was shot five times. I guess you could say I took five bullets for them.'

I was about to tell Buddy more about my life with the Trembley's, but that's when I hear the sound of hurried footsteps and what sounds like Colin's voice. I have the idea of using

Buddy to help Colin not see me but hint that I'm here in ghost form and have come home.

I don't know if it'll work out, but I have to try something. I look at my old box of toys and instantly know what to do.

'Tell you what, see that lime and grey pull-rope toy?' I ask, watching the Doberman puppy look over to the wooden box with my name on it.

'Yes. Was it yours?'

'Yeah, it was my favourite toy. Can you do me a favour and pick it up? Then when Colin comes down, can you drop it in front of him?'

Buddy starts panting and wags his tail. 'I can do that!'

I watch as the tiny puppy wanders over to my old toybox and drags out my old favourite toy. Seeing it makes me want to cry.

'Thank you, Buddy. You're a good pup. And you'll grow up to be an even better dog.'

I hear the footsteps reach the bottom of the stairs. My body was frozen, tears rolling from my eyes when I see Colin again for the first time in two years.

Even though I know he can't see me. I sure can see him, and it's so good to see him again. I'll never forget that face...

'I've come home, Daddy...' I whimper as my tail wags.

***

DAD AND I are downstairs. As soon as we make it into the living room, we both see Buddy. Thank goodness, he's perfectly fine. He's happily wagging his little tail.

'What is it, Buddy? What were you barking at?' I say, leaning to pet the puppy around his ears, his tail wagging faster.

'See, Col, he's alright. There's nothing to be worried about, so come up back to bed,' Dad says, as he holds the cuff of my blue Japanese-style pyjamas. But I instantly pull away when I notice what's inside Buddy's mouth. I throw my hands to my face and tear up when I see the lime and grey pull-rope in his mouth.

Buddy then drops it at my feet, nudges it forward with his nose, and steps back, his tail wagging. I pick it up and examine it like it's a museum exhibit piece. I look at Buddy, who's happily panting at me paw-dancing and hopping with pride. His tail is wagging and he's yapping happily like he's trying to tell me something.

'Dad, look!' I say, holding the toy up to Dad. He takes it from me and studies it for about five seconds before dismissing the toy as being one of Buddy's many toys, which I partly can't blame him for, because Mom and I did buy a lot of toys for Buddy when we went to the pet shop two weeks ago.

'No... this isn't Buddy's toy. He doesn't like pull-ropes that much, remember? Buddy likes the squeakers. This was Atlas's favourite toy!' I say before turning back to Buddy, looking around him, wondering what made him decide to rummage through my old dog's toybox and take out his favourite toy.

There's something strange about this action, because Buddy liked the squeakers and not the pull-ropes. Is he trying to tell me something? Is Atlas here in some way? Did Atlas tell Buddy to drop his favourite toy in front of me?

I watch Buddy for what feels like a long time; maybe he's trying to tell me something. Maybe he's trying to tell me that my old dog has returned?

Has Buddy been talking with Atlas's ghost? Has Atlas returned from the dead for a visit?

I can feel tears beginning to form in my eyes. Without thinking straight, I kneel down to Buddy and start talking to him like a person.

'Is Atlas here?' I ask the puppy, even though I know it must sound stupid to Dad— to see his thirteen-year-old son, who started junior high this year, ask his Doberman puppy about whether the ghost of his first dog is in the room.

Whatever Dad's thinking, he's doing well to hide it; he just yawns, saying that he's going back to bed, that he'll let me have this moment before telling me that I shouldn't be too long because I have school in the morning. He yawns again. 'Goodnight, Col,', he says and heads back upstairs. I hear his bedroom door opening and closing behind him. So now with Dad back in bed with Mom, I stay with Buddy, and possibly the ghost of my old dog Atlas. I hope Atlas is here and that he's come back for a visit. I don't care if the whole idea of ghosts seems crazy or if I look crazy doing this; if my dog's come back as a ghost, I won't be able to keep the smile from my mouth. Atlas was my very first and best friend. But he was cruelly taken away from me by that horrible man who I hoped would get prison time.

I pick up Atlas's old pull-rope and hold it before Buddy, who continues to wag his tail and pant his tongue happily.

'Did Atlas tell you to get this and drop it in front of me?' I ask. I knew that dogs can't talk like us humans, but at times, I'm sure I can tell what they're thinking just by their actions. And every time I mention 'Atlas,' Buddy seems to get more excited, running around in circles and getting down low to do the play bow.

I wipe my eyes as tears begin to spill from them. But these are tears of joy. I feel a smile spread across my face. I rub Buddy's head around the ears. I'm hopeful and overjoyed at the prospect of Atlas being in this room somewhere. I think about the idea of Atlas's ghost coming home again to see his family that he loves so much.

'Can you show me where Atlas is? Can you walk over to him if he's here in this room?'

I'm right here, Daddy... I'm right here.

I watch Buddy as he makes a slight yapping noise, which I have to shush (because I don't want to wake my parents.) Buddy hops over to the middle of the living room in between the couches and coffee table. I recognise the spot instantly as the place where I sat two years ago, with Atlas's head on my lap, his blood pooling from his chest, out of five different bullet holes.

I drop the toy and cup my mouth; the tears now really falling down my cheeks. According to Buddy, Atlas was sitting in the exact same spot where he'd died.

Please don't cry, Daddy Colin... I don't like seeing you sad... Oh, I wish I could lick those tears away.

Sniffling and wiping at my eyes with the sleeves of my pyjamas, I glance at Buddy, who stops panting and wagging his little tail. He's now tilting his head up at me with confusion (bless this little pooch) like he's trying to understand the reason why I'm so emotional. I let out small chuckles mixed with sniffles as I wipe my ears, feeling so incredibly happy that Atlas has come home.

Even though I can't see Atlas, I can feel his presence. I pick up the lime and grey pull-rope again, holding it close to my chest. I shuffle over to him on my knees and tried to pick him up and hold him to my chest along with the toy. I hug Buddy, kiss him on the head, which makes him start licking my face, near the eyes, as if to lick the tears away.

'You're such a good puppo!' I sob as I give Buddy another kiss on the head, hugging him tightly, laughing while sobbing, calling him a good dog. I manage to wipe my eyes with the hand that holds the toy. I look ahead of me, sitting on my knees, and keeping Buddy and the pull-rope to my chest, not daring to let them go even for a second, as at this moment, they both mean the world to me. I close my eyes for a brief moment, sniffle, and when I open them again, I imagine Atlas's ghost; transparent and glowing with an ocean shade of blue, sitting there on the place of his death and staring at me with the face he always made when he wanted to know if I was okay. Like the days, I'd come home with a black eye and crying from getting into a hassle with Cole and his jerk friends.

'Hi, Atlas,' I say through heavy tears to his ghost. I feel goosebumps on my arm as if there's a light breeze, like a tail wagging near me. Even if I can't see him, I can feel his presence. He was here! I can almost imagine myself having a conversation with him, even though he's a dog, and I'm human and I can't see him.

'Hi, Daddy! It's been so, so long... I've really been missing you.'

'I've been missing you too, Atlas,' I blubber. 'So, so much.'

'I wanted to come down here to see you again. Because I've been missing you. I wanted to see how my family's doing. In case you were wondering, Heaven is a lovely place. I've met a lot of animals like me and have a lot of friends up there. I get to do what every dog dreams about! But despite all the fun and joy I have up there. I'll always remember this as my home, and I'll always remember you as my Daddy. I love you so much, Colin. But at least you have Buddy here to make you smile like I used to all those years ago.'

'I love you, Atlas.'

'As do I, Colin. Take care of the family, Buddy, and of yourself for me.'

'I will. Thank you so, so damn much for everything, Atlas... I wouldn't be who I am today without you.'

As much as I want to stay and talk with my old dog's ghost, I know that my parents will get angry at me for staying up too late. Dad might even think that I'm having a mental breakdown. I don't want to have to explain this to someone who I know won't be able to understand. Either way, as much as I want to continue talking with my dead dog, I know I have to wrap this up because like Dad says, I have school tomorrow.

'You will always be my Daddy. I love you!'

And with that, I stand up, holding both Buddy and the toy. I wave goodbye to Atlas's ghost, watching him give me a nod before standing up and turning away where he seems to walk right through the furniture before disappearing. And even though I'm a sobbing mess, I smile because I know that I've been talking to Atlas's ghost, - even if I couldn't see his actual body without using my imagination. It feels nice to witness his ghost and to know that he's in peace up in animal Heaven.

I looked at Buddy and hug him again, smooching his head, calling him a good boy before getting up and wiping away my happy tears. I walk up the steps carrying both my puppy and Atlas's pull-rope up to my room. After the talk with Atlas's ghost, I know I won't be able to go to sleep by myself, so I take Buddy up with me. And, I'm sure the puppy will like to sleep in bed with a human rather than spending the night downstairs by himself in his tiny little dog bed. Besides, if Buddy is going to grow up into a fit, healthy, happy, and loyal Doberman, a good start is for him to sleep on my bed with me and get to know what it's like to sleep with a human. Get him used to the years to come.

When I put Buddy down at the foot of my bed, I hop in, clutching Atlas's toy close to my chest. Buddy snuggles up to my feet. I pull the covers over me and get myself comfortable. I stare into the darkness, eyes still wet but I'm smiling to myself thinking of just one thing as I go off to sleep:
Atlas had come home.

-Wolfgang Buchenwald-

IN THE EIGHT years since Tiger had been put down, age had finally caught up with me. I turned eighty-seven a month ago. It's currently the middle of August. Those eight years marked by a mix of stress and significant events, starting with the overwhelming emotions after losing Tiger in 2013, followed by the heavy confusion and joy that came with going to Carina's wedding in Stockholm, Sweden.

I resigned from work as an accountant on my eighty-sixth birthday in 2020. The job had started to take a serious toll on my body and health; I simply couldn't manage the workload anymore. This was compounded by the challenges having two strokes: one in 2015 and another in 2018.

Now, back here in my hometown, Frankfurt, Germany, I find myself lying on my death bed. Around the same time as my recent birthday, I contracted pneumonia. I saw my doctor at the visiting Westend Praxis clinic and complained about frequent chest pains and fatigue. The doctor told me I wasn't going to make it to the start of 2022, that I was going to die at some point during the year.

But even with that diagnosis, my doctor recommended I take things easy but try to do things that bring me joy, like going to the park, feeding the birds pieces of bread, and taking short walks. The doc also suggested that if I had any lingering milestones or wishes I wanted to achieve, then I should get them done before my passing.

So, not long after receiving my prognosis, I hired a personal carer, named, Agathe Adler. I employed her to help me get to the toilet, cook meals for me and generally take care of me during my final moments on Earth. Agathe worked six hours a day, and despite the nature of her job, Agathe says she likes caring for me and hearing stories about my life with Tiger.

Being bed-bound does feel restrictive and dull at times. The only times I get out of bed are to be escorted to the bathroom or for Agathe to give bath in nice warm water. Agathe is a young brunette, in her thirties with smooth features and a lovely disposition. We have had a good relationship with each other.

She's noticed the photographs of Tiger displayed around the house and expressed that she, too, has cats: a black male cat named Phantom and a white female cat named Frau. I shared with her how Tiger died eight years ago after he had to be put down because he was too sick. Agathe expressed her sympathy, saying it was always hard to lose a pet. She then said that she used to have a Dogue de Bordeaux named Munchy who had tragically ate some chocolate bars that the local kids had fed him. Muncy had been in so much pain that he, too had to be put down. I told her I was sorry for her loss, but she said that it was okay because it happened twelve years ago, and now she found comfort with two cats, Phantom and Frau.

As I lie in bed watching returns of *Der 90 Geburtstag*, a sitcom I loved in the '60s. Agathe enters my room carrying a glass of orange juice and my mobile phone. I usually prefer to leave my phone charging in the downstairs kitchen, because that's where I've charged it for years. Besides, the only power outlet in my room was occupied by the TV.

'It's your daughter, Carina,' Agathe says as she hands me the phone. I nod, take it from her, and hold it to my ear.

Ever since Carina's wedding eight years ago, a miracle has happened: Dorothea and Carina have started calling me daily. They finally understand the hurt they caused by neglecting me for years, abandoning me as if I was never part of their family. But that's all changed. They've both apologised for all those years of neglect and silence. They've even invited me to play golf with them when they visit, remembering that I used to like playing golf in my free time.

Everything is back in balance, back to the way I always hoped it would be. My family is whole again. Even the news Dorothea shared a few years ago, in 2019, about my ex-wife, Irene, passing away from heart complications hasn't shaken the newfound sense of peace I feel. Although I no longer have Tiger to keep my lap warm, everything else in my life seems just as I dreamed it could by.

I often still wish I had Tiger here with me, cuddling by my side during my final days. But I know that's just wishful thinking because it's been eight years since I said goodbye to my beloved Sphynx cat. But I do believe that wherever he is, he's happy and at peace with all the other kitties who've passed away... just as he did.

Lying here on my deathbed my mind drifts to the beautiful memories I have of my hairless little boy. I think back to the day I adopted him as a kitten in 1999 from that kind family. I recall the year 2010, when he started to show signs of deterioration, and in 2013, when I made the heartbreaking decision to take him to the vet to end his suffering. I still miss his wrinkled little face and often wish I could pat it.

In bed, waiting for my time to come, I feel at peace. My once sad, lonely life finally has meaning to it, and for that, I'm grateful.

'Hello, Carina,' I speak into the phone.

Carina's voice comes through thick with tears. I know someone must have told her the news—possibly Dorothea or Agathe— about me being on my deathbed. As my personal carer, Agathe often keeps my two daughters updated on my condition.

'Hey, hey, what's wrong, my sweet? This happens to everyone, remember? It happened to your mother, and now it's my turn. I'm actually at peace with the idea of dying and welcome it without fear,' I say, trying to calm and ease her worry.

'I know you've been sick, and I just want you to know that Doro and I still feel very sorry we neglected you. We're in Hamburg now, waiting to catch a plane to Frankfurt. Please hold on until we get there,' Carina pleads.'

'I know, Carina. I look forward to seeing you both when you get here,' I reply.

After all these years, Carina still calls her sister Doro. It amuses me, as it always had, to hear that childhood nickname slip from her lips. Back when my daughters were growing up in this very house, it was just one of those small things that warmed my heart. I almost chuckle at the memory but hold back; Carina is already too upset.

Even without my loyal cat to keep me company I have my daughters back. It's as if Tiger himself had gone to Carina and Dorothea and whispered to them their father is suffering: that this flawed old German man named Wolfgang Buchenwald needs his girls, no matter the distance or estrangement. Because family, like it or not, remains family. We can choose our friends, but not our family... not our blood.

Knowing I don't have long to live... I know because I can feel it: the angels from Heaven are beckoning me, their harps playing, their wings softly fluttering in the distance.

Before I go, I wish to see my daughters' faces one last time before I slip away. That would be enough to bring me peace. Yet, if I could wish for just one more thing, it would be a final visit from a certain ghostly feline. To see my Tiger one last time before I slip away would be a gift beyond measure.

Agathe has looked after me well during the past six months, and I can tell she's been preparing herself for the crucial moment when my heart eventually stops beating. When that time comes, I know I will close my eyes peacefully, ready to embrace the arms of the angels above.

'We love you, Dad, and we'll see you very soon when we both arrive in Frankfurt', Carina sniffles. I hear some muffled sounds, like the phone is being handed over, perhaps to Dorothea.

'We'll stay by your side until it's time for us to leave,' Dorethea says, sounding more in control than her sister but her voice is shaky. Love you, Dad'.

'I love you both, my girls. I'll see you when you get here. Just knock, and Agathe will let you in. See you soon.' With that, I end the call and hand the phone back to Agathe, who's been waiting patiently by the door.

'Both Carina and Dorothea will be here soon,' I tell her. They're currently in Hamburg.

She curtsies, takes the phone, heads downstairs to place the phone on its charger. Moments later, she returns to my room, stands at the doorway.

'Would you like anything else, Sir?'

I think for a moment. 'A glass of water, please. And, if it's not too much trouble, could you fetch me a photo of Tiger from the mantelpiece downstairs?'

'Of course, Sir. Which one in particular?'

'Agathe?'

'Yes?'

'Please call me Wolfgang. You're my friend as well as my carer.' I say.

Her hazel eyes widen slightly, and her cheeks flush a soft shade of pink. She dips into another curtsy, her voice tinged with a hint or surprise. 'O-of course, Wolfgang. Any particular photo of him?'

'Nope, surprise me,' I reply with a gentle smile, trying to keep an air of warmth despite the dwindling time I have left to live.

'Certainly Wolfgang. I'll be back shortly.'

True to her word, she returns moments later, placing a glass of water on my bedside table and handing me the photograph.

'Thank you, Agathe,' I say, taking the frame from her hands.

As soon as I see the image, my eyes well up with tears, and an involuntary smile creeps onto my face. Agathe had chosen well. She picked the very first photograph I'd ever taken of Tiger back in 1999: a tiny, wrinkled kitten gazing up at the camera with those large, curious eyes, one yellow and one blue eye.

I hold the frame gently in my hands, just as I had when I said 'Goodbye' to him all those years ago. But this time, there's no grief. Instead, I feel a sense of warmth and gratitude.

Though Tiger has left this world, I like to believe, with all my heart, that he's at peace and living in another world. And soon, I'll join him there. I can almost hear myself whisper, 'It's my time now. I'm coming to join you, Tiger. We can be together again for as long as we want'.

Realising the TV is still on, I pick up the remote and turn it off, wanting a moment in silence. The room is suddenly still, save for the sound of my breathing. I sink deeper into the pillow, letting my gaze drift to the ceiling. My lips curled into a soft smile as I hold the photo to my gaunt chest. Memories, of my hairless boy, my loyal companion, Tiger fill my mind. I close my eyes, waiting for my two girls to arrive.

When I arrive in Wolfgang's home, more specifically, the living room, I see that he isn't around. I start to feel a little frightened. Then I see a woman I've never seen before walk down the stairs.

Wolfgang must be upstairs! So, without thinking of anything else, I run up the steps. At the top I hesitate and wonder where he could be. Then it comes to me. Bedroom!

I head to Wolfgang's bedroom. Once inside, I find my old human lying peacefully in his bed. His chest is rising and falling with shallow breath but he's still breathing. Thank God! I see a faint smile on his wrinkled face.

Quietly, I approach the bed and leap up onto it. As soon as my paws land on his bed covers, he jolts awake and glances around with a puzzled expression.

'Agathe?' *He calls out, his voice thick with confusion. I tilt my head, wondering who on Earth this Agathe is. My question is quickly answered. The woman I'd seen a few seconds ago walks up the steps and into the room. That's when I understand who this strange woman is: she's Wolfgang's loyal servant.*

'Did you leave something on my bed that I don't know about?' *Wolfgang asks, his tone puzzled.*

The woman, Agathe shakes her head. 'No,' *she simply replies.*

'Oh, really? Huh! Must have imagined it,' Wolfgang says.

It's strange, Wolfgang looks at where I am—the spot on his bed where I've made myself at home like I used to when I was alive. I notice his eyes; they seem to broaden. His mouth forms into a slight grin of surprise.

Can he see me? Or feel my presence? Does he understand that I've come home to visit him?

'Tiger?' *He whispers.*

Yes! I realise he can see me! My tail flicks up and I knead the blanket over his leg., I'm amazed! I want to know what else he can sense of me.

I wander up to his chest, sitting on the frame he holds so closely. The entire time, he stares at me with perplexed and teary eyes, as if he isn't sure if he's dreaming or if my ghostly presence has come as a result of his asking for it. Whatever the reason, I don't care. As long as I'm here in front of my old human again, seeing that smile on his thin lips, that's more than enough for me because he deserves happiness.

Without taking his eyes off me, he speaks to his servant.

'Agathe, could you please leave me for a moment? I think someone has come to see me before I slip away, but I'll still cling on for my daughters.'

Slip away? No... Wolfgang can't be dying, not now that I've been allowed to come and see him again! Sure, I haven't been able to visit him in eight years. But he can't already be on his deathbed! Can he?

Agathe takes a bow, purses her lips and says, 'Of course, Wolfgang, Sir, I will be right downstairs if you need me and when Carina, and Dorothea arrive.'

Have his daughters contacted him after I passed on? Oh dear, so much has happened during my eight years in Heaven. So, much stuff that I never would've guessed could happen. But either way, I'm glad Wolfgang finally has his daughters back in his life again. I'd suspected that my passing would've hit him like someone dropping a baby elephant on him. So, even if I had missed a lot during those eight years, it sure is a blessing to see him again -, even if he is on his deathbed. At least I'll be able to see him before he passes, spreading his wings just as I had done when I died.

***

I can't believe what my eyes are seeing: a faint blue aura of a hairless cat sitting on my chest. I wish to God that they aren't deceiving me because they've been playing tricks on me lately. After all, that's to be expected when you know you're dying. Hallucination or not, I'm happy -, the happiest I've felt in quite a while. I have my cat here with me. It seems impossible, but he's sitting here right in front of me. He looks like he always did when he was young and full of life! The only catch is a slight translucency, which tells me he's a ghost. But I'm not afraid of this ghostly feline apparition in front of me. How could I possibly be scared? It's the ghost of the cat I've been missing for eight years, the cat whose ashes sit on top of the mantelpiece, surrounded by old photographs I'd taken all those years ago. I feel no fear, only comfort.

I want to lift my hands to rub the ghostly form of Tiger, but I reconsider because my hands will just go through him, and besides, I'm far too weak to really move. So, I keep my hands where they are and let tears of joy fall at the very sight of his ghost.

'Hello Tiger. How is Heaven with all the other animals?' I say to Tiger's ghost, watching him lie down and curl his paws under his chest, looking like what the local kids call "a cat loaf." The image of his ghost brings great tears of joy to my eyes, particularly as I watch him and hear him speak… a cat actually speaking? If Agathe could hear me from downstairs, she'd think I've lost my sanity, but even so, I bet she'd secretly smile, knowing that I was happy.

'Hallo Wolfgang, Heaven is a beautiful place. You can make friends immediately, even with animals that are usually sworn enemies, such as dogs and cats. But enough about Heaven and me, how are you? You mentioned that you're going to slip away...'

'Indeed Tiger, I'm dying. I've got a sickness called pneumonia, and quite a deadly version of it. But even as I lie here on my deathbed, I can't help but smile. Do you know why, Tiger?' I ask watching him blink slowly, something he often did when he was curious about something.

'No, please tell me, Wolfgang.'

'Because I have my family back. After you passed on, I was close to tying the rope around my neck when Dorothea rang me and gave me her condolences. Then I was invited to Carina's wedding in Sweden, which they even paid for. After that, Carina and Dorothea swore to contact me daily to check up on me, which I'm grateful for. My ex-wife Irene died at one point, which was a downer and quite heartbreaking because even though she left me, I still loved her. I never remarried. But other than that, things have been going wonderfully. I only wish you could've lived longer to see it. Six months ago, I employed my personal carer, Agathe Adler, who's very kind and consistent with me. But out of all those things that have happened over the eight years, there's something that makes me even happier.'

'What's that?' Tiger asks, placing his head in front of him. His multi-coloured eyes never leave mine, not even to groom himself. He keeps his full attention on me. He was always an attentive listener.

'You're here. You came to see me, and that makes me really happy! You being here has provided me with my final dying wish. I love you for that, Tiger.'

Tiger shuffles forward a bit.

I've never been happier.

'Tiger?'

'Mmh?'

'Will you stay with me until I pass on? And when I do, will you lead me into Heaven?'

'You know I would, Wolfgang, I may be a cat, but I'm as loyal as a dog. I'd do anything for you because you're the best human a Sphynx cat like me could ever want. I love you, Wolfgang Buchenwald.'

'I love you too, Tiger Buchenwald. I'll see you again in Heaven.'

'I'm sure you will.'

With that, Tiger's blue translucent ghost falls asleep on my chest. I can't help but stare at him as I wait patiently for my daughters to arrive so they can say their final goodbyes. Then, I'll wait for my eyes to close for the last time.

Luckily, I don't have to wait. My daughters arrive just after Tiger's ghost has settled for a nap on my chest. I hear the door open downstairs, followed by the mingling voices of Agathe, Carina, and Dorothea. I hear Agathe's calm voice—ever the professional. Quite the opposite, I hear Carina sound like she's bawling. In contrast, Dorothea sounds like she's trying to keep herself composed despite her younger sister being in a fragile state.

'Where is he?' I hear Dorothea ask Agathe, who simply replies, 'He's upstairs in his room.'

'Thank you, Agathe. Come on now, Sis. We're going to see Dad. You've got to be strong for him. Remember to take deep breaths,' Dorothea says to Carina, who still sounds like a complete wreck; knowing that this is the last time she'll see me alive. It's going to be extremely hard for her... for both of them.

But even through the pain, she must be feeling, Dorothea is commendably playing the role of a good, older sister, trying her best to keep a brave face and stay strong for Carina and me. I can't help but smile. For once, I have everything I can possibly want. I have my Tiger back. Even though he isn't alive, his presence—his ethereal residue —is snoozing on my chest, comforting me in preparation for when my heart eventually stops beating. To have Carina, Dorothea, and Tiger with me in the same room is all I could ever want,

I stare at the sleeping transparent feline on my bed and cry tears of joy. I look over and see my two daughters standing in the doorway. Dorothea is holding Carina's hand. Carina's face is red She's holding a handkerchief to her face. Dorothea's face is a little pink but in control of her emotions.

'Hello, my two beautiful girls.' I smile at them, offering a weak hand. Carina kneels in front of it. Dorothea stands at the opposite side of my bed and gently takes my other hand in hers. I watch Carina take my thin fingers in hers and kiss them. I feel Dorothea do the same to my other hand.

'Oh my god, Dad, I'm so, so sorry!' bawls Carina as she shuffles closer, placing my skinny hand on her chest where I can feel her heart beating.

'For what?' I ask, though I should've expected what she'd say. But I'm curious nonetheless.

'Remember to breathe, Sis,' Dorothea says. I feel her squeezing my hand a little, but not enough to hurt it. I glance at my eldest daughter briefly, watching her wipe her eyes before I turn to look back at Carina, who takes a few deep breaths before answering.

'For everything. I realise that Doro and I haven't exactly been kind to you for a long time, and now that you're lying here, I regret everything... I wish I could take back all those years. We both do.' I see Carina glance at Dorothea, prompting me to do so.

'She's right,' Dorothea says. 'Ever since Ma told us about Tiger's death and how it must have affected you, we have both been reflecting on how we acted and how selfish we were. You needed us, and we weren't there...'

Thank you,' I sniffle. 'That makes me really happy,' I say weakly. I can feel my heart starting to slow down... but even so, I keep on smiling my thin smile.

'You're crying... don't cry...' both my girls say, leaning over and wiping my cheeks with their thumbs. But that just makes me tear up even more because I'm so close to the end now. But before I go, and even though, at this point, talking has become difficult and I have one more request of them.

'My girls... Carina... Dorothea... I.' I take a breath and regain some composure. 'I have one final request of you both.'

They take my hands again and look at me eagerly, wishing to know what my dying request is.

'When I pass on, please take the photos of Tiger with you, so, while I'm no longer living with his memories, his memories will be living on with both of you. Can you do that for your old man?'

'Of course, we will. We know how much Tiger meant to you. So, yes, we'll do that for you,' Dorothea says. I smile and cry simultaneously, doing my best to hold onto their hands. They didn't know Tiger, but I'm glad they've accepted my request. It makes me a very happy man.

I stare at Tiger's ghost, who is now awake and looking back at me with eyes that tell me it's time - and that he's happy that Carina and Dorothea will be taking his photos with them. I suspect they already have pictures of me, but I want more than just my legacy in their lives; I also want Tiger to be a part of it.

'Thank you. Now, I can die peacefully as a happy man. I love you,' I say as I close my eyes for the final time. The last thing I hear is my daughter's and Tiger's ghosts saying, 'I love you too.'

-Paula Lahey-

BETH AND I made several phone calls and spent countless evenings browsing Gumtree ads, hoping to find Jack Russell puppies available for adoption. Jackie even helped us with the search. Although it might've been too soon to consider getting a new dog, Beth and I decided we needed a four-legged friend in our lives, someone to make us smile again. However, Jackie recommended we adopt an older dog rather than a puppy, and perhaps a breed that isn't as naturally energetic as a Jack Russell. A Rat Terrier was one we considered.

The price didn't matter. It was about finding the right bundle of joy to add into our lives. After Lilly's impact on us, we knew we couldn't just call it quits on dog ownership, despite initially believing we might. The impact Lilly had on my family was something special; her ability to make friends and bring joy to anyone she met was truly a wonderful trait. She was just a very special dog. She left behind a legacy that deserved to continue.

At eighty-seven, I'm fortunate to still be in relatively good shape. I believed I have the energy to care for a new dog. But this time, Beth and I decide not to get a puppy. Puppies require constant attention: they're hyperactive, cause a racket at night and need to be toilet trained, not to mention their desire to chew on furniture instead of their toys. I understood that all this might be too much for my old bones, so an older dog is better suited to us both.

Jackie and Jacob came over one day after Jackie had called to tell me she had something for me. Since Jackie doesn't drive, Jacob had to bring her out whenever she wanted to visit. Jackie has a habit of going out of her way for people she likes; like the time she drew that stunning portrait from a photo of Lilly for my birthday.

When the knock comes, Beth answers it and I stand up with anticipation of Jackie's "little surprise." Jacob enters the house first, comes over and greets me with a hug and a 'Hi, Mum.' I welcome him with a smile. After I let him go, he moves over to Beth and plants a small kiss on her cheek. Then Jackie appears. She gives me a quick one-armed hug because she's holding her other hand behind her back. With a smile on her face, she displays the hand that was behind her back.

'Here, this is for you and Beth,' she says.

On first glance, what she's holding looks like a book of some sort, a photo album. I take it from her with a 'Thank you' and proceed to sit in my chair to take a better look at the gift. I run my hand over the smooth plastic covering of the book. All the while, Jackie, Jacob, and Beth are in the kitchen, discussing politics and other topics relating to the news.

'Our Prime Minister is a real drongo,' I hear Jackie say to Beth, and I can't help but agree: I believe our PM's a few screws short of a lightbulb. But then their chatter becomes background murmurs as I turn over the first page of the teal-coloured album that Jackie's just given me and see these words in Jackie's handwriting: *This book belongs to Paula and Elizabeth Lahey*, along with three other distinct words that read: *Book of Lilly*.

Flipping to the next page, I see a collage of photos—printed snapshots taken throughout the years. I can't help but smile. Among the photos, two specific pictures stand out: one is the photo that Jackie had drawn, the other is of Lilly sitting on the floor, tilting her head curiously up at the camera, with a tennis ball at her paws. This has always been one of my favourite photos.

I continue flipping through the album, each page filled with memories of Lilly— her charm, her boundless energy, and her unmistakable ability to win hearts everywhere she went. When I reach the end, I close the album and hold it close to my chest, just as I'd done with Jackie's drawing the day we received word that Lilly hadn't made it. This album is now a precious memento, alongside her ashes.

The voices from the kitchen grow clearer as I stand, still clutching the album. They're reminiscing about Lilly and the other dogs we've loved: Mindy; Molly; Chloe, and finally Lilly. I join them, placing the album gently in Beth's hands.

'You'll want to see these,' I say softly. Beth smiles at me, opening the album to admire the collection.

I then ask Jackie how much money she wants for the album. But she and Jacob glance at me in unison. Jacob is quick to explain that Jackie isn't expecting any payment, but I'm not going to take 'no' for an answer. I can't bear the thought of letting her leave without offering her something in return.

Jackie, however shakes her head and firmly says she doesn't want any money because creating the album was something she wanted to do out of the goodness of her heart.

But I still want to repay her in some way, I reach into my wallet, pull out a $20 note, presenting it to her, which she politely declines.

I really don't need the money, Nan,' she says firmly. 'I made the album because I want to, not because I expected anything in return.'

I try again to insist, determined to give her the money, but she gently pushes my hand away. *Please just take it*, I think to myself.

Eventually I give up and accept defeat when she insists for the tenth time that she doesn't want my money. 'Oh, well, okay, I just thought I should repay you,' I say meekly.

I see Jackie's face light up. 'Just enjoy those memories and continue to be happy; that's how you can repay me,' Jackie says.

'Which reminds me, Nan,' Jackie says. 'Can I see her?'

At first, I'm confused about what she's asking me, but then I understand that she's talking about Lilly's ashes.

'Oh, right, sure,' I reply. She's in the top right drawer in Beth's room.'

Jackie leaves the table and heads for Beth's room. I take a seat where Jackie had been moments before. Beth, who's finished going through the photos, has closed the book, and is wiping at her eyes.

'That's lovely,' she blubbers, her voice catching as Jacob gives her shoulder a reassuring rub.

'She's a good girl,' he states. *And isn't that the truth,* I think to myself. Jackie's thoughtful gesture has only deepened my love and appreciation for her. Her genuine kindness in comforting those grieving and her willingness to go the extra mile for others never ceases to amaze me. I feel incredibly fortunate to have her as my granddaughter and Jacob as my son. They were the constants in my daily life now, especially since my eldest daughter, Michelle, lives in Sydney and rarely visits.

Jackie soon emerges from Beth's room, wiping her eyes, faint streaks of tears still visible. I know seeing Lilly's ashes would make her tear up, just as it did for the rest of us. Lilly had left a mark on everyone who had the pleasure of getting to know her, her endearing charm and boundless affection earnt her a special place in all our hearts. Wherever she is now, I hope she's happy, finding joy and making friends with dogs like her.

'Well then, suppose we had better make tracks,' Jacob says, standing up and grabbing his wallet and his cap. Jackie joins him, slipping the strap of her red purse over her neck and shoulder.

'Leaving us so soon?' I ask them, unable to hide my disappointment.

Jacob nods and explains that they have things to do at home and that the reason for visiting was for Jackie to give us the photo album.

Jackie adds, 'I've also got to work on my writing project. It's called *Franklin's Flower*: a short horror story.' Her eye lights up as she describes it. 'It's about this beautiful but cursed flower that blooms on a man's grave and anyone who tries to pluck the flower is met with grave misfortunes or even death. '

I can't help but smile at her enthusiasm, though horror isn't exactly my genre. Still the fact that Jackie is writing it is enough reason for me to support her.

'Well, I'll have to get a signed copy when it's done, ' I tell her. 'Even if it's not my kind of book, I'll proudly have it on my shelf. Who knows? If it becomes a best seller, I might even give it a read. '

Jackie laughs clearly touched and says, 'Thanks Nan. That means a lot.'

'Well, alright,' I say resting a hand on her shoulder. 'I wish you all the success in the world with it. Just know I'll be cheering you on from here.'

As they prepare to leave, I feel a pang of longing to keep them here a little longer. But I also understand they have their own lives to tend to. Watching them head out, I feel a quiet pride. No matter where life take them, Jackie and Jacob carry the values of kindness, creativity and love that will always keep our family close.

'Thanks, Nan. You and Beth look after yourselves for Dad and me,' Jackie says with a warm smile.

'We will, Jackie, don't worry,' Beth replies.

Jacob steps forward, giving me a light kiss on the cheek. 'Goodbye Mum, ' he says.

Jackie lingers for a moment, tilting her head as if she wants to double-check something.

'You really liked the album, right, Nan?'

Now, it's my turn to chuckle, shaking my head at the question.

'What kind of silly question is that, Jackie? Of course I do! It's one of the best things a grandchild of mine has ever given me.'

Jackie smiles brightly and follows her father outside. Jackie gets in the car, but not before giving Beth and me one last wave.

***

I'm back at the dining table, looking through the photo album. The glossy pages are brimming with fabulous snapshots of Lilly spanning the eleven years of her life. There she was a shy little puppy in 2009, clearly a few weeks old, looking hesitant but full of potential. It's still hard to believe that Lilly, a timid pup blossomed into the spirited, loving companion who charmed not just our family but the whole neighbourhood.

The later pages brought bittersweet memories. By the time Lilly turned ten, she began to show subtle signs of deterioration. She'd stopped eating or drinking; her boundless energy noticeably waning. And last year, at eleven years old, things had gone from bad to worse for Lily. Beth and I had taken her to the vet to see Dr Elliot Prendergast, a kind and empathetic man, who understood how much Lilly meant to us.

Dr. Prendergast explained to us that Lilly's kidneys were failing and while they could try to stabilise her at the clinic, her prognosis wasn't good. He said treatment might buy her some time, but it wouldn't cure her or ease her suffering. We couldn't let her life a life of pain. And after long and tearful conversations, ultimately, Beth and I came to the heartbreaking decision, we'd give Dr. Prendergast permission to put her down and end her suffering.

The memory of that day still stings, but I find peace knowing we did the right by Lilly. And while we still miss her dearly, and we know that there will never be another Lilly, we can rest knowing that our little dog with the upside-down love heart on her side is being well cared for and is possibly watching over others with her special brand of love. The thought of this gives me comfort.

God Bless you, Lilly.

***

I'M BACK! IT'S been a year and a few months up in Heaven. But now I'm back home! Back to Paula and Beth where I belong! Everything is exactly how I remember it. It's dark though, so I guess that it's the middle of the night. Beth and Paula must be sleeping in their beds. I wonder if I should jump up on either of their beds and let them know I'm here. I could lick their faces and bark in their ears to tell them that I've come home to see them.

But then I decide against that idea because what if they can't feel or see me? That will create a problem, and I know that if I'm going to make them both understand that I'm here and I've come to visit them, I have to be innovative. I have to be creative. So, I wander around the living room for a bit, then into the kitchen, looking at the objects around me, trying to work out how I can create a lot of noise so either Paula or Beth come into the living room to investigate the source of the strange noise.

I realise I can't jump on the dining table or counter; it's high up, and I'm too small a dog. The highest my little legs can reach is the couch or the bed, not the furniture in the kitchen.

Then it comes to me like someone's dropped a toy on my head! How had I not thought of it sooner? Heaven told us that as angel pets we can still play with our owners and our old toys, even if we're ghosts, and our owners can't see us. So, with this thought, I wander over to the corner, between the main lounge and Paula's couch, where my toybox is. I tip it over with my paw, spilling toys everywhere. I flick a few of the ball-shaped toys into the middle of the living room.

Then, for my plan to really work, I have to make some noise to wake them up. I know exactly how to do it. I go to the toy box, pick up a squeaky lion in my mouth, and start chewing on it. The squeaks echo throughout the house. If this doesn't wake them up, I'll be at a loss. But I'm optimistic. After all, my name is Lilly Lahey, and it's my job to make those around me happy. Even if they can't see me, I'll make them delighted, one way or another.

***

For some weird reason, I find myself tossing and turning in my bed and unable to sleep. I'd been dreaming about Lilly meeting her sisters: Mindy, Molly, and Chloe up in Dog Heaven, where suddenly, I'm kicked out of the lovely dream by a squeak-squeak-squeak from the lounge room. At first, I think it's just my mind playing tricks on me. At almost ninety-years-old I don't believe in fairy tales or strange things that go bump in the night. So, I put my hands over my ears, trying to block out the squeak. But it doesn't help much, so I pinch myself on the wrist. If this really is part of my imagination or another dream, pinching will wake me up. But when I doesn't I'm even more surprised: I can still hear the squeaking and it sounds close… really close, like it's coming from the lounge room.

It can't be outside, and I don't remember the neighbour having a dog. I think about waking up Beth to ask if she's hearing the unexplained squeaking. But then I remember that Beth is a heavy sleeper. She might be hearing the squeaking, but she'd most likely be far too tired to get up and investigate the source behind it. I guess that I'm alone in trying to figure out the mysterious noise. I hope that maybe if Beth needs to go to the toilet, she could help me figure it out. For now, it's just me.

I get out of bed, wondering, what the heck is going on. I put on my white slippers and matching dressing gown and leave my room to look for the source of the strange squeaking sound. I listen carefully and confirm that the squeaking is indeed coming from the living room. I put a wrinkled hand on the door handle, turn it, push the door slightly forward to open it when the mysterious squeaking abruptly stops!

At this point, I'm more than a little shaken up by this anomaly. I wrap the dressing gown cord around my waist and tighten it. I take one timid step into the living room, turned on the light, look around and see Lilly's old toys scattered across the carpet. I'm startled, I can't make sense of this. I want to wake up Beth so she can see this, but my legs won't move; they just tremble on the spot. First, the squeaking, and now, Lilly's toys are everywhere? What's going on? *What's next?* I think to myself.

As I stand there, trembling, I notice something that freezes me in place: one of Lilly's tennis balls is rolling around all by itself! Then it rolls towards me as if someone invisible has pushed it. I blink, looking down at the ball for a few seconds before kneeling and picking it up. I examine it carefully, trying to figure out how it had been moving, but there's no explanation for how it was moving. It's just a normal-looking tennis ball.

I toss the ball into the kitchen, expecting it to bounce off the wall and eventually roll to a stop, but it doesn't! Something I can't see picks up the ball just as it hits the wall. The ball then hovers in the air, floating back towards me, then drops at my feet. I pick it up again, and my eyes start to tear up. It can't be...

I don't believe in anything supernatural, like Jackie does, but at this moment with the ball hovering in front of me, I feel something shift in my heart, the hairs on my arms stand up. I'm convinced that I'm playing fetch with Lilly's ghost; that she's come home to see the family that she left behind.

I examine the ball again, still needing to comprehend how it's been moving. There aren't any magnets attached to it, and I'm sure my slippers don't have any magnets in them to attract the ball. No, the ball isn't moving closer to my slippers, so I rule out the outlandish theory of my slippers having magnets inside them. I look down at my ankles half expecting Lilly's ghost to be there, wagging her tail, tongue lolling out, waiting for me to toss her old favourite toy into the kitchen for her to fetch.

'I'm here, Mummy, I'm here!'

I feel silly, but I can't stop myself. 'Lilly? I ask. Have you come home?' I speak softly while asking the floor, feeling silly. But if Lilly's spirit is there, I have to find a way to make contact, even if I can't see her.

I know that if I keep throwing the ball into the kitchen, Lilly will bring it back to my feet. It's her favourite game, after all. Without hesitation, I throw the ball into the kitchen, watching it bounce off the kitchen counter and disappear behind the wall. I wait, wondering if it will come back.

At first, I think maybe the ball won't come back to me; perhaps I'm just too tired, and I've been imagining things… hallucinating: a side effect of being exhausted. Maybe that's what's happening, but then I hear the ball's squeak again and I know Lilly's spirit has truly come home.

Then I see the ball appear again! And like it did last time; it hovers just above the ground. Once again, the ball is dropped on my feet, another confirmation that Lilly's here. that she's returned home from Heaven to play ball with me, and to let me know she's happy. I really believe she wants to tell me that she still thinks about me and loves me dearly as I love her.

So, I pick up the ball again, wave it in the air and imagine Lilly's ghost getting excited, bouncing up and down like she did when she was alive.

'Mum?' I hear Beth's voice behind me. I see her standing there, in her own blue dressing gown, rubbing her eyes. She looks as tired as I feel. 'What are you doing? She asks. 'It's like one in the morning.'

'It's Lilly,' I reply, even though I know I probably sound crazy to her.

'What? Lilly?' She says, rubbing her eyes again and stepping forward, making me move out of her way.

I sit on the couch, and I beckon my daughter, patting the side of the couch, gesturing for her to sit down next to me.

'What are you doing, Mum?' she asks again while I continue to tap the couch, but she wouldn't budge.

'I just went to go to the toilet. I saw that the lights were on in the lounge room, then find you standing in the middle of the doorway softly sobbing to yourself. What's going on? Are you sick? Should I call 000?'

'I'm not sick, Beth. I feel fine. You don't need to call the ambulance.' I say, wiping my own teary eyes.

Beth takes another step forward, her eyes both tired and questioning. 'Then what are you doing? You're freaking me out.'

'It's Lilly,' I say. She's come back. Even though we can't see her, she's come back. Please, sit with me. I've been playing with her. Join me.'

Beth's eyes dart around in a confused manner. I can see the hesitation on her face. She doesn't know what to do or say. She's confused about what I'm doing. Heck, I don't know what I'm doing. I guess the idea that Lilly's ghost is here and wanting to play with us is overwhelming.

I blink just as Beth yawns, giving in to my request. She sits on the couch next to me. 'Now, what do you mean that Lilly's back, Mum?' She asks. 'You know that she's been dead for a year and a few months and that her ashes are in my drawer, right? You're talking nonsense.'

'Look, I know how this must sound, Beth, but believe me... Lilly's returned... as ... as a ghost.'

Beth's eyes widen. She knows I don't believe that ghosts are real; preferring to believe there's usually some logical explanation behind most alleged "phenomena."

'But I thought you said you didn't believe in ghosts or anything like that?'

'I know, I know. But trust me on this one. Pick up one of Lilly's old tennis balls and throw it. Even though we can't see her, she brings it back. Trust me.'

Not wanting to argue with the words of her silly old mother, Beth does as I ask and picks up one of the balls lying on the carpet. She sighs, then tosses it into the kitchen, where it rolls under the dining table.

'See? I think you are just tire...' Beth starts.

'Look!' I whisper, pointing to the ball that's hovering above the floor and heading in Beth's direction. Then Beth's eyes really widen. Lilly's ghost drops the ball in front of her. Beth simply stares at the ball, baffled.

'Did that just...' Beth tries to speak.

I nod, tears of happiness dripping down my cheeks. 'Yep! She brought it back to you. Throw it again,' I encourage.

Beth picks up the ball and tosses it into the kitchen again. I watch as her mouth drops when the ball's returned to her yet again.

'Lilly? Is that you?' Beth asks.

'Yes! Yes! It's me, Beth. It's me! I've come home to see and play with you both!'

This time, I pick up the ball instead of Beth and look at the space where I imagine Lilly is standing, tongue happily panting and tail wagging back and forward. I say in a weeping but happy voice.

'Lilly, we want you to know that you're the best dog Beth and I could ever have. You gave us so much joy. Even if you, at times, were naughty, you still gave us joy. And knowing that you've come home in ghost form just to play with us and let us know that you're happy makes us happy. We love you, Lilly, and you'll always be in our hearts.'

Then, I pull Beth in for a hug. I toss the ball one more time, watching it float straight back to me. Beth and I sob on each other's shoulders, knowing that Lilly's ghost is right here to comfort us. We eventually say 'Goodbye' to Lilly's ghost and head to our rooms to go back to sleep. We both now have something nice to dream about and something twice as magical to tell the rest of the family in the morning. But before I go to bed, I give Beth another big hug, grateful that both she and I helped to raise such a beautiful little angel.

-Marian Kushner-

MY BIRTHDAY IS tomorrow. I'm going to be fourteen, and I have no blooming idea what's going to happen or what's going on as my parents keep teasing me by saying that it's going to be a surprise and that they're sure I'm going to love it. But the catch is that I have to be patient and wait until the seventh of July 2021: tomorrow.

My parents got me a bird last year. It's a cockatiel called Peachface.

Their teases are killing me…They knew I love surprises but when I tried to get at least some idea of what it's going to be, like a hint of some kind, they won't give me any, and I'm left to keep on guessing and guessing. Normally I'd shrug it off and try to concentrate on something else like reading a book like *Watership Down* (the book I'm currently reading) or trying to teach Peachface to talk. But there's something about this surprise that's itching at me. Why do I have to like surprises so much?

'Can you at least tell me if Sheila or Eric are coming?' I ask them, crossing my arms and pouting at them, wanting them to at least give me one straight answer and at least fill me in on that one thing as I sit beside Dad at the kitchen table where my homework is.

'You'll have to wait and see tomorrow,' Dad winks at me. I stamp my foot in response. 'Oh, bollocks!' I stomp away, still with my arms crossed and a scowl because Dad won't answer my simple question! It isn't like I', asking what kind of cake I'll be getting. So, I go into the living room, sit down, pouting, and think about the two people I hope are coming tomorrow.

Sheila remains my best friend, even though we are both in our second year of high school. As for my boyfriend, Eric Dyer, I met him on the first day of high school. He was from Bray in Ireland and had a handsome accent that sounded similar to my

Scottish one. Eric said that his parents and younger brother Brandon, who's currently nine, moved to Scotland for a change of scenery in 2018 and because Scotland is a pretty place in the equally appealing country of the UK. We became boyfriend and girlfriend about three weeks into first year, when Sheila and I were on our phones in recess, discussing botany for our gardening classes. Eric came from behind us, cleared his throat to alert his presence while holding his hands behind his back and kicking away an invisible rock. We turned to look at him, and I remember Sheila giggling at the blush on his cheeks. She asked him why he was blushing, and he told her that he wasn't blushing (which he clearly was) and that it was just hot (it was that, too). He looked away trying to hide the idea that he was obviously blushing. 'Can I spend some time with Marian alone, please?' he spoke to Sheila, blinking quickly, biting his bottom lip and kicking a nearby rock away.

Sheila 'Oooo'ed' at me before giving me a wink, getting off the bench we were sitting on to go somewhere else, possibly to find the boy she liked, Greg Reznik, a disabled boy in a wheelchair.

With Sheila gone, Eric stared at me. With his hands behind his back, he gulped and said in a heavy stammer, 'H-Hi, Marian'.

'Hello, Eric,' I greeted him politely, 'what's behind your back?' I asked him. With a trembling hand, he brought out a single sunflower that he had gotten permission from the gardening teacher to get out of the garden for this purpose. Th-this is fu-for you, he said'
I stared at the flower and blinked at him, asking him why he'd had come to me of all people. He said, his cheeks going even redder, and he spoke with an even greater stutter. 'Because I like you... a lot... and I was hoping you... would be my girlfriend...' He kicked another invisible rock away. 'I've kinda had a crush on

you and never knew how to approach you.' He said bashfully, looking away as if embarrassed. I stood up, put my arms around him, and hugged him for a few seconds before letting go and taking the sunflower from his hand. 'No one has ever asked me to be their girlfriend. Even in primary, I had never had a boyfriend,' I had said, telling him the one thing that I'd always wanted to tell him, but always never had the courage to, because I always got red in the face whenever I saw him. Eric looked at me and stammered. 'So, does that mean you will?'

'Duh!' I said, staring dreamily into his eyes. 'What do you think!' Eric's face lit up when I said yes, and he threw himself into my arms, kissed my neck, and showered me with 'Thank you's,' and 'I'm so happy's.' We've been a thing for more than a year. Eric's a total gentleman and is very loyal; he holds doors open for me, brings me daises he finds around the school grounds and offers to help me with science homework. In some ways, he reminds me of a classical depiction of a dog, showing how loyal and loving he is towards me; if there was ever a Labrador in human form, it would be Eric. Sheila laughs at him whenever he goes out of his way for me, but he doesn't show much care about her teasing him with her laughter. Because as long as he has me and I'm happy, that's all that matters to him.

I look over at the mounted digital clock on the wall above the flat-screen TV, seeing it's only 4:12pm. I groaned, throwing myself backwards on the couch and letting out a frustrated sigh. My birthday is still HOURS away, and I have all this time to kill. Birthdays are an exciting time for any child, and mine indeed are because my parents spoil me with presents, so no wonder why I'm excited and want to know the details about what's happening.

What's a thirteen-year-old supposed to do? I think to myself. I look at the bookshelves and remember something that had happened four years ago, when my first kitten, Mittens, had died. 'Speaking of my old kitten...' I say aloud to myself. I stop thinking about my surprise birthday tomorrow and sit up. I go up to my room to look at the framed photograph of Mittens playing with one of her mouse toys Mum got around a month after Dad came back with Mittens' ashes. I pick it up and smile at it as a small tear dribbles down my left cheek. Considering I only got to have Mittens for a few months, she was my very first pet, and the impact of her death still meant a great deal to me. No ten-year-old girl wants to wake up one morning to hear her neighbour talking to her parents about finding her kitten's lifeless body somewhere outside his lawn. Because I could tell you that I wasn't ready for it. I wipe my eyes, even if they aren't crying, and murmur, 'Miss you, Mittens,' before my mind goes back to Peachface, the cockatiel we have in a pretty big cage downstairs. A bird is entertaining nonetheless, and if we train Peachface right, he should be able to fly out of his cage, sit on my shoulder, and possibly peck at my hair or tickle me with the feathers on his crest. Sometimes I even hear Mum scolding Dad for trying to teach the bird to swear. But, as the saying goes, good things come to those who wait. And that could be said about me waiting for my birthday tomorrow.

    'Hmm, what's a girl to do to pass the time?' I whisper to myself as I put the photo of Mittens on my bedside table and stare dreamily up at the ceiling, trying to think of something to do to make this day go quicker. I think for what seems like forever until I decide to go back downstairs, go through my schoolbag, and try to work on my science homework about plant and animal cells (I'm not a fan of science class and wish I had Eric to help me). I sit at the dining table, study books and exercise books on the table, when Dad's voice calls out to me. I looked into the archway and saw him peek his head in. 'Oh, there you are. Listen, your Mum and I are going to go out to get some takeout for dinner. You want to come?' He asks me, and I shake my head, replying with, 'No, thank you, I'm going to try to work on this week's homework. It's due this Monday.'

He smiles at me. 'Alrighty then, if you're still struggling with it when we get back, don't be scared to ask either Mum or me.'

'Okay. But I should be done by then. I only have about six more questions to answer, and I got books to help me with them.'

'That's my good girl,' He smiles. After Dad gives me a kiss on the temple, my parents leave the house, leaving me home alone with Peachface, who's happily nibbling on his seed stick.

***

OWWIE! I landed on my bum when I returned home and realise, I'm sitting on the hard table in the living room. That's why my landing hurt; I'd landed on something hard instead of soft, like a pillow or bed. And as I lie here on the table, I look around me and, for once, realise just how massive my old home is: it's giant! It makes me think back on my reaction when I first saw that Mummy Millie was a big tiger, especially compared to little me and my friends in Heaven: Milo, Yuki, Princess, Peter, Bakari, Zoila and Berry. The furniture is precisely how I remember it to be the last time I was here. How long ago that? What did Mummy Millie say the year was again? 2020? Nope, 2090? Heavens no! 2021? Yes, that was what she had said. The thing is, when did that mean animal get me? How long have I been away from this house? Was I even in the right house? Oh! I don't know! I need help to think straight... But I suppose it's a long time...

'Cat!'

Eep! I hear a strange, yet funny voice. I hop off the table to look around for the funny voice, I come to the living room doorway. I see an enormous birdcage with a colourful birdie that I've never seen before sitting on a twig inside it. I think this bird is friendly, and the way it said cat to me, like it was trying to get my attention and wants to become friends. So, being friendly myself, I decide to speak to the bird, hoping that it isn't going to tease me like Mr Bird did whenever I wanted to ask him to play with me. I watch the birdie look down at me, open his wings, and flap them. 'Hello, Mr birdie! Down here! Hi!'

'Cat! Cat! Hi Cat!'

'Peachface, will you please keep it down? I'm trying to think of the answer to this question.' *I stop trying to talk to Mr Birdie because I know that voice... is that, Marian? Is that the voice of my old mummy before Millie? I have to find out! I have to see if it's really her and that I haven't, for some reason, ended up in a house that only* looks *like my old home. So, ignoring the funny bird with the equally funny name "Peachface:" (just thinking about it makes me want to laugh), I wander out of the living room, and my little paws stop when I look up and see her... my hooman Mummy: Marian Kushner! I know what I have to do. I can't just sit here and stare at Marian because the purpose of me being back here is to "reunite" with her, as Heaven had said, and because I'm here, I plan to do just that! So, I go on carrying my little fuzzy legs towards her.*

'Cat! Cat in house! Cat!'

'Oh, shut up, Peachface; there isn't a cat in the house and hasn't been for at least four years. I get that you're probably thirsty and need a water change, but I need to finish this homework, so I'll be right with you after that, so for the second time. Be Quiet!' Once I've told him to shut up, Peachface stops squawking, leaving me to peacefully finish the rest of my science homework, for which I now only have two questions left.

I started teaching the bird to talk as soon I got him for my birthday last year. He knows a few words, but I still can't have a full conversation with him. Sometimes I think that teaching him to talk was a bad idea, especially when I have homework to do and he's there squawking and distracting me. I look back down at my homework now that it's quiet. When my parents get home, I could ask them any questions I'm not sure about, rub out the answer, and rewrite it based on my parents' information. But as soon as I'm about to write the answer for the second last question, Peachface commences squawking his little feathery head off with 'Cat' and 'Cat' and 'Cat,', and I know that I'd better not keep the bird waiting. If he wants water, I suppose I'll have to get up and get him his water. I get off the chair, go over to his cage to look at his water bowl and see if it's empty, as I assume is typical of most birds, they scream and make a racket when they want attention or something. To my surprise, his bowl is still mostly full! So, I stare at the cockatiel with confusion, wondering what on earth he's carrying on about if he isn't thirsty or hungry for another seed stick.

'What's up, Peachface? (Idiot) You've got my attention, so tell me, what's up? And don't you star…'

'Ceiling! SQUAWK Ceiling!' I throw my palm to my face, and the bird laughs. Peachface loves that joke, and I should've said something better than, 'What's up. ' Because every time someone asks him that, he always says ceiling. The joke had been funny at first, but now it's become annoying because it happens daily. Every. Single. Bloody. Time! Peachface just wants some attention and to say the punchline of his infamous ceiling gag, 'You daft bird,' I told him and turn to go back to my studies.

But my eyes don't go to the books on the table. Instead, they go to a ghostly outline of a fluffy little kitten sitting on my opened exercise book. My first thought is to trip over my own feet and fall on my backside, but I end up doing such a thing. Instead, I rub my eyes and pinch myself to ensure that I'm not dreaming. I quickly find out that I and that the ghostly kitten before me is as natural as goose pimples on my arm. But how could this be? Ghosts aren't real, are they? At least that's what Mum says.

'Mummy!' The kitten squeaks, and I throw my hands to my mouth. I feel like crying when the kitten speaks and calls me, 'Mummy' in perfect English! I pinch myself again and rub my eyes, but the ghostly image of the kitten remains. I'm not dreaming this; this is actually happening!

'Cat!'

'Shush you!' I snap at the bird; he's distracting me from this moment that's happening in front of me.

I watch the kitten stand up, flick its fluffy tail, and knead on the papers in my exercise book, but to my relief, the kneading paws aren't doing anything to ruin the pages of my book. I stare at the kitten, unable to do anything, taking in the patches of brown-on-white fur and how the kitten calls me Mummy. That can only mean one thing. This ghostly kitten stands on my work is my first pet, my first cat, my first four-legged friend. My Mittens!

'Mummy! Hooman Mummy! Heaven said I could come to see you again and said that you wouldn't be able to see me, and I was worried that you wouldn't and that I would have to do something to make you see me. But I don't have to do anything: you can see me; you can see me! Oh, I was so scared that you wouldn't be able to! Mummy... why is there water coming out of your eyes?'

I'm speechless. My hands slowly move away from my mouth. My eyes continue to stare without even so much as looking away for a mere second. Then I moved my hands to my hair and ruffled it up, still not believing what I'm seeing. My parents aren't going to believe this when I tell them.

'Maybe coming back here was a bad idea... I made hooman Mummy sad...'

'N-no, it's fine, Mittens, It's just...' My legs start to move again, and it isn't long until they powerwalk over to the table. My arms throw themselves out without my control, and I wrap them around the ghost of my old kitten. She feels cold... like freezer cold... but that doesn't bother me or drive me away. I attempt to pick up the ghost kitten, not caring how cold she is and hold her up to my shoulder so I can hug her like I've often did four years ago when I was only ten years old.

'It's just...' I blubber. I know that right here and now I won't be able to hold in the emotions, and that I'd let out everything that I want to say at this moment without hesitation. 'I thought that I'd never see you again. I thought that I would never get a chance to see your ghost again. Days and nights, I prayed in front of my bed, begging God to give me a sign that wherever you were, you were at peace and that I could have just one chance. *Would I be able to see your ghost?* To tell me that everything was going to be okay and that you were happy where you were in Heaven and making a lot of friends. The water in my eyes are tears, Mittens, but not because I'm sad. Goodness... no! I'm crying tears of joy! Because God has finally answered my prayers and delivered your spirit to me.

Despite being four years ago when that feral cat with rabies attacked and killed you, I never lost hope that perhaps, one day, I'd see your ghost and that everything will be alright again. Because I've seen it; I truly know that you're happy and living peacefully up in Heaven with all the other angel pets, such as yourself. Because, as I'm sure you've been told a lot, you were far too pure, too young and innocent to go out in such a horrible and scary way. But despite leaving me really early, I never lost hope that you'd return as a ghost. I still remember you clearly, and I keep your photos in my room to remind me of all those adorable and precious times I had with you. So, thank you, Mittens. Thank you, thank you, thank you for coming back to me. Thank you, God, for giving you to me. And most importantly, thank you, Mittens, for all those sweet memories. I love you so much, Mittens, and couldn't have asked for a better kitten!'

When I finish, I place Mittens' ghost back on the table and wipe my eyes, as I won't stop ugly crying. I know I shouldn't be this emotional around a kitten I have only owned for a few weeks. Still, I can't help but feel this way because Mittens was my very first pet, and first pets always mean a lot. Not only that, but Mittens was utterly adorable and had the softest fur and the sweetest little face I've ever seen on a white tabby kitten, especially when she made those big, innocent eyes that I always fell in love with. She was a dream come true, and that's why I have such a deep connection with her because she had meant too much to ten-year-old me. I'd never throw away her photos and will always keep her short-lived memories in my heart and mind. Even as an old woman knitting in my rocking chair, I'll remember Mittens and every other animal that I would come to own. Yes, even Peachface will have a place. As annoying as he can be, Peachface will still have a special place in my heart. Now that I think of Peachface, he kept saying 'Cat'. Did that mean that he could also see Mittens and was trying to tell me that she'd come home to see me? I can't know for sure, but I darn well hope that's the case and if it is: thank you, Peachface!

    I glance back down at Mittens, ensuring all my tears are gone, before asking her how long she'll stay with my parents because I hope that she can stay long enough to see my birthday tomorrow morning and the big surprise that my parents kept teasing me about. I'm sure Mittens has missed the smiles I'd make every time I saw her running into the kitchen, mewing for food.

    'Heaven didn't say how long my visit would be, but Heaven did say that I could visit as many times as I want to. So, do you think that means I can stay for as long as I want?' Mittens asks.

    I smile gleefully at the ghost kitten when I hear a car pull up in the driveway. Mittens seems spooked by the sudden noise and the yellow lights behind the curtain as her back arches up and her tail fizzles up, indicating that she's scared. But I reassure her that it isn't anything to be scared of because I instantly know that my parents have come home with dinner.

'Hey, uhm, Mittens, it's my birthday tomorrow. I'll be fourteen, and my parents are organising a big surprise for me. I'm wondering if you could be here with me when I wake up tomorrow morning.'

I watch as Mittens' ghost becomes somewhat like a puppy and hops around on the spot, tail in the air and running around in circles as if to chase said tail and make herself dizzy. *'YEAH, YEAH! Of course, I will be here tomorrow morning! I'd very much like to see my hooman happy again! But...'* Mittens suddenly turns sour, her tail falls, and she stops running around in circles and looks down at her front paws as if something sad has just crossed her mind. I ask her what's wrong, and Mittens stares up at me with those delightful little eyes that never failed to melt my heart.

'No one will be able to see me... only you, so I won't be able to play with anyone... like Sheila,' Mittens says. I smile at her, laying out my hand to pat her on the head, to which she reacts gracefully.

'It doesn't really matter if no one can see you but me,' I say calmly. 'With me being the only one to see you, that just makes it more special; knowing that you're still here for me,' I tell her. I look over at the front door and then at the ghostly kitten. 'Sure enough, my parents will be coming through the door with food. Can you hang around and go upstairs when I do?' I ask Mittens' ghost, who nods instantly; I never once doubted her. I smile, and sure enough, right on cue, my parents open the door, my dad holding a white bag wrapped with clear tape. Fish and chips are what we're having for tea.

'Sorry we're late, Marian; the shop was packed,' Dad apologises, rubbing the sweat from his forehead. I tell him it's okay and go over to help him and Mum set up the table. Still smiling, I walk over to the cupboard, get out the plates, and ask Mum if she'll be able to help me with my homework after tea, to which she, of course, agrees. After that, the three of us sit down and have dinner. All the while, I make glances towards Mittens, just to make sure she's still around.

Thankfully, she is. I bite my lip, trying to force myself not to have the biggest and stupidest grin on my face as I eat my food. I have to hold my wrist to stop my hand from shaking because of how giddy I am that my kitten's come back to me and is going to be around for my birthday tomorrow. I guess having her here with me is part of my surprise. I can't stop myself from grinning and taking a few glances at my parents, making sure that they aren't looking at me and noticing the stupid grin on my face.

***

When I wake up on my birthday, Mittens' ghostly face is staring right at me. Her cold paws are on my nose, and she's lightly patting them onto my nose as if to wake me up in the most adorable way possible.

'Happwi berthday, Marian! Happwi berthday!'

'Hello, Mittens!' I giggle, taking my arm out of the covers to rub the ghost kitten around the ears, much to Mittens' delight. Soon after, I get up and get dressed. I stare back at Mittens, who's under my feet, her tail perked and staring up at me curiously. I smile a wide grin at her and open my door. I head downstairs when my parents jump out from the corner of the hallway shouting, HAPPY BIRTHDAY!

'Thanks, Mum and Dad,' I grin as I hug them both. I get some breakfast and sit down on the couch with my parents, who are smiling joyfully. Mum scoots over next to me and puts her arm around my shoulder. Dad smiles down at me and reveals my surprise to me.

'Welcome to being fourteen, my little sweetheart. Guess what you'll be doing today? We'll be taking a trip down to Landmark Forest Adventure Park, and it's not just the three of us that are going, we've invited Sheila, Alanna, and Eric to come with us. And after that, we'll come back here and party. And we've already discussed it with his parents, Eric will be sleeping over tonight!'

I'm lost for words, but you can bet that I'm absolutely elated, so much so that I throw myself into the arms of both of my parents. Today's shaping up to become one of my best birthdays ever! And Mittens will be a part of it—as a ghost, yes, but she'll still be here on my happiest birthday!

Dedication

And with that, my humble pet owner and reader concludes the story of *Angels with Tails*. I dedicate this story to all the pet owners out there who have lost someone close who had four legs, a tail, feathers, or scales. It was quite a challenging book to write as I tried to create different scenarios for my characters. But now that we are here, I want to take this moment to say that we cannot change or help what happens to our pets when they pass away, but the important thing is that we do them a favour by keeping their memories alive and cherish all those wonderful times that they bless upon us humans. Because nothing is more special than a connection between pet and owner. The saying may be, 'Dogs are man's best friend,' but that isn't strictly welded to just dogs. If you take the time to train and love your animal, regardless of whether it's a cat, bird, or guinea pig, that animal will become your friend for life and never leave you as you hold a special place in their hearts as much as they in yours.

Animals are truly unique and beautiful creatures that we often take for granted. Just like us humans, animals deserve to feel loved and cherished because they fill a place in our hearts that no other person can ever fill and can make us feel a sense of belonging and love. Dogs may be the masters of loyalty and dedication to their Masters, whilst cats are the Masters of our lives and never fail to crack us up with their antics. This, my friends, is why we love our pets dearly; they keep on giving right up until their time comes. They will always be in our hearts, and their flames will never be extinguished because they are the pets that just keep on giving, so we commend them and say thank you for everything they've done for us. They may not talk or understand things as well as we humans, but the one thing that they know all too well is how much we love and adore them just for being themselves. Love is a universal language and is something that is shared with everyone, not just with humans but with animals. So, love your pets, give them a hug, and tell them you love them.

My inspiration for writing *Angels with Tails* came as an idea after my Nan and Aunt lost their own dog back in 2020, who wasn't just a simple dog. She was family, and she had meant so much to my family that when she died at the vet, the entire family was in mourning, as if we had just lost a human member of the family. Because that's what our pets do, they make their way deep into our hearts; so much that they become family, and when they die, it's profoundly devastating and harrowing. And that was precisely what my Nan's dog Lilly did. Yes, Lilly was a real dog, and Paula and all the other characters featured in her chapters were based on actual members of my family, with Jackie being based on myself!

Rest in peace, Lilly Lahey, 2009-2020.

We love you so much, beautiful girl!

Spread your wings.

Acknowledgements

There are a few people I want to thank for the development of this book. Let's start by saying thank you so much to my developmental editor, Flavia Young, who helped me throughout this journey of loss and grief. My proofreader, Robin Clark, who had to pause throughout due to non-stop crying. My mum, Natasha Wiggins who has always remained my biggest supporter. My nan Patricia and my dad Gregory Lahey who supported me during my writing.

Thank you to the people whom allowed me to borrow photos of their animals for this project. But mostly thank you to Lilly who had filled most of my childhood with endless joy with just her very presence. Thank you, nan, for bringing Lilly down to comfort me whenever I needed it, thank you for raising such a beautiful and wonderful dog who I would write as a main character in this book. Thank you everyone who ever had the pleasure of meeting Lilly in person and knowing just how much of an amazing dog she was.

But mostly, I want to thank everyone who took the time to pick this book up and make it through to the end. I know reading about a lot of animal deaths isn't a nice thing, but in the end it all comes together to create a bittersweet tale of legacy and loss of our fur babies.

About the Author

Chantelle Jacqueline (also known as Madelyn Elisa Lahey) was born in Hobart in March 1999. She is the only child of Gregory and Natasha. Her parents separated when Madelyn was just 3 years old. During her upbringing she didn't have a lot of support around her Autism, due to lack of understanding from others. She found this quite difficult and struggled with many things growing up, which left her with her own imagination most of the time. As she got older people started to understand her more and encouraged her to use her imagination as best as possible – writing. Since 18 she has been constantly writing and is always inventing new book ideas.

Although Chantelle (Madelyn) suffers with social anxiety alongside her Autism she strives to overcome the barriers these things bring. She strives for success in her writing and is passionate about using her gift of imagination to create something readable for her readers.

www.ingramcontent.com/pod-product-compliance
Lightning Source LLC
Chambersburg PA
CBHW051421290426
44109CB00016B/1390